From Bataan
to Freedom

From Bataan to Freedom

The World War II Odyssey of Errett Louis Lujan Through the Death March and Five Japanese POW Camps

Judy Reed

McFarland & Company, Inc., Publishers
Jefferson, North Carolina

Unless otherwise noted, all images are from the author's collection.

LIBRARY OF CONGRESS CATALOGING-IN-PUBLICATION DATA

Names: Reed, Judy, 1951– author.
Title: From Bataan to freedom : the World War II odyssey of Errett Louis Lujan through the death march and five Japanese POW camps / Judy Reed.
Other titles: World War II odyssey of Errett Louis Lujan through the death march and five Japanese POW camps
Description: Jefferson, North Carolina : McFarland & Company, Inc., Publishers, 2024 | Includes bibliographical references and index.
Identifiers: LCCN 2023057534 | ISBN 9781476692418 (paperback : acid free paper) ∞ ISBN 9781476650586 (ebook)
Subjects: LCSH: Lujan, Errett Louis, 1922–1992 | United States. Army. Coast Artillery Regiment, 200th. | World War, 1939–1945—Prisoners and prisons, Japanese. | Prisoners of war—Philippines—Biography. | Prisoners of war—United States—Biography. | BISAC: HISTORY / Wars & Conflicts / World War II / General
Classification: LCC D805.J3 L787 2024 | DDC 940.547252092 [B]—dc23/eng/20240117
LC record available at https://lccn.loc.gov/2023057534

BRITISH LIBRARY CATALOGUING DATA ARE AVAILABLE

ISBN (print) 978-1-4766-9241-8
ISBN (ebook) 978-1-4766-5058-6

© 2025 Judy Reed. All rights reserved

No part of this book may be reproduced or transmitted in any form or by any means, electronic or mechanical, including photocopying or recording, or by any information storage and retrieval system, without permission in writing from the publisher.

On the cover: Errett Lujan's POW label (55, with his name in Japanese); Lujan after liberation in 1945; *background* prison fence © Shutterstock

Printed in the United States of America

McFarland & Company, Inc., Publishers
  Box 611, Jefferson, North Carolina 28640
    www.mcfarlandpub.com

To all Allied military personnel and civilians
who perished during World War II in the Pacific theater

Acknowledgments

Paramount to the contributions of those I interviewed were Matthew Braun and Dick (Richard) Daly. They provided valuable details and insights into my father's experiences. Others who graciously provided their time for interviews, for which I am extremely grateful, were Betty Lujan, Claire Guentz, Howard Houk, Donnell Hester, Tony Reyna, Bill (William) Overmeir, Richard Gordon, and Francis VanBuskirk.

Perhaps the greatest turn of good fortune came my way when General Jack Fox, then-director of the New Mexico National Guard Museum in Santa Fe, allowed me access to everything in their archives and included a treasure trove of information, not the least of which was an entire box of World War II correspondence donated by my father.

Another stroke of luck was when Jean Naughton put me in touch with Mine Takada, who doggedly tracked down the identity of the boy in the photograph my father kept all the years after the war. I would not have been able to link the boss of the Showa Denko carbide plant to that picture on my own. It filled in a small but very important piece of the puzzle I was attempting to solve. Both Jean and Mine provided translations of the writing on my father's papers.

I entrusted the first draft to a few people once it was complete. I have the following people to thank for taking the time to read it: Jack Fox, Marvine Fox, Doug Peterson, Patsy Peterson, Mike King, Jennifer Amyx (who also helped with some Japanese translations), and Paul Reed. Paul went above and beyond encouraging me every step of the way through this lengthy undertaking. He is my pillar of strength on whom I can always depend but have inadequate words to appropriately thank him.

McFarland has my utmost thanks for taking this book under their capable wings. The people I worked with there helped me negotiate every twist and turn of the process.

Table of Contents

Acknowledgments	vi
Preface	1
Introduction	5
1. The Far East Before World War II	7
2. Sign Me Up!	11
3. Antiaircraft Training at Ft. Bliss	18
4. Deployment to the Philippines	27
5. Combat Begins	39
6. Retreat to Bataan	52
7. Losing Ground	62
8. The Lull	69
9. War News Stirs the Home Front	75
10. Surrendered	82
11. In Enemy Hands	91
12. Wrestling with Defeat Stateside	97
13. A Parade of Death at Camp O'Donnell	102
14. Life at Cabanatuan and Bilibid Prison	108
15. Entering Japan	117
16. Settling into Camp at Mitsushima as a POW	125
17. The Worst Winter	134
18. Remaining Months at Mitsushima	147
19. Changing of the Guards	156

20.	The First Leg at Kanose	168
21.	The Last Leg at Kanose	190
22.	Liberation	203
	Epilogue	220
	Appendix	223
	Chapter Notes	227
	References	239
	Index	243

Preface

This rendition of the life of Errett Louis Lujan during World War II as part of the 200th Coast Artillery (Antiaircraft) Regiment is a passion I am most grateful to present. I am his daughter. His experiences include a brief quarantine in Santa Fe, training at Ft. Bliss on antiaircraft guns, deployment to the Philippines in September 1941, combat in the Philippines, the Bataan Death March, and as a POW for three and a half years at Camp O'Donnell, Cabanatuan, Bilibid, Mitsushima, and Kanose POW camps.

Errett was laid to rest at the Santa Fe National Cemetery in New Mexico forty-seven years after the Japanese capitulation that ended World War II. A neatly engraved marble headstone marks the spot. The week of his funeral, my mother pulled open a drawer, carefully slipped two small books from it, and held them out to me. "These are your father's diaries he kept during the war," she said. "I thought you, most of all, would like to have them."

Errett had chronicled some of his thoughts during his captivity using the stub of a pencil on lined and fuzzy paper that resembled my Big Chief Indian tablet in first grade. One diary was small, about two-by-three inches, and the other five-by-seven. The larger of the two was authorized and read by his Japanese captors, which is why he did not record all of his thoughts or what he saw or what happened to him. The other he had secreted away writing in it when he could. The secret diary was never discovered.

I knew my father was in the military during World War II. I knew he was in the Pacific theater. I knew he had been a prisoner of the Japanese, but this was the first I had heard of the diaries. The discovery flung me into researching his travails during that time of his life.

The first thing I did was transcribe his diaries. In no time at all, the facts dispelled my initial concept of him entering World War II that was in my mind for so long. For years, I imagined a poignant scene in which he and three of his school chums decide to enlist. The four are in their respective Santa Fe, New Mexico, homes that fateful day Pearl Harbor was bombed. The Lujans had just finished eating when the startling news in Franklin Roosevelt's firm, bold, and outraged voice emanated from the radio to inform stunned listeners that our naval fleet had been attacked in Hawaiʻi. There is little else talked about in the following two days. Mothers huddle in groups in their neighborhoods spreading news as fast as it arrives. Fathers and older sons go to the plaza (town square) as an impromptu meeting place. Every face is dazed and every conversation is about current events. The drone of conversation fills the streets, shops, homes, churches, and schools.

By the third day, my imaginary scene unfolds among the escalating pitch of voices from the men in the plaza, and their dazed faces become more animated. Errett and his three closest friends are in the crowd and form a pact with one another to enlist. They are committed to carrying out their decision even knowing it may cost them their lives. They run the two miles uphill from the plaza to the National Guard Armory, never stopping to talk but talking all the way. They are some of the first to arrive at the recruiting office that day and they enlist without hesitating. I imagined this to be the pivotal moment when the camaraderie of these particular soldiers forms.

My thoughts of this, however, were fantasy and proven so when I looked at his military discharge. It was as if a big red circle with a diagonal slash, the international NO! sign, was forcefully stamped down on my mental preconception. The problem? He enlisted well before the day of infamy in December 1941. The reality? He was deployed to the Philippines before the attack on Pearl Harbor.

I quickly realized I did not have adequate knowledge of certain events to appreciate his circumstances while in the military. My goal was to correct this deficiency and, as it turned out, produce a worthy history. Obviously, all experiences during wartime are unique and important to tell, but as I discovered in my research, memoirs are usually confined to a single person without benefit of the bigger picture. This book provides such a benefit to the reader: a synopsis of the Japanese doctrine that led to their attack on Pearl Harbor, the Philippines, and other places in the Pacific, as well as references to events during the war, especially in the Pacific theater, as Errett slogged through his days as a POW without having to recall or look up historical facts. As generations progress beyond World War II consciousness, a lack of understanding the historical context of what any one individual endures diminishes. This book is hopefully enlightening for these people less familiar with that era.

The history of his war days is incomplete in some instances, but what I included in this book is accurate. World War II in the Pacific is an enormous topic, and so few remain who can provide firsthand accounts of what my father experienced. I wish I had explored the topic with him, but that never happened because, like most POWs of the Japanese, he said very little about his captivity in my presence. Instead, I researched those places, people, and events surrounding him, allowing me to put my father's diaries into a greater, more understandable context.

I personally conducted almost all of my research through reading publications, investigating archives, and conducting interviews. Many key facts I obtained from the New Mexico State Archives and Records Center and the Fray Angélico Chávez History Library and Archives. Probably the most surprising and beneficial archival research was at the New Mexico Military Museum Archives, where I carefully examined all of their holdings. To my astonishment, I came across an entire box of letters written during World War II between Errett and his family and the pencil stub he used. All of these archives are located in Santa Fe, New Mexico.

I was also fortunate to talk with many veterans of the 200th Coast Artillery (Antiaircraft) regiment as well as two ex–POWs not part of the 200th but who were in the same camps as Errett while in Japan. Interviews of the 200th veterans mostly took place in New Mexico at their residences, although one was at the last convention of the American Defenders of Bataan and Corregidor held in San Antonio, Texas. I interviewed the two ex–POWs who shared experiences with Errett in Japan by telephone several times over the course of about six years. A few questions needing answers were fulfilled via e-mails with other people, like the identification of the picture of Shotaro Kanagawa that Errett brought home from Kanose. Mine Takada accomplished identification through her own research.

It is at this point that I should admit my biases. The characterization of the World War II generation as the greatest generation of the twentieth century is not contestable in my opinion. I subscribe to this characterization not because of how they handled their trials during war but because of how so many of them made a conscientious effort to live a life of character rather than live as victims after the war. This does not mean, however, that none were victims, true or perceived. Also, I am an unabashed admirer of my father. I do not suggest that he was flawless, nor do I suggest that all World War II veterans were sterling examples of character during or after the war, but I believe most were.

To be sure, tragedy scars the hearts of the battle weary and war prisoners, but it is my premise, based on personal experience and observation, that however it comes, tragedy will either strengthen or diminish one's character. Questions tumbled through my mind in a loop early on in my research. Did my father's character get him through the ordeal, or did the ordeal shape his character? When was Errett's hope diminished, and what were the causes? Is there any evidence that some events during this horrific part of his life improved his character?

My assessment is that yes, the war gave him lasting nightmares and he saw and endured things no one should, but his character seemed to be built on the same moral values both before and after the war. He seemed the same type of person going in, judging by what those who knew him said, as he was when I knew him. Yet the grueling conditions of war and imprisonment by a heavy-handed enemy is bound to define, redefine, or exemplify one's character. I believe his was exemplified. We all experience tragedy in our lives, but few will be tested to the degree of my father and the tens of thousands of others held prisoners by the Japanese. From enlistment to returning home after the war, Errett's character was tested minute by minute, oftentimes with his life hanging in the balance. I think what resonated with him was something on the order of but for the grace of God, he too might have been among the half of his regiment who did not return home. The truth of his ordeal is captured in this book.

Introduction

Errett Lujan faced death three times in his life. All were situations beyond his control. In the first, he escaped the death grip pneumonia had on him shortly before his first birthday. Second, he experienced the indiscriminate onslaught brought on by the dust bowl of the 1930s as he lived in the heart of the disaster, including Black Sunday in April 1935. His lungs, probably from his early bout in life with pneumonia, seemed more susceptible to problems from the great dust storms periodically plowing through where he lived. The storms devastated livelihoods, and Black Sunday prompted the Lujans to relocate to Santa Fe, New Mexico, to earn a living.

Upon arriving in Santa Fe, Errett leaped to the ground from the bed of the truck, scowled, and gave the place a cursory glance. Then he blurted, "I hate this place, and I'm going to run away and go back to Clayton as soon as I have the chance!"[1] His disgruntled attitude toward Santa Fe was short lived, and he embraced the city as his forever home.

The third threat to his existence, which seared incomprehensibly graphic and horrific memories into his soul, was being a prisoner of the Japanese. The time Errett spent in Japanese POW camps may oddly have rendered the worst and best effects on his life. The depravity he witnessed, the cruelty he sustained, and his constant hunger are horrible experiences he and others suffered. There were a few touching moments of kindness Errett received that could have ended in murder but did not. The final effect, though, was that he considered every day after the war a gift for which he was truly grateful.

Errett Louis Lujan was born on Mother's Day in May 1922 into a ranching family in Mexhoma, Oklahoma, and the only son of Jess and Louis Lujan. But with the help of his mother who corroborated a false claim, he obtained a delayed birth certificate stating he was born in Clayton, New Mexico. His age lay between older (Merle) and younger (Claire) sisters. The family raised cattle and chickens and grew a variety of vegetables on a spread of about forty acres near Boise City in the far west end of the Oklahoma panhandle before moving to Clayton, New Mexico. Hardships and working hard were constant in the Lujan family.

He enlisted in the New Mexico National Guard on March 28, 1940, two months short of his 18th birthday, and his regiment was activated into the U.S. Army in January 1941 and trained at Ft. Bliss near El Paso, Texas, where he became engaged to a young woman with "exotic eyes." He returned to New Mexico in October 1945 a different person after three and a half years as a POW, met and fell in love with another woman immediately after coming home, and married her, my mother, before New Year's Day 1946.

1

The Far East Before World War II

The Lujan family, like many Santa Feans and perhaps many Americans, paid little attention to world events of the 1930s and early 1940s. Their lives and livelihood had been at the mercy of the dust bowl and Depression. Life was difficult enough during those times without concerning themselves with the troubles and problems facing people across the globe. What little about the world they read or heard about seemed irrelevant to their futures, but an inescapable connection would soon present itself and its roots went deeper than the twentieth century.

In 1823, Satō Nobuhiro wrote a widely accepted proposal in Japan to make the whole world provinces and districts of Japan, beginning with the territory the Japanese referred to as the Middle Kingdom, or China, and specifically Manchuria. His treatise was called *Kondō Hisaku*, in English, *A Secret Strategy for Expansion*.[1] Its clearly stated vision was to annex the world under Japan.

Japan encountered Western culture when Admiral Matthew Perry led an expedition that forced Japan in 1854 to accept and actively engage in trade and diplomatic relations with the West after more than two hundred years of isolation. The Japanese not only acquired many of the artifices of Western culture but were also introduced to democratic rule. The exposure put the Nobuhiro doctrine somewhat at odds with the People's Rights movement that began in Japan in 1880. People's Rights was based on a vision of a world without aggression, war, armaments, and possibly military forces, all directed under a single world government. The first tenet toward achieving this utopia was to establish democracy in Japan.[2]

The Japanese government envisioned themselves becoming a great world power through a strategy closely aligned with Nobuhiro's plan of conquest with China in the crosshairs. However, rather than invading China directly, they began with Korea, a prize coveted by both China and Russia at the time. The Japanese military prevailed bringing them complete control over Korea by first defeating China (1894–1895) and then Russia (1904–1905) for the island prize. Their first real choice between siding with democracy or dictators presented itself during World War I. In 1914, Japan entered the war on the side of democracy despite their rule to the contrary over Korea. Japan sent a few small destroyers to the Mediterranean, occupied German island possessions, and patrolled the Pacific trade routes in the war.

In 1929, three years into Emperor Hirohito's reign over Japan, forty-seven nations met in Switzerland to improve on the principles and minimum standards of treatment of POWs put forth in the Hague Treaty formulated in the Netherlands in 1907. Japanese delegates objected to the final version of the Geneva Convention treaty but signed it anyway. Their objection centered on a perceived lack of fairness in what countries must do for POWs. In their way of thinking, it was unfair for Japan to provide amenities and abide by certain standards of treatment of POWs because Japanese POWs were unlikely to exist since their warriors were to follow the Bushido code of suicide over surrender. In the end, the Japanese government refused to ratify the Geneva Convention their delegation had signed and refused to recognize it as binding on them. Concurrently but written as a separate document was the Red Cross Geneva Convention, which specifically dealt with the treatment of wounded, sick, and dead POWs. Both Japan and the United States signed and ratified this treaty.

A multitude of Asian immigrants moved to West Coast cities of the United States after World War I. As a cheap source of labor, West Coast companies and businesses encouraged their immigration until their overwhelming numbers were deemed a problem for the country. The U.S. Congress's solution was to pass the Exclusion Act in 1924, prohibiting Oriental immigration. Humiliation Day, as the Exclusion Act was known in Japan, followed by a series of U.S. embargos on natural resources into Japan, hardened the Japanese leadership's perspective against the United States. In the first decade of Emperor Hirohito's reign of Showa, or enlightened peace, a campaign of heavily weighted propaganda and revelations of discriminatory U.S. laws against Orientals, such as the Exclusion Act, bombarded the people of Japan by factions that disdained the West. The goal was to foster anti–U.S. opinions. Hirohito was twenty-five when he ascended the throne as emperor. He preferred many Western concepts and material things but was pressured into maintaining and promoting traditional Japanese culture and quest for world dominance. In fact, he backed his cabinet's proposals for Japanese aggression and war until he surrendered in the fall of 1945, when he was at last convinced Japan had lost the war.

Citizens of the United States in the 1930s generally supported an isolation posture with regard to world events, but this was not shared by most in the U.S. government. One of the preeminent names of World War II in the Pacific theater is General Douglas MacArthur, but his larger-than-life reputation was built during World War I. He was decorated nine times for heroism while fighting in France. At thirty-eight, he was promoted to general and became superintendent of West Point the next year. After a stint as Army Chief of Staff, MacArthur retired from the army in 1936, a requirement before accepting the position of Philippine field marshal. His first time in calling the Philippines home was when General John J. Pershing posted MacArthur to the Philippines in 1922.

Japanese ambitions as a world power did not wane after its takeover of Korea. A secret strategy for expansion lingered with little impetus behind it for some time until the invasion of China. Part and parcel of the dream to become a world power was the reality of the Japanese people's needs. Japan's population density threatened total consumption of the country's natural resources, making it necessary to obtain them elsewhere. Japan set its sights on oil, rubber, and other minerals in Indochina. The new twentieth-century plan to facilitate this, the Greater East Asia Co-prosperity Sphere, sprouted from Nobuhiro's seed. The first foreign land taken into the fold of Japanese expansion under this plan was in Manchuria, where Hideki Tōjō gained prominence as commander of the Japanese military policy.

Japan began its invasion of China in 1937. This was a far greater endeavor than Korea and required far greater resources and compliance from its citizens. To this end, Japanese children were taught a three-pronged curriculum in schools beginning at an early age. They learned to worship the emperor, be completely self-sacrificing, and think militaristically. Tōjō was appointed Japan's Minister of War in 1940 and was by far the most powerful cabinet member and most ardent advocate of Japanese aggression.

Japan's march through China from Shanghai, a military effort we have come to know as the rape of Nanking, made headlines in the Western world but was largely ignored by Americans who were reeling from the Great Depression and dust bowl. In places closer to the action and controlled by Western countries such as the Philippines, the daily papers kept the news of Japan's incursion into China out of the columns or gave the story short shrift in a single line that was oftentimes inaccurate. By 1939, Japan occupied all the cities of coastal China, north China, and the Yangtze Valley up to Hankow.

It was not until decades later that scholars attempted to accurately quantify Chinese casualties inflicted by the Japanese. Nineteen million is Iris Chang's estimate, and that number lacks an accounting of tortures, rapes, and other atrocities that did not end in death.³ At the time, the bigger headline news about war came out of Europe. Adolf Hitler's unbounded appetite for power moved his troops through countries neighboring Germany. His aggressive Nazi military methodically captured one European community after another. U.S. President Franklin Roosevelt wanted to join in the defense of Britain and other Western European nations facing Nazi domination. However, a divided and mostly isolationist citizenry pressured Roosevelt into keeping American troops out of the early years of World War II.

At the same time, Tōjō and other influential military men were busy modifying the Bushido code of the highly revered samurai to "whip the Japanese people into a war mentality."⁴ They inserted rape, murder, and torture into the code. Repugnance for surrendering to an enemy was highly praised and not expected to occur. The Japanese military liberally applied the new aspects of the code as they advanced through China.

The Greater East Asia Co-prosperity Sphere was published for the world to see in March 1941.⁵ It states Japan's ambition for cooperation and social harmony of the five races (i.e., the Chinese, Manchus, Koreans, Mongolians, and Japanese). Not surprisingly, Japan assumed they should be in the lead role over the five races as well as the responsibility for guiding those people who lacked capacity for independence. Also, and not very surprising, is the assertion that Japanese interests take precedence over those of any other country.⁶

Roosevelt and his cabinet kept abreast of the world's circumstances as a heightened sense of impending danger seeped through the administration in Washington, D.C. The U.S. Naval fleet was ordered from San Pedro, California, to Pearl Harbor in May 1940, probably much to the displeasure of Britain's new prime minister, Winston Churchill, who wanted U.S. resources sent his way. But for all its foreign policy maneuvering, the United States was impotent as a world power while Japan and Germany callously pursued their dreams. Nonetheless, the United States began preparing for the worst in the Pacific. All military dependents were ordered to leave the Philippines amid a modest number of U.S. regiments arriving in Manila in the first half of 1941.

2

Sign Me Up!

President Roosevelt pondered the situation in Europe and the Far East for a seemingly interminable time. How could he convince Americans not to ignore the tragedy striking out against democracy in other parts of the world? After six months and on the precipice of his third term as president, Roosevelt delivered his State of the Union address replete with his most alarming rhetoric to date. It was January 1941.

Americans listened as the New Yorker's aristocratic voice called for U.S. industries to manufacture arms that could be provided to democratic countries under siege and bolster our own arsenal to protect the United States. Undoubtedly, his prediction was influenced by watching England's struggle for survival against the backdrop of the Allied evacuation from Dunkirk, France, in May 1940, German takeover of the country the next month, and the air blitz on London that began on September 7, 1940.

Army Chief of Staff George Marshall continued exposing U.S. military deficiencies trying to convince Secretary of War Henry Woodring of the problem.[1] The message: The United States was unprepared to fight any battle of consequence. The conclusion: The United States was vulnerable. Roosevelt incorporated need for U.S. military preparedness into his next radio address on January 6, 1941. Not until he reached the tenth page of this twelve-page address did he mention nonmilitary programs for Congress to fund.[2] It was imperceptible if his ardent arguments swayed popular opinion on the war in Europe, but the Japanese invasion of China definitely sat on the back burner of world concern. Even the sinking of the USS *Panay* by a Japanese air attack a few days before the Nanking invasion did not incite the people of the United States.

It seemed that in New Mexico, the idea of remaining isolated in a hostile world was not a foregone conclusion. A large number of New Mexican enlistees were among the approximate 1,800 troops on the New Mexico National Guard roles by the end of summer 1941. Errett Lujan enlisted on March 28, 1940. Alongside him were Bill Brown, Jimmy Lopez, Francis VanBuskirk, Jesus Silva, Bob Duran, Richard Daly, Charles Safford, Eloy

Ruiz, Jim Sadler, Tony Reyna, and Gabby Rivera, to name a few. The primary reason behind most of the enlistments, though, was not necessarily to join against aggressions by other countries but to earn a decent wage. The 14-percent unemployment rate in prewar Santa Fe[3] was a discouraging prospect for landing a job. Joining the National Guard gave one a secure income. Sadly, nearly half of the New Mexico troops would not return home except as memories.

At the time, Santa Fe's population was just over twenty thousand. In a town that size, everyone knew everyone, and Errett tended to know the girls his age better than the boys. He simply enjoyed female companionship more than the boys.[4] The girls had a reciprocal attitude toward him often while he jerked sodas at a downtown store. The manager, Mrs. E.P. Moore, said he was "the most charming employee I had."[5] He was also the youngest at seventeen. The boy Errett probably knew the best was Jimmy Lopez, although Bill Brown turned out to be the person who weighed most heavily on Errett's mind in his postwar years. Billy, as he was called then, had a sister two years his junior. The Brown family lived in Tesuque on the northern outskirts of Santa Fe.

Nothing much was discussed about the world situation or U.S. policies at the Lujan dinner table or any other time. They received most of their news via the radio as most people did. Jess listened to news and programs during the day as she cleaned house, baked pies, and washed clothes. The radio was usually turned on at suppertime, too. The whole family listened to the evening broadcasts, feeling safely isolated from world events and could not imagine how they could be affected since they did not believe the war in Europe or anywhere else would affect them. The attack on Pearl Harbor, the Philippines, and other Pacific islands drastically changed their connection to the radio and their stakes in world events.

Germany's invasion of Poland and abuses of Jews within Germany itself made headlines in the newspapers and prompted newsreels on the subject that were shown in theaters across the United States. Even Americans who were more aware of world news were at a loss as to what the United States realistically could do to help. The skepticism was valid. Domestic affairs and the American economy were still suffering from the one-two punches of the Great American Depression and the dust bowl of the 1930s. Families who lost their livelihoods as farmers moved into nearby cities or set out for California trying to outrun the great dusters of the western Great Plains while holding on to the few scraps of belongings they did not have to sell.

In the mid–1930s, the downtown Washington Avenue National Guard Armory in Santa Fe was declared to be inadequate in size and scope of facilities needed to conduct proper training. In its stead, plans for a new

2. Sign Me Up!

compound on nine acres of land already owned by the National Guard and located two miles south of downtown were finalized on April 22, 1938. Governor John E. Miles managed to overcome the financial constraints imposed on federal monies for military projects, such as the newly proposed New Mexico National Guard buildings, and the needed funding to proceed with construction solicited bids for a new armory.[6] National Guard construction and camp training activities drew many a young man's attention, including Errett's. It was a signal of hope and prosperity.

The architecture was to conform to the new Santa Fe style popularized by engineer-architect John Gaw Meem. Construction commenced on the heels of closing the bidding process. Planners incorporated a caretaker's quarters along with the normal amenities of an armory. The relatively new National Guard rifle range built in 1935 augmented the new facility. It was situated in hilly, undeveloped land about three hundred yards

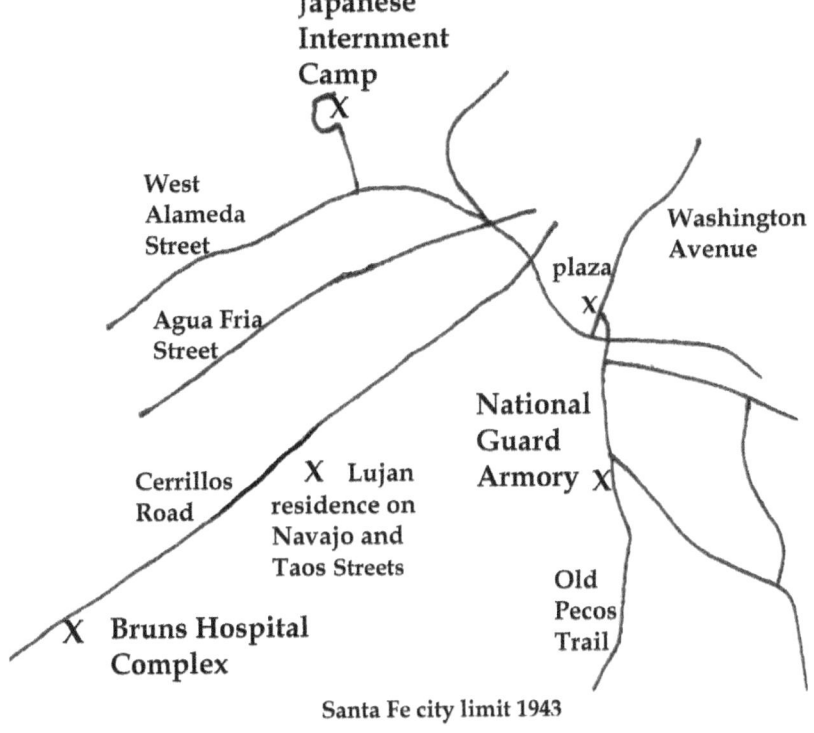

The major streets in Santa Fe, New Mexico, in 1943, showing the locations of the second National Guard Armory location, the Japanese internment camp, Bruns Army Hospital, and the Lujan residence on the corner of Taos and Navajo Streets.

northwest of the Santa Fe National Cemetery on the north edge of town and a stone's throw from what was to be the Japanese internment camp later in the war.

In spite of the lack of a formal declaration of war, the National Guard leadership felt war was inevitable as evidenced by their drive to train recruits in combat as quickly as possible. In the summer of 1940, the U.S. Army and National Guard initiated a series of training classes in the use of coastal artillery equipment at Fortress Monroe in Virginia. Within six months and continuing through the summer of 1941, Colonel Charles G. Sage along with more than twenty officers and a considerable number of enlisted men of the 207th New Mexico Coast Artillery regiment who were under his command successfully completed six months of antiaircraft operations training there as well.[7] The tall, mustachioed Colonel Sage had "the natural bearing of a general,"[8] a rank he later achieved when war broke out in the Philippines. The Deming, New Mexico, native was well respected by his men. Colonel Sage was equally, if not more, impressed by his men and would genuinely be shaken by their fate as POWs. Upon their return from Virginia, the freshly trained marksmen of the 207th, now redesignated the 200th, led by Sage were called on by Governor Miles to demonstrate their skill. It was a choreographed media event at the guard's annual encampment, Camp Luna, just outside Las Vegas, New Mexico, some seventy miles from Santa Fe.

With the stage set with a small number of national guardsmen, six brand-new antiaircraft guns, and Governor Miles sporting an eye-catching double-breasted suit and dressed completely in white from hat to shoe, the event went forward. Adjutant General Russell Charlton stood in the July heat next to the governor as the gunners ran through their paces with the new equipment. The antiaircraft guns were mounted on a boardwalk with barrels angling skyward and protruding ten feet in the air. Three soldiers were trained as a team to operate one gun. Usually, the biggest soldier was given the task of loading the ammunition into the barrel opening.

Although war raged on in two continents, the United States had not yet felt the financial cost of war, especially in Santa Fe where such trends were felt much later than in other parts of the country. The devastation abroad, however, was considerable. This prompted New Mexico governor Miles to record radio spot messages that began playing on October 29, 1939, calling on New Mexicans to support the American Red Cross European war relief. With New Mexico's help, they could reach the nationwide goal of $10 million. Governor Miles was a popular politician and inspired most New Mexicans to donate. He was first elected as governor of New Mexico in 1938 and again in 1940. He had the ability to persuade people toward his way of thinking and was a tireless socialite. He was as good at

2. Sign Me Up!

staging a media event, like the one at Camp Luna, as he was at dealing with connecting with people one-on-one.

Government officials in Washington, D.C., were becoming more and more convinced that entering the war would be inevitable. On September 16, 1940, the U.S. Selective Service Bill became law, and registration for the draft began one month later. Around this time, President Franklin D. Roosevelt called General Douglas MacArthur out of his fifth year of retirement and back into the U.S. Army to command troops in the Philippines and activate War Plan Orange-3.

War Plan Orange-3 was the code name of a defensive plan for the Philippine islands against a Japanese invasion. Although the name "War Plan Orange" is a 1940s label, its concept stretches back to 1907 and Theodore Roosevelt's presidency when he asked his joint chiefs of staff how the United States could best defend itself against a Japanese military attack. Their answer was to hold the Philippine islands until the navy could send reinforcements there, thus giving birth to the concepts of what would later be called War Plan Orange (WPO).[9]

Orange was the code name for Japan. Other countries were indicated by other colors.[10] WPO assumed the Japanese would target Manila to capture and control Manila Bay and its all-important docks. Even with the details of the plan superbly carried given available resources, the Japanese military was likely to be superior to the U.S. defenses. The authors of the plan recognized the situation and agreed that engaging Japan head-on to keep Manila Bay in U.S. hands would be doubtful. Therefore, the strategy was to abandon Manila and withdraw to the Bataan Peninsula where defenses would be established until help arrived.[11]

At home, Errett was making his own strategic plans. On March 28, 1940, and while a junior at Santa Fe High School, he enlisted in the New Mexico National Guard, 111th Regiment of Cavalry. He was called into active duty the next year, when the regiment was renamed the 200th Coast Artillery (Antiaircraft). There were no discussions with his parents about whether it would be the right or wrong thing to do. Errett decided that the twenty-one-dollars-a-month salary to join the guard was something he could agree to. He simply stated the obvious. His only reply was from his father.

"Well, if that's what you want,"[12] Louis said. Jess and Louis escorted him to the armory. He was not of legal age to enlist without their consent since he would not be eighteen for another six weeks. Without reservations or pause, Jess and Louis signed the papers allowing their underage and only son to join the military. Errett was not unique in his action or his reasoning. Other young men in Santa Fe slowly and steadily volunteered throughout 1940.

New Mexico National Guard units were called to active service in early January 1941 for the purpose of an intense, yearlong training on antiaircraft guns. Battery C of the 200th was formed by eighty-seven Santa Feans. Other towns and cities comprised other units. Initially, 216 men from Albuquerque were organized into Battery A, Battery B, Headquarters Battery/First Battalion, Medical Detachment, and the Regimental Band; 114 from Gallup formed Battery D; 83 from Clovis formed Battery E and Headquarters Battery/Second Battalion; 189 from Carlsbad and Artesia formed Battery F; 91 from Silver City formed Battery G; 98 from Taos formed Battery H; and the Regimental Headquarters and Headquarters Battery all hailed from Deming.

New recruits to the 200th as well as their comrades already serving were directed to arrive at the new Santa Fe armory on January 6, 1941. The gangly group of mostly high school students and recent graduates who agreed to serve in Uncle Sam's army in the 200th Coast Artillery (Antiaircraft) were sworn in. Activation of the regiment was officially one minute past midnight.[13] One of their first official group gatherings was to listen to President Roosevelt deliver his State of the Union speech via radio.

The newly activated personnel were housed in the new armory where they had an ample, albeit windowless, drill area. But the facility was an inadequate space for honing their skills with antiaircraft weaponry. For a complete retinue of their yearlong training in both equipment use and army regulations, they would move to Ft. Bliss outside El Paso, Texas.

Jess and Louis Lujan, Errett's parents, in the front yard of the house they purchased in the spring of 1943. This photograph was taken between 1944 and 1947.

2. Sign Me Up! 17

Certain precautions were followed in activating and sending entire regiments to army posts. First, tetanus shots were given to each recruit and an immediate ten-day quarantine imposed. Quarantines were standard preventive measures taken to stem the spread of communicable diseases. The north side of the drill floor was to be their home for the next ten days. Given the quarantine, practice at the rifle range on the north edge of town was out of the question. Firearms training would begin at Ft. Bliss. The newness of the place was obvious. Piles and scatterings of sawdust, carpenter's glue, and wood shavings dotted their new home.

For the most part, Santa Feans and the rest of the United States were unaware of the Greater East Asia Co-prosperity Sphere much less that they had in store for them the day that will live in infamy. So while the community carried on the normal course of living—taking care of family members, working, visiting with friends, going to dances, and enjoying *Gone with the Wind* at the Lensic Theater in cushy swivel seats where one could smoke cigarettes—the 200th remained in quarantine. At their around-the-clock home at the armory, Errett and fellow recruits Evans Garcia, Francis VanBuskirk, Richard (Dick) Daly, Vicente Ojinaga, Jimmy Lopez, Bill Brown, and others had no other social activities beyond enjoying the radio, cleaning up the construction mess, learning what they could about their new jobs, and pretending to be draftees for the purpose of honing interview skills of the newly formed unpaid Selective Service Board in Santa Fe.[14] The guardsmen contented themselves the best they could and grinned ear to ear on payday.

Finally, the slow-paced, endless days of quarantine passed. Battery C was taken down to the plaza in the town's center where they were regaled by friends, family, and dignitaries in the afternoon before leaving for Ft. Bliss. The mood was celebratory and spirits were high as they headed to their accommodations for the night before their morning departure. The few without family in Santa Fe were put up in the Montezuma Hotel.[15] Errett and the others from Santa Fe went home for the night. They rose before daylight, dressed, ate, assembled at the plaza, and marched back to the armory one mile away.

3

Antiaircraft Training at Ft. Bliss

They loaded their equipment onto trucks and a small number of soldiers hopped on while Errett and the remainder of the 200th were sent by train, arriving at five the next morning at Ft. Bliss, their U.S. Army installation destination. A several-hour layover in Albuquerque added half a day to their travel time. After such a long trip, Errett was anything but crisp in his new army uniform. Before going to their barracks for a few hours of sleep, they formed a line to receive their dog tags. Errett paused to read his serial number before slipping the 25½-inch silver chain over his head and around his neck. He looked them over never suspecting that the other information on the tag suspended on the chain, next of kin, would come into play in just a little over a year.

During the day, he practiced reciting his serial number from memory—20843147. Unlike those whose number began with "1" indicating a post–1939 regular army enlisted status, Errett's number began with "2," which identified him as a national guardsman activated into the U.S. Army. Later, in the heat of battle in the Philippines, he would learn other hallmarks of a serial number. Those beginning with "6" were given to pre–1940 army enlistees, "3" indicated someone who was drafted, and the second number in the series represented the army unit from which one originally came.

"We got off the train at 5:00 am and came to camp," he wrote home to his mother. "We all have been working all morning and still have lots to do. I am sure hungry. We stayed till 7:30 in Albuquerque. The wind is blowing here at Bliss along with a little dust, but it is warm." He concluded his letter with a request to his mother and the rest to not "worry about me because I'll be all right." He and everyone else were to have the thought of being safe banished from their minds by the end of the year.

His next letter a few days later showcased a clever plan. The first week at the post, he arranged to earn a little more money to supplement his

3. Antiaircraft Training at Ft. Bliss

$54-a-month pay. He loaned out most of his money at an interest rate of 50 cents on the dollar. "Not bad, no?" he boasted in a letter to his mother on January 22, 1941. In Santa Fe, Errett's father, Louis, was now making a little more money at a new job at the state prison working the graveyard shift.

Immediately upon arriving, the soldiers of the 200th were confronted with their stark accommodations. Ft. Bliss, just outside El Paso, conveys a misleading moniker for a post in the middle of the arid Chihuahua Desert, especially in the summer when temperatures soar into the hundreds seemingly as often as the bugle sounds. There was no mistaking Ft. Bliss for anything other than an army post. The barracks that dotted the flat landscape were crowded with men, and other barracks already under construction were identical. The 200th was assigned to their quarters straightaway. Errett wrote home that his bunk mates were "all a swell bunch of boys—Bill Brown, Charles Safford, Jack Rogers, Don Higgins, and Connie Phillips." Bill was five years, six months older than Errett and died overseas, as did Charles and Connie.

The desert landscape was swept away of brush and grasses as new buildings were quickly assembled. Although lacking, little did anyone know then how luxurious the conditions at Ft. Bliss would seem compared to the next five years. By early March 1941, it was decided by senior military officers to reduce the training underway at Ft. Bliss from one year to seven months. They also determined to station the 200th in the Philippines as an integral part of WPO. The information, however, was top secret and not shared.

The 200th's barracks were in a section of the fort named Logan Heights. Four other regiments were simultaneously stationed there for training. The men of the 200th were filled with a sense of purpose and were eager to become involved with their training after their dull days of quarantine. They identified Logan Heights as theirs by constructing three concrete markers in front of the 200th Headquarters Battery. Two were identical circular medallions each displaying the Zia sun symbol and planted in the desert soil above the official insignia of the 200th Coast Artillery (Antiaircraft) regiment. The crimson Zia sun symbol displays radiating lines from a circle set against a yellow backdrop, a motif that has been New Mexico's state flag since 1925. The regimental insignia is that of two crossed artillery guns overlain with a circular patch sporting a round of ammunition. In the space on top between the gun barrels is "200," "AA" on the right, "CA" on the left, and "HQ" below. The 200th CA (AA) insignia was moved to the state capitol grounds in Santa Fe in the spring of 1943 where it remains today, although a newer capitol complex has since been built across the street.

What little there was in the way of grasses and shrubs around the barracks and other buildings was soon stomped into oblivion from the repeated footfalls of the constantly drilling troops. Those repetitive steps were the first in making the men think, move, and act as one—an advantage every military force hopes to have over an enemy.

Errett, at his new rank of corporal, and his battery buddies headed out on a convoy in mid–March as part of their training. It was his first. They drove twenty-five miles out, set up tents and equipment, took it all down again, loaded up, and headed back to Ft. Bliss. Errett crowed about how fast they put up their tents in three minutes and complained when the brass told them it needed to be faster. He was confounded and wrote to his mother on March 12, 1941, "What is going to be good enough?"

Their guidebook, the 1941 *Basic Field Manual of Military Training*, contained the official protocols and goals for a well-disciplined soldier within the structure of three levels of training—basic, technical, and tactical/logistical. In it, the overall purpose of their training was clearly spelled out as "the assurance of victory in the event of war" through "conditions which may face the Army of the United States" that "cannot be definitely foreseen."[1] This basic underpinning, it states, was to guarantee domestic peace and international security of the people. Basic training goals were itemized for instructors and recruits alike. The men were to become well disciplined, physically hardened, qualified to march, proficient in the use of weapons, and learn to care for himself and his transportation in the field in order to have the ability and desire to take offensive action in combat. They were to achieve this through following their leaders. Their leaders followed their progress at Ft. Bliss by monitoring their ability to follow instructions and pass training and tactical inspections.

Momentum to shore up military prowess was also building on the national level. The U.S. Navy was organized into the Atlantic, Pacific, and Asiatic fleets on February 1, 1941. By mid-month, the War Department issued a call for more than 34,500 national guardsmen to be activated by June, and by February 20, more than five hundred U.S. troops from places other than New Mexico carried aboard the USS *Grant* arrived in Manila. Governor Miles issued his own encouragement to this end by proclaiming February 12 through 22 as National Defense Week in New Mexico.

As fresh recruits at Ft. Bliss, the 200th were given an orientation to their post surroundings, listened to lectures, learned what was expected of them, and were told other administrative information they should know. In short order, they knew when paydays were scheduled, how to get a furlough pass, where they slept, ate, and showered, the general rules of the post, and developed some animosity toward the troops from Chicago

3. Antiaircraft Training at Ft. Bliss

along the way because "they all think they're a bunch of big shots," as Errett described them in one of his letters.

Some occasions were splendidly celebrated, like Army Day, April 6. The pageantry stunned Errett. "It sure was a big day for the Army and people of El Paso. I never saw so many horses, trucks, and men!" he wrote his family. He quickly learned that Army Day was not the army's birthday, as he assumed. Its birthday is June 14 and would be another post-wide celebration. Originally May 1 was chosen as Army Day in an effort to counter the Communists' celebration of Workers' Day. In 1929, Army Day was shifted to April 6, the day the United States entered World War I.

In the mornings, the time of day when they presumably possessed their greatest mental concentration, trainees at Ft. Bliss were usually in the classroom. Anyone prone to nodding off in class was cured in the afternoon during their next phase—physical training designed to increase their stamina, endurance, and strength for morning classes. According to the manual, physical training drills were practices that were to follow a standard procedure and be formal, precise, and brief and augmented by practicing with weapons and equipment. Those who went on to the intermediate level of instruction studied articles of war, orders, military courtesies, and military customs. Upon proficiency in the basic and intermediate training programs, a recruit could request or be considered for technical training.

Training was supposed to be varied and avoid monotony. The scope of training in discipline, first aid, sanitation, physical training, marching, countermeasures to elude detection, chemical weapons, camouflage, signal communication, weaponry, equipment, tactics, team building, and taking care of one's own shelter, supplies, movement, and security implies that there was, indeed, variety.

New recruits and draftees trickling into Ft. Bliss swelled the original New Mexico National Guard contingent. Eventually, the 200th more than doubled in number, from about eight hundred men to eighteen hundred. One who trickled in was Harry Steen, a buddy to many already in the 200th. He was living in Albuquerque at the time and registered for the draft in 1940. He thought his number 264 would not be called up for a couple of years, but by the end of March 1941, he received his summons. He reported for duty in Santa Fe on April 3, 1941, and was sent to Ft. Bliss. In two weeks, he joined his buddies of the 200th Coast Artillery.[2]

Errett, like all of the soldiers, took a turn at guard duty. May 5 was one of those days for him. His shift was thirty-six hours, from 4:00 a.m. on the 5th to 4:00 p.m. the next day. "It's not as bad as it sounds," he wrote in a letter home on May 6. "I had two hours on and four hours off."

The brass announced to the press that the 200th would be training in southern New Mexico for several days beginning on May 9 in the vicinity of Black River. Kept a little closer to the chest and out of the press was the deployment of more soldiers to the Philippines when two thousand landed in Manila on April 22, 1941.

While trainees were in the field, Major General Innis P. Swift was installed as the new commanding general of Ft. Bliss. Led by Swift, the senior officers at the army post created a more intense field training schedule, including night convoys, to meet the still-undisclosed timeline and place to send the regiment. Training the men to move convoys as efficiently as possible was deemed extremely important with respect to WPO being a withdrawal plan. Most deemed it merely as a succession of simple road trips. The intensified training was slated for July 20 through August 8.

The stepped-up training pace interfered with visitors who would have otherwise visited Errett at the post. He looked forward to these, saying in a letter to his sister Merle that it was those face-to-face times that he got "all the inside dope" about what was happening at home. He also left behind a girlfriend he stole from Frank Gomez but did not take that relationship too seriously since he was now dating a blonde who worked at the post canteen.

Colonel Sage, commander of the 200th CA (AA), recorded the number of the New Mexico regiment to be comprised of 77 officers and 1,954 enlisted men. It was about to expand quickly. With two days' warning to the public, President Roosevelt ordered the induction of nine hundred thousand men from the draft beginning July 1, a few of whom would be added to the 200th.

During the intervening weeks before resuming convoy maneuvers, the 200th practiced shooting their antiaircraft equipment without ammunition since it was in such short supply. With the arrival of Brigadier General Spiller, commander of the country's entire antiaircraft training program, a twenty-one-day practice ending in a firing competition between the 200th, 206th, 260th, and 63rd regiments was scheduled using live rounds. The target was a long cloth sleeve about the size of a bomber fuselage. For the competition on June 4 and 5, a large airplane towed the target at the end of a five-hundred-yard cable. Spiller was unabashedly fond of his home boys from the state of Washington antiaircraft regiment who happened to be simultaneously training at Ft. Bliss with the 200th and openly ridiculed the "boy scouts from New Mexico."[3] He was looking forward to what he believed to be the superior marksmanship of the D.C. boys.

During the live firing, Company C of the 200th shredded the target with four rounds, an impressive feat since it usually takes two or three shots just to hone in on a target. Companies B and D of the 200th showed a high degree of accuracy, too. The other three regiments had different results, much to the chagrin of General Spiller. As he looked on in disbelief, he watched his boys take control of their guns only to miss the target completely. In fact, their aim was so poor that the shells exploded closer to the airplane than the target. In an act of self-preservation, the pilot ditched the cable with its target and left the area. Spiller's expectations also vanished. At the end of the day, Batteries B, C, and D of the 200th had the highest accuracy.[4]

The achievements of the 200th probably catapulted them to the Philippine islands. Spiller may have had his favorites, but he was going to recommend posting the best in the Pacific. Their reputation for being excellent cavalrymen was now enhanced to include being the best anti-aircraft regiment, regular or otherwise, then available to the U.S. armed forces and it prompted their early departure five months prior to completing their training. The 206th, 260th, and 63rd were not sent to the Philippines.

Antiaircraft guns were not simply pointed at a target and shot. Operation required a team working on a twenty-four-foot-long height finder, a director (analog computer), and the guns themselves. Four men worked the height finder—one observer looking into the binocular eyepieces,

Official photograph (partial), Company C of the 200th Coast Artillery (Antiaircraft) regiment while at Ft. Bliss. Errett is the fourth from the left in the front row; on his right is Felipe Trejo and on his left is Bill Brown, both of whom died in the Philippines in 1942.

two men to rotate gears to adjust the scope, and another man to record a series of numbers once the target was in its crosshairs. The numbers went straight to the eight-hundred-pound director. Another three—the gunner, fuse setter, and trainer—loaded and operated the gun as directed by the gun sergeant. Francis VanBuskirk, Tony Reyna, and Errett Lujan were among those trained as height finder readers or stereo observers. Looking through the lenses of the height finder, the observers' job was to match up vertical and horizontal patterns in the reticle when viewing the target through the lens. When the points aligned properly, the observer shouted, "READ!" This was the signal to the reader to enter the numbers and press the button that sent the coordinates to the director. When the points from the director matched those on the gun, the command was given to fire the three-inch bored gun. Each director had the capacity to process information for four guns simultaneously.

A lasting memory occurred in June, a particularly dry month in the arid Southwest, yet this year was worse. A drought had settled over the area. The Taos Pueblo Lujans in Battery H took it upon themselves to relieve the situation. They did a rain dance. Soon, it began to rain, then pour, and the dancing continued. It rained so much that Colonel Sage was compelled to order them to stop.[5] They danced another time to exorcise an outbreak of meningitis that required several batteries to be quarantined.[6] Errett was glad he was not stricken and simply enjoyed the mesmerizing sounds of footfalls and Indian song rolling across the desert.

Soon enough, the troops at Ft. Bliss once again left the army post for maneuvers in the southern New Mexico desert. They headed out the same day Errett's one-month confinement to the post ended—the result of having been picked up by the military police (MP) for joining in a brawl in town. Although his confinement had ended, his reduced rank to private first class was still in effect. The Franklin Mountains, located just behind the Organ Mountains in the Southwest, were included in the route at the last minute to give the men practice in areas similar to the mountainous zones of Mt. Samat in the Mariveles Mountains and Mt. Silanganan in the Bataan Peninsula of the Philippines that would likely be traversed in a withdrawal from Manila. These similarities scrapped the alternate training venue of Louisiana, which was not a place Errett wanted to be at the height of summer.

Training on this outing began with forty-eight hours of war games followed by overnight stays in Deming, Albuquerque, and Carlsbad to practice quick convoy maneuvers. Before heading back to their home base at Ft. Bliss, the men were treated to a tour of Carlsbad Caverns. Their arrival on Saturday in Albuquerque brought out unprecedented crowds. Thousands of people lined Central Avenue from the Old Town Bridge to the fairgrounds to watch the 200th regiment parade past them.

3. Antiaircraft Training at Ft. Bliss

In fact, each town they came through garnered cheering crowds issuing accolades to the guardsmen. Due to the enormous turnout of support, the field exercise was extended a few days in hopes the press would continue to cover their popularity. The troops finally returned to Ft. Bliss around August 14. Less than one week later on Tuesday, August 19, Errett wrote Merle that the men of the 200th were told "we have until Friday to send all of our own clothes home because we're to leave for California where we will board ship on August 27th."

During their training at Ft. Bliss, the men routinely requested and received furlough passes for a night out on the town of El Paso. Errett, never one to pass up the opportunity to mingle with the ladies, met Miss Lilly Bodillo during one of these outings. Between returning from the field maneuvers and leaving Ft. Bliss for the Philippines, he had proposed to Lilly and she accepted. The grapevine worked well, and Jess was soon told that her son was going to be married. She wrote him asking if it were true. He strongly denied it, beginning his defense in his responding correspondence with "you think I have gone nuts?"

At last on August 19, the men were told their training was to be cut short. Their reputation as one of the best, if not the best, antiaircraft regiment caught up with them. Bill Brown received some bad news around this time. His twenty-one-year-old sister, Betty, and only sibling had been killed in a car crash about three days before Bill shipped out.[7] Billy knew his mother was strong but nonetheless had a sense his deployment would add to her distress.

Errett was certain, and correctly so, that the news of him being shipped out to places unknown would be taken hard by his own mother. To soften the blow, he wrote his sister Merle first so she could break the news in person and provide whatever comfort she could render. She synopsized the information to Jess and Louis and then handed the letter to her mother. Jess read her son's words in his August 19 letter: "Everything is going to be all right. Those bums over there are just about all pooped out and it can't last much longer. Don't think we are going over there to get ourselves all killed. That is the last thing the U.S. is going to do. They are not going to fight for a long, long time. I don't think they will. They don't need any more men to help them, all they need are guns, food, and all that stuff and I know every man and woman over here will say the same."

The men were to leave for their new and as-yet-unknown destination in two staggered groups beginning August 22. Errett and the other Santa Feans completed a little over seven months of training by then, but many others who joined the regiment during the summer had far fewer weeks under their belts. During their few days in preparing for their departure, they speculated about where they might be going. Most had never heard of

Bataan, or Manila, or Pearl Harbor, so among the guesses, those places did not rank among likely destinations.

Many of them thought it a good time to visit with one of the sixteen chaplains stationed on base. Given the advance notice, several of the men's families were able to be at Ft. Bliss when the men left. Jess drove herself, Merle, and Carmen Saddler there to send off their loved ones. Carmen was married to Jim Saddler who was part of the 200th regiment. Louis could not get off work, so he stayed behind with Claire.

Errett departed with the first group. His most extensive traveling to date was riding in the car his mother drove to Waco, Texas, to visit Sam Naylor, his maternal grandfather, and convoy training out of Ft. Bliss. He loved his sisters and father, but he had an abounding love for his mother. Each felt a tightening of the heart and it was a difficult goodbye for both. The 200th regiment's band began playing the state song, "Oh, Fair New Mexico," as the wheels of the train slowly began to turn. Jess, Merle, Carmen, and other families stood on the platform engulfed in mixed vibrations of music and horsepower, waved farewell to the westward-bound train until it was out of sight, and then solemnly slid into their cars and drove home.

4

Deployment to the Philippines

The train left Ft. Bliss on August 24, 1941, heading for San Francisco and stopping frequently to allow the men to get off and walk about during the two-day ride. As Errett and his friends stepped off the train about halfway to their destination, they speculated if Hawaiʻi is where they would end up. It was a stark contrast to where they stood now—in the desert near Yuma, Arizona, with the noon sun beating down on them spiking the thermometer to around 112°F. Then, to their surprise, a bellowing drill sergeant ordered them to do calisthenics. Their visions just moments before of basking on tropical Hawaiian beaches evaporated in the surrounding heat waves.

Errett tried not to put too much energy into the workout. The parched earth reflected heat that radiated through his shoes in a matter of seconds. He caught a glimpse in his peripheral vision of someone to his right out of sync with the group followed by an uncoordinated scuffle of feet and a puff of dust. The same thing happened again to his left. About five minutes into the drill, the guy in front crumpled and fell in the same manner.[1]

Catching sight of the men collapsing like rag dolls, several officers bolted off the train and toward the group. "Hey! Hey! Let's stop this. Stop this! Get back on the train."[2] Each sweating heap of khaki-clad soldier splayed out on the ground was helped to his feet by those closest, a scene that was to be replayed many times under even more dire circumstances in the next few years to come.

The military ports at San Francisco were humming with personnel on August 25 and they took center stage in Errett's head. The new arrivals from Ft. Bliss dressed in their khakis noticed all the other soldiers wearing their woolen winter uniforms. The men from New Mexico thought these guys were perhaps headed for colder climates. The 200th moved from the train to a baggage ferry that dropped them off at Ft. McDowell on Angel Island located next to Alcatraz Island where they were to be detained for a short spell. As Errett stepped aboard the ferry, he was struck with the realization that it was his first time ever on a boat. They tried to get a good look at the twenty-two-acre island of Alcatraz. Some of the men had inklings of its history as a federal prison. It served as a military installation from 1850 to 1934, after which it was redesignated as a federal prison and remained in that system until 1963. American Indians occupied the facility a couple of times, once in 1964 and then again from 1969 to 1971 in unsuccessful attempts to acquire ownership.

Braving the elements on deck was unpleasant and the short boat ride to Angel Island solved the mystery of wearing winter uniforms in August. It was freezing! Before the goose bumps could retreat, the men received a series of inoculations, such as for yellow fever, and were then led into the chow line. By many accounts, the food on Angel Island was the best they ever had. Errett had the added pleasure of gaining his corporal stripes back.

The day before departing the West Coast, the stevedores loaded their transport, the USS *President Pierce*, while it was docked at Angel Island. The cargo was basic necessities of mostly oil, water, and food along with equipment and supplies. Errett was astounded at the amount of fuel the *Pierce* burns when underway. The oil alone had to be enough to fuel the *Pierce* at the astounding rate of "1,000 barrels a day," he wrote to his mother on September 2. After eight hours, the job was done. The *Pierce* was an American president liner chartered by the army and obtained from the Dollar Steamship Line on August 3, 1941. Its function now was to transport troops across the Pacific.

The following morning, August 28, various rumors spun through the men of the 200th aboard the USS *President Pierce* regarding their still-undisclosed new post. They weighed anchor at nine that evening, cruised under the Golden Gate Bridge, and headed west into the open sea only to encounter mechanical problems that necessitated their return to Angel Island. The problem was fixed that night, putting them back on course the next day. The second battalion was shipped out a week later aboard the USS *Coolidge*, the same ship General MacArthur and his wife sailed to Manila on when returning from their honeymoon in 1937.[3]

The trip from San Francisco to Honolulu lasted nearly a week. Errett described the voyage in several letters he wrote his mother while on board and readied them for posting once he reached Hawai'i. "The water is just as blue as if someone put bluing in it. And there sure is a lot of it, believe you me. I haven't been one bit seasick," he conveyed in an August 30 letter. He slept in what looked like a hammock, and each man in the regiment was assigned a job while sailing. Errett was a runner, or page boy, delivering messages from one officer to another.

4. Deployment to the Philippines 29

On September 2, the day before the *Pierce* reached Honolulu, Errett penned another letter in which he laments, "Have had about enough of this boat ride. If I ever have enough money to decide to take an ocean trip I hope someone shoots me. It's not that I have been seasick or anything, it's just too much damn water." The *Pierce* stayed in the Honolulu port one full day to allow the guys a little sightseeing time and load the cargo holds with supplies, equipment, and vehicles once again. They had a little more help this time from the 14th Bombardment Squadron who joined them in Honolulu for the rest of the trip.

They were met with a heightened sense of seriousness when they returned to the ship at nightfall and got underway. The USS *Phoenix*, a cruiser in the near distance but barely visible because both ships were following blackout orders, escorted the *Pierce*. The *Phoenix* was bought by Argentina after World War II and reconfigured into a battleship that they used to invade the Falklands in an attempt to wrest the colony from the British. The English sunk the ship during battle in April 1982.

Long after Hawai'i receded from Errett's view, he found a comfortable place on deck to write another letter on September 11. "I did not think much of Honolulu. It has rained now for seven days. It has let up now so I washed my clothes and hung them over the railing to dry. I washed four pants, four shirts, three underwear, two towels, twelve pairs of socks. I am not very good at washing so I was surprised when I saw they were clean."

It was a few days of wandering around the ship before the 200th discovered where they were headed when they came across their artillery pieces clearly labeled MANILA. Crates and windshields of what turned out to be P-40 airplanes were likewise labeled. The bombardment squadron insisted they were told that their deployment was for six months. Errett happily conveyed this information home to his mother on September 14, adding, "I will be back before you have time to miss me."

Word spread quickly, but few knew their geography well enough to have a sense of where they would be stationed or what the climate had in store for them. Diseases such as malaria, dengue fever, amebic and bacillary dysentery, skin mold, and flatworm and roundworm infections ran rampant in the Philippines. The peninsula of Bataan had on record the highest incidence of malaria in the Philippine islands at the time.[4]

Blackout conditions lasted the entire voyage to the Philippines. This held true even when they encountered a typhoon on the night of September 12–13. The storm started innocently enough with just a little rain. Then more rain came, lots and lots of it. Errett could not see fifty feet in front of him. They spent thirty-six hours, mostly in the dark of night, battling ninety-mile-an-hour winds and sixty-foot waves that covered the whole ship when they crashed down. Even with the portholes closed,

Luzon, the main island in the Philippines. Errett was stationed at Clark Field, which was part of Ft. Stotsenburg.

water seeped below deck. When the storm subsided in the early hours of the 14th, the "sea was just as smooth as glass, just like looking into a mirror."[5] The typhoon added perhaps two days of travel time to their schedule. Now they had only 689 miles to go to get to the Philippines according to information Errett wrote home on September 14. Seasickness was pervasive with or without the storm, but Errett continued to escape that malady. Some were still bent over the side as the *Pierce* approached Luzon, the main island of the Philippines, from the southwest through the San Bernardo Strait on a relatively calm day.

The *Pierce* reached Manila Bay on September 16, 1941. It was an exotic place to the men of the 200th. Dawn had not yet cast the day's first light,

4. Deployment to the Philippines

and a blackout was imposed while Errett and the others were trucked to Ft. Stotsenburg. On occasion, they would spot the leader of the Filipino aborigines, the Negritos, dressed in top hat and loin cloth. Upon arrival, Errett wrote home on September 16 that "when I get home I will have a lot to tell everyone. I think I will like it here. I can say I have been half way around the world and still like the good old U.S.A. the best."

Three days later, he wrote home in a little more detail. "This is a very nice place. A little warm. The people here look very poor. There are about twenty people to each [and] they all live in little grass huts. We don't work but a half a day here on account of the heat in the afternoon. We get paid in Philippine money. An American dollar is worth two in Philippine money," he wrote his grandmother on September 19. Indeed, his paycheck on September 30 was 158 pesos, and after paying off his loans, he had 30 left. "Things are cheap to buy here," he wrote Merle the same day and postulated, "we might be here one year at most. I am going to try and get a letter out on every clipper."

They found other things not quite so amusing and encountered some trouble in trying to adjust. The most notable was the climate. New Mexico is part of the greater arid Southwest where the rainy season is three to

Errett, the newly arrived soldier standing outside his barracks at Ft. Stotsenburg around October 1941.

five weeks of afternoon downpours. In contrast, the guys were now living in a place where the rainy season was sixteen weeks of constant rain. The winter garb that they acquired after the bone-chilling excursion to Angel Island was now soaking wet and plastered to their bodies from the sweat coursing from their skin from the excessive heat.

The remainder and majority of the 200th regiment put into the Manila dock aboard the USS *Coolidge* ten days later and carried the bulk of the 200th's equipment in addition to another tank battalion and air corps they picked up in Hawai'i. The *Coolidge* followed the same route to Manila as the *Pierce* without encountering a typhoon. Their trip was comfortable and enhanced by the many luxuries still on the ship that were remnants of its cruise liner days. The battalion received inoculations while sailing to help protect them against the tropical diseases common in the Philippines.

Like those on the *Pierce*, most of the men had never been on a ship or seen the ocean. At Pier 7 in Manila Bay, the *Coolidge* passengers disembarked, hopped onto the open-air Combusto buses, and started out for Ft. Stotsenburg just before sunset to join the smaller group of the 200th who were already there. The horizon was a brilliant red and the most beautiful Errett had ever seen. The peace surrounding him at the time lasted long enough for him to receive three paychecks.

Manila, capital of the Philippine islands, is on its largest island of Luzon. The well-trained Thirty-First U.S. Infantry Regiment had been stationed in the country for many years and was the only army infantry regiment there when the 200th arrived.[6] The United States maintained five army posts and one navy base in the Philippines. The installations included recreational facilities. Those stationed there and their families could play tennis, badminton, and polo and bowl.

The army established Ft. Stotsenburg, one of the five army posts as a cavalry base a short distance from Clark airfield as well as the main base of the Army Air Corps in the western Pacific. Weekly polo matches were held there since that is where the horses were kept. The Philippines in general is mostly mountainous. Peaks in ranges were used as landmarks in describing one location or another. Clark airfield lay at the midpoint between Mt. Arayat to the east and Mt. Pinatubo to the west. The Ft. McKinley firing range was seven miles from Manila and Camp John Hay lay north of Manila near the Cordillera Central Mountains next to Baguio. Sangley Point airfield and hospital, part of the Cavite Naval Base near Mariveles, was across Manila Bay and south of Manila. Cavite had long been recognized as one of the finest ports in the bay. Ft. Mills, south of Bataan, was on the protruding land mass of Corregidor Island in the mouth of Manila Bay. If one draws a straight line southwestward from Ft. Stotsenburg to the Bataan Peninsula, then due east to connect Manila, and

4. Deployment to the Philippines 33

finally northwest back to Ft. Stotsenburg, the result would be a symmetrical triangle with the fort anchoring the top. Field artillery training was concentrated at Ft. Stotsenburg.

Men aboard the *Pierce* were also unfamiliar with their new station. The place could not be more different than the high-elevation environment of the arid Southwest. The 7,100 islands comprising the Philippines are a few thousand more than the total number of towns and cities in New Mexico. The area of ocean that contains the Philippines is more than five times the size of New Mexico. The voyage across the Pacific Ocean had some effect on acclimatizing the men to the higher humidity of the tropics, and they soon learned some of the nuances of living so close to the equator. Unlike their hometowns, there was no twilight or dusk. It simply went from daylight to dark as if a light switch was flipped off at night and on in the morning. They would not, however, experience the rainy season until they were embroiled in a battle for their lives.

Of course, what caught the men's attention first were the trees, so different from the piñon, juniper, and pine of their homes. Their eyes were met with an abundance of giant hardwood timbers, a variety of smaller softwoods, and bamboo and rattans too plentiful to count. It was easy for Errett to sense that considerably more than half of the land was covered with forests and was, for him, as opposite as could be from the desert of southwest Texas, the tail of the Rocky Mountains surrounding Santa Fe, or the Great Plains of eastern Oklahoma.

Dense tropical forests covered the volcanic mountains jutting dramatically upward adding height to those four-thousand- to six-thousand-foot peaks that looked like they were pulled up by a giant's hand from the surrounding lower elevations. The flat lands not being cultivated were blanketed with thick, coarse grasses, most of which was the noxious, weedy cogon grass that could grow to ten feet. The other predominant vegetation in those areas was mangroves growing in swamps.

Vague shapes of the jungle growing up to the road he was on were beginning to take on shape and color as dawn neared. He had never seen even pictures of such beautiful flowering plants. A profusion of ferns and plants had stuffed themselves in the spaces between adjacent tree trunks forming a fantasy tapestry. He sensed a light breeze blowing from the north as he took in the view developing with the approach of morning. The prominent direction of the wind would change twice more with the seasons, but he would be a POW before he experienced all three.

It was the job of the 200th to protect Clark airfield from enemy air attack using the type of antiaircraft weapons they had trained on at Ft. Bliss. The infrastructure of Ft. Stotsenburg was inadequate, even more so than what greeted them at Ft. Bliss in January, but Errett had a nice Kodak camera that he intended to use a lot. They slept in a tent camp nestled between Clark airfield and the fort grounds and, by day, built their own barracks using "wood and woven bamboo sides that went up only half way to the roof, creating an opening to aid in air circulation. The barracks were about half a block long and housed thirty men," as he described it to Merle in a letter of September 30. The makeshift quarters did not disrupt their daily routine. Prompted by the first bugle of the day, the men rose, dressed, stood for roll call, washed, shaved, made their bunk, cleaned their area, and ate breakfast before beginning drills. Weekend passes could be had. Errett asked for one on October 4. It would be his first trip to Manila.

Live ammo was issued as part of personal field equipment within four days after arriving. Standard prewar field packs contained a blanket, half shelter with tent poles and pegs, raincoat, socks, leggings, gas mask, canteen, weapons, and some hand grenades. In the ten weeks before the Japanese attack on Pearl Harbor, Clark airfield, and Ft. Stotsenburg, the 200th set up camp, received field gear, unpacked equipment, acclimated to their new surroundings, socialized on and off base, and practiced shooting the antiaircraft guns without live ammunition. The last antiaircraft gun practices the 200th did with ammo before they were attacked was at Ft. Bliss.[7] No practice rounds for their three-inch guns were available. The lack of equipment, ammunition, men, and training was pervasive in the first few years of the 1940s. Ft. Stotsenburg, for instance, was protected by one-fifth the number of men required for its size and strategic location.[8] To give the illusion of a stronger force, the army contracted with some local Japanese men to build several decoy P-40 airplanes out of straw. "They were lined up on the tarmac at Clark Airfield with the real airplanes."[9]

Occasionally, they engaged in night drills. Tracks around the airfield supported eighteen-inch searchlights that operators moved around. The antiaircraft teams would chase the lights. The guns were loaded onto trailers and pulled by trucks from one location to another. Selecting a good gun site was to pick advantageous locations suitable for firing but obstructed from clear view. Each height finder required a ten-foot pit up on a ridge. The guns themselves were situated below. At one point, a B-17 fell out of the sky when a searchlight temporarily blinded its pilot during a night practice. Everyone held their breath, but as it turned out, the pilot was able to safely land his plane and no one was hurt.[10]

Complaints among the men were few. Everyone was enjoying being in the Philippines. The four army posts and navy base in the Philippines came with tennis and badminton courts, bowling alleys, and polo fields that the men referred to as playing fields.[11] They were buying tailor-made clothes for the first time in their lives and drinking beer, gin, and sometimes rum. The availability of alcoholic drinks was unprecedented in their lives. Most had never drunk gin before, but it was appealingly affordable. About thirty-five pesos would buy a fifth of gin. It instantly became the "drink of choice."[12] Overindulging was not uncommon and sometimes done to steel the nerves to sample unusual food delicacies of the island. A favorite among the locals were baluts, those half-term duck eggs buried in the sand at the shoreline and left to rot over a few weeks, then soft boiled before being cracked open and consumed. One could also try the chocolate-glazed, crispy fried, extra-large locusts.

Troops in the Philippines by October 1941 gave no indication or received any signs from the chain of command that war was imminent. Correspondence centered on family. In fact, Errett began his last letter before his status changed from free man to POW, with condolences on the death of Andres Lujan, one of his father's six brothers. Each of Errett's other uncles had sent him letters, which he read all the while crying. He was determined to answer them all. He added he had grown to a thirty-two-inch waist size, then he concluded in a nothing-to-worry-about manner and wrote to his father on October 18, "If we have to show those Japs how to behave, us boys from New Mexico can do it."

In Japan, aggressive military action was being planned by Hideki Tōjō, the new premier. There were a few Filipino civilians and fewer Japanese civilians working on the army bases in the Philippines. As it became known later, some were part of a fifth column or spies for the Japanese. Interactions with them were pleasant. The men had no inkling of what they were up to.

What was to be the last shipment of supplies into Manila before the war started arrived on November 10, the same day Errett's family posted a Christmas package to him in which Merle included a nice wristwatch. Was it bombed, burned, lost, stolen? At any rate, it never arrived, nor was it returned.

Equipment, ammunition, and weapons just off the assembly line arrived. Ordnance personnel organized the shipment according to standard procedure, and its newness bolstered confidence in their ability to answer an attack if it did ever come. In the heat of the battle when the shiny new grenades were plucked, triggered, and tossed, that confidence evaporated faster than the water boiling in a machine gun cooling apparatus. Most were absolutely no good, and it cost some of the men their lives.

Michael Gilewitch, a supply officer, promptly received word of problems with the ammo from the new shipment that he had distributed. He picked out a couple of grenades and .45 caliber bullets. He unscrewed the top of a clean and supposedly flawless grenade "and found to my horror, not one grain of powder in it!"[13] He had been told that the .45 caliber bullets sounded like a pop gun when fired. He took a pair of pliers and carefully pulled it apart only to find a minute amount of powder in the cartridge. He spent the next few moments raging about the situation to his superiors and then set about trying to remedy the problem.[14]

A couple of weeks before war started, the commanding officer at Ft. Stotsenburg canceled all leave. It was a Saturday afternoon and several men were enjoying themselves off base. They were searched for, ordered back to base, and told to dig in because war was expected any minute. The men got busy. They set up six different searchlight locations encircling Clark airfield. Each one was about fifteen miles from the field. The men stayed at ready in their positions around the clock for a week. Normally, an "at the ready" order would be the green light to set the accuracy of the antiaircraft guns. To do this, five rounds of ammunition would be shot to set the accuracy of the guns. But orders from Washington to save ammunition and forgo this step were still in place. By the end of the week, around November 23, no enemy appeared, nor were any approaching as far as they could tell. They were to stand down for now, so they moved back to their tent camp at Ft. Stotsenburg.[15]

There was certainly something afoot in Japan despite the lull at Ft. Stotsenburg. Hirohito convened the first meeting of the Japanese Diet since Japan's invasion of China in 1937. Army General Masaharu Homma moved his command post to Formosa. Activity stirred within the Japanese navy, too. Japanese submarines left their home bases and headed for Hawai'i on November 18, 1941. Their plan was, of course, to attack Pearl Harbor, a seemingly contrary move to Hirohito's proclamation that his was a regime of Showa, or enlightened peace. Something violent, indeed, was well underway.

Newspapers back in Santa Fe were picking up some of the innocuous movements of the Japanese and of U.S.-Japanese relations. The better part of four pages in the *Santa Fe New Mexican* published in late November were dedicated to Japanese-U.S. relations. It was reported that Japanese representatives met with the American ambassador and secretary of state. Japan seemed committed to economic and, if necessary, military domination of the Orient just as the United States was clear that Japanese expansion could go no further without risking war. Such newspaper articles may have added to the worry of the Lujan family. They had not heard from Errett for some time, so they wrote him on December 3 wondering what was happening around him. That letter never made it to the Philippines. Mail service was suspended after the attack.

Japan issued seven demands that most felt would put the United States under Axis domination if agreed to. The first two dealt with our interference with Japan's invasion of China. We were to stop sending aid to China and leave China free to deal with Japan alone. Three other

4. Deployment to the Philippines

demands concerned recent U.S. actions that stymied Japan's economy. They insisted that the United States remove the blockade around Japan, release Japanese funds frozen in the United States, and restore all trade agreements. Additionally, they insisted that the United States recognize Manchuko and acknowledge Japan's priority right to rule a Greater East Asia Co-prosperity Sphere in the Pacific.

Perhaps the most crucial news anticipated was that from a meeting between U.S. Secretary of State Cordell Hull and the Japanese envoy concerning the ever straining relationship between the two countries. The outcome of the meeting was reflected in the November 18, 1941, headline on the front page of the *Albuquerque Journal*: "ALL SILENT AFTER PRESIDENT TALKS WITH JAP ENVOY." The feeling echoed across the country, but Admiral Nomura of the Japanese navy summed up the one-hour-and-twenty-three-minute meeting with this quote in the paper: "Many things said." What was left unsaid is probably the grandest omission of all—Japanese submarines were already headed to Hawai'i. Orders to attack Pearl Harbor were issued on December 2, and with that, Japan had made a fateful decision. The 200th, now at a level of 1,809 men (1,732 enlisted men plus 77 officers) along with the other troops in the Philippines and Hawai'i, were soon to pay the price. On the U.S. side, it was clear that talks dodged all queries as to the growing crisis between the United States and Japan. A measure of optimism was inserted with a reference to another meeting between the parties. Secondary articles brought news from the European front concerning war waging between Germany and Russia. In the private talks with Hull, it was made clear that the United States was not interested in meeting any of Japan's seven demands. Within a few days, Japan announced that the U.S. terms were unacceptable. Whether the 200th and other U.S. troops stationed in the Philippines thought Japan's announcement was relevant to them is unclear, but senior military officers were quick to take stock of their defenses in the Philippines.

On December 3, 1941, General Jonathan Wainwright was named commander of the northern Luzon force. Approximately twenty-three thousand American troops had arrived in the Philippines by this time.[16] Wainwright ordered ammunition for the antiaircraft guns issued to troops at Ft. Stotsenburg and for gunners to resume their stations with their equipment. The crews placed their guns in position in the sugar cane field around Clark airfield making sure to encircle them with plenty of sandbags. With all of this going on, most of the men sensed something big was about to happen but were nonetheless surprised when it did. Radiomen at Clark airfield stuck close to one of their newest pieces of equipment, the 268, the forerunner of radar.

News updates in New Mexico continued to focus more on the Pacific where a large portion of their male population was stationed. Within a couple of days of the 200th digging in once again, their families and loved ones were informed that they had been put on alert. Most did not worry so much about it, though, because indications were that negotiations with Japan were still in play and had a good chance of reconciling the problems. President Roosevelt also weighed in sending an appeal to Hirohito to maintain the peace on December 6, 1941.

5

Combat Begins

The Imperial Japanese Navy attacked Pearl Harbor, sinking or damaging nineteen ships and killing 2,300 people on December 7, 1941. It occurred at 1:00 a.m., December 8, Philippine time. Errett Lujan, Harry Steen, and others of the 200th Coast Artillery slept in their barracks at Ft. Stotsenburg. Those on guard duty were among the few awake at the time. It was a strike of historical magnitude unimaginable at the time. It would not be the last one of the day.

The Philippines was acquired by the U.S. government through a treaty with Spain concluding the Spanish-American War of 1898. The treaty was ratified by Congress in February 1899, making the Philippines a commonwealth of the United States. It was critical to the Japanese to capture and control those islands to eliminate the effect U.S. blockades were having on oil shipments coming to Japan from the East Indies. General Homma's orders cascaded down the ranks of officers. Some three hundred Japanese airplanes took off from the general's base and staging area in Formosa, resolute in their mission. Their bearing was almost a due south route to Luzon in the Philippines. Hours later, Hong Kong and other British possessions, Guam, the Philippines, and Wake Island were hit and hit hard. The Philippines was bombed nine hours and forty minutes after the Pearl Harbor attack began at locations miles from where Errett and the 200th were at Ft. Stotsenburg. The loss of life did not begin to reach that at Pearl Harbor, but it was the first step in a succession that created a Japanese stranglehold on American interests in the Far East.

Night shift office workers at American military installations in the Pacific usually tuned their dials to Don Bell's radio program, a favorite among the American soldiers. This morning, however, casual attentiveness gave way to shock and drama. Bell cried and was nearly hysterical. His words bellowed from the radios: "Those dirty little bastards have struck Pearl Harbor! Reports remain sketchy." He continued, "But there is no doubt! Oh, God!"[1] The soldiers in the Philippines were stunned. Shortly before Bell's report, Tony Reyna of the 200th answered a ringing telephone at his field post. The captain speaking from the other end of the line relayed the shocking news.²

The horrifying turn of events passed through the night duty shift like embers of a wildfire. A guard coming in to replace Harry Steen said, "The Japs hit Pearl Harbor last night."³ Steen found it difficult to process the magnitude of the information. He had never heard of Pearl Harbor, nor had most. Steen abandoned his usual stroll to his tent. Instead, he ran to his barracks. He hollered and shook everyone awake. With drowsy faces and eyes blinking from interrupted slumber, they followed his directions. Radios clicked on simultaneously moments before the fort's alarm sounded. They were to man their positions and stay on high alert. The men at Ft. Stotsenburg would not have another peaceful day in their lives until September 1945.

The allocation of U.S. Army forces in the Far East was concentrated in the Philippine islands across three defense zones. The north Luzon force under General Wainwright was to defend the main island of Luzon from Manila northward using four divisions and one regiment. Wainwright's zone also hosted two divisions that comprised the reserve force. The defense of the southern portion of Luzon, which included a sliver of the northern coastline of Mindoro, the closest of the large islands to Luzon, was known as the south Luzon force and assigned to Brigadier General George Parker and his two divisions. The bulk of Mindoro and the remaining eight other large islands of the Philippines were left to the Visayan-Mindanao force under General William F. Sharp and his three divisions.

Errett Lujan and his buddies of the 200th Coast Artillery (Antiaircraft) regiment had the distinction of being the largest American military unit in the Philippines when the fighting broke out.⁴ The 200th was part of the north Luzon force and responsible for protecting Clark airfield, which was tucked into the southernmost edge of the north Luzon zone. There were four other coast artillery regiments. The others were strategically scattered throughout the islands. Two were Philippine scouts (91st and 92nd regiments) and two were U.S. military (59th and 60th regiments). The 200th is, in fact, credited with being the first unit in MacArthur's command to fire on the enemy and probably the last to fire before the battle for Bataan ended.⁵ Two kinds of other American artillery were on the battlefield. One was armor piercing and sent shock waves through the ground like small earthquakes when they hit. A near hit by these guns chased Japanese out of caves later in the battle where they hid. Antipersonnel weapons were the others. They flattened all vegetation they were shot through.

Flying in from the west from behind the looming Mt. Pinatubo,

5. Combat Begins

ninety-six Japanese twin-engine bombers first pierced the morning skies in their "V" formation high over the heads of the 200th around seven. They flew too high to readily identify. As they drew closer, the men working the height finders soon verified they were enemy planes. Captain John W. Turner gave the order to fire when the targets were within range. Richard Daly clearly remembered thinking "the war was on!"[6] At the time, the United States had fewer military personnel than either Portugal or Greece.

The first wave of Japanese planes came and went. Errett and the others standing ready to protect Clark airfield spent the morning on high alert in their respective defensive positions. They peered through the lenses of their height finders scanning the sky for incoming enemy. Suddenly, the distinctive drone of airplanes coming in from a distance broke the silence, and tension among the soldiers became palpable. The sound grew from a buzz to a roar while spotters looked the planes over. A collective sigh soon went up. The planes were some of the seventy-five P-40s that lifted off from Clark airfield around 6:30 a.m. to patrol the region. They flew in long bunches in circling patterns like vultures hoping to pounce on some morsel to relieve their empty stomachs. For the pilots, the hope was revenge and the morsel was a Japanese plane. The airmen continued their patrol flying over the gun emplacements off and on all morning.

The predawn news that tightened every fiber of Errett's body a few hours earlier relaxed incrementally as the morning wore on. Others felt the same. Chatter elevated and smoking cigarettes helped pass the time although Errett did not have any on him to smoke. His were in his footlocker with the rest of his gear. Soon, a pack of cigarettes being passed around came his way. He plucked a couple, lit one, and leaned against an incline pot marked by large dollops of shade. The twenty-six or so fully loaded B-17 bomber pilots were ordered to remain grounded until there was confirmation of a potential target. The planes sat side by side on the tarmac enveloped by an eerie quiet throughout the morning.

The all-clear signal broke the monotonous waiting at 11:30 a.m. Needing a break and low on fuel, the P-40s returned to Clark airfield after five hours of patrolling the sky. Pilots and ground troops filled the mess hall to grab something to eat. Most had missed breakfast to answer the callout alarm. On their way out of the mess hall, troops were issued gas masks, but only part of the men received them. Incoming enemy planes were spotted, and once again, the alarm blared. It was 12:35 p.m.

Men outside when the alarm sounded snapped their heads back to look up. They strained their necks and squinted into the noonday sun trying to make out the silhouettes flying in their "V" formation toward them. Harry Steen counted fifty-four Japanese bombers[7] in the first wave of the attack, a little over half as many as Daly counted earlier that morning.

Tony Reyna recalled being in the chow line. He did not get a meal, much less a mask.[8] Others bolted from their lunch without having taken a single bite. Men exiting the mess hall reached for masks, then ran in every direction like marbles rolling on a hard surface.

Winston Shillito spotted two groups of high-flying bombers, still too high to see any markings, leading the attack.[9] Even though they had been on alert for the past two weeks and had seen the Japanese bombers a few hours earlier, many of the men's first reactions were to think the planes were American. Reality clipped short their thoughts as the whistling of falling bombs emerged from the drone of the plane engines. Then the whistling sounds gave way to that of fully loaded, fast-moving freight trains.

Men dived into trenches and clambered to their weapons waiting for a chance to take a shot. The 200th's guns were essentially useless against the first wave of bombers. The American gunners had three strikes against them: most of the Japanese bombers flew higher than twenty-seven thousand feet and out of their range, the men did not have time to properly set their shots for accuracy, and the aged ammunitions were largely duds. By the time they fixed the shot to improve their aim, the bombers were out and the Japanese pursuit fighter planes, Zeros, were bearing down on them. Notwithstanding these difficulties, Corporal William "Shorty" Coleman from Santa Fe and Sergeants Joseph S. Smith and Paul "Doc" Womack of Carlsbad managed to each shoot planes down later on in the afternoon.[10]

Japanese Zeros came in crisscrossing each other and strafing one transect after another over Clark airfield and its adjoining army base. Although moving at speeds considerably faster than the bombers, they had to come in low on a target to inflict damage. It was the time the 200th had waited for. With lightning speed, the elevation men began reading their height finders, traversing men made sure the information from the directors was sent to the correct guns, and the others fed the guns with what they hoped to be deadly ammo, but the damage inflicted was minimal. The small indistinguishable markings on the undersides of the wings took shape as big red dots as they neared. That simple symbol seemed to fill their whole field of vision and an unfamiliar feeling of fear mixed with anger penetrated Errett's very core. It was a feeling that was to last a lifetime for him and many other survivors of the war.

The stomach-turning feeling temporarily evaporated just as quickly as it had come when, one by one, the order rang out. Fire! Every gun of the 200th fired repeatedly. It was not long before VanBuskirk found it difficult to see through the lens of his height finder given the density of smoke, dirt, and debris in the air. He pulled a cloth from his trouser pocket he had

5. Combat Begins

tucked in there, rubbed off the film, took one reading, rubbed again, and repeated the process over and over.[11]

The menacing "V" of bombers appeared over other places in the Philippine islands, dropping their lethal payloads on Iba airfield, Aparri, Davao, Nichols airfield, Cavite Navy Base just south of Manila, Baguio, Camp John Hay, and Tarlac. Total allied casualties on Philippine soil reached into the hundreds on this first day of World War II in the Far East Pacific.

Toward the end of the pummeling at Clark airfield, a couple of pilots flying P-40s were able to take off, but they were too few against vast odds. The pilots knew they were considerably outnumbered but no doubt concluded that it was better to use the planes for what they were intended rather than let them be sitting ducks on the ground. Errett watched the deadly game play out overhead. A Zero was on the tail of the first one up before the P-40 gained enough altitude to maneuver well. The chase lasted only seconds before the P-40 was riddled with bullets from the Zero. First Sergeant John Gamble of the 200th put his sights on the Japanese fighter, forcing it to abandon pursuit of the P-40, but that still left the P-40 pilot in the air in a crippled machine. Gamble's crew tracked the damaged P-40, their hearts pounding louder, it seemed, than the explosions surrounding them. At last, the pilot ejected, parachuted to safety, ran toward Gamble, and thrust out his hand. Still shaking from the episode, the pilot thanked him for saving his life.[12]

The pilot of the other P-40 did not last much longer in the air. The melee was intense. This time, unfortunately, the plane was shot down by friendly fire. Much to the relief of the team who shot it, the uninjured pilot managed to land his plane in a nearby field. The pilot scurried to the nearest wall of sandbags. As VanBuskirk followed the pilot's trail alongside the tarmac, he noticed something quite interesting. The straw bale P-40s made as decoys by the Japanese contractors were completely intact—an unbelievable coincidence. "I figured the Japs had been told they were fakes."[13]

Errett checked his watch when the shelling stopped and the smoke began to clear. They had endured the bombardment for over an hour. From what he could see in the smoke-dimmed light of the sun, the men around him were okay, but the scene on Clark airfield and Ft. Stotsenburg told a different story. The attacks were devastating. Everything was on fire or engulfed by thick clouds of smoke. Burning rubble replaced the barracks, mess hall, and headquarters.

Sergeant Richard Daly returned to his barracks with a detachment of men to recover what was left of their personal gear. It was not much. The only salvageable item from Daly's partially burned duffel was a pair of shoes that were serviceable only after he pulled shrapnel from the heels. The devastation depressed him, but his mood was lifted by an unofficial report from the MP. Apparently the rapid-fire 37-mm gunners shot down about five Zero fighters. One of the pilots bailed before crashing and floated down onto the slopes of Mt. Pinatubo, the jungle home of the Negritos, the dark-skinned aboriginal people of Luzon. The Negritos captured the Japanese pilot, lashed him to a pole, and carried him into Ft. Stotsenburg like a trussed pig to barter with the Americans. A deal was struck, and the Negritos returned to their homes with a sack of rice and some beer.[14] The Japanese pilot was one of the first POWs held in the Philippines.

Spies operating in the Philippines were reportedly aiding the Japanese by guiding their pilots using flares and lights in houses during blackouts. Intelligence may have been sent to Japanese ships using signal lights before the bombing.[15] Other Japanese spy networks discovered that roughly half of the Japanese men in Manila were well prepared to join in on the invasion of Luzon when it came. Many were incarcerated in Bilibid Prison in Manila.[16]

Back at Clark airfield, those who were able searched the bombed-out installation for wounded and dead. The bad news of what was found on the road between the airfield and buildings circulated among the 200th that afternoon. The first of the 200th to be killed in action were Privates First Class Roy Schmid and Private Douglas Sanders from the neighboring towns of Roswell and Hagerman, respectively, in southern New Mexico. They took a direct hit while driving their trucks.[17] Eight more from the regiment would be killed in action before their surrender.

Two days later, the war in the Pacific intensified. The Japanese landed at Aparri and other places along the northern Luzon coast. Six Japanese transports were bombed off Vigan, with one sunk and serious damage inflicted on the others. Although the United States experienced some success off Vigan, the Japanese inflicted heavy casualties in the bombing of Cavite Navy Base, Nichols airfield, Nielson airport, Ft. McKinley, and the Manila suburb of Pasay.

Some distance from Clark airfield, other U.S. casualties were adding to the statistics of the first day. A Japanese force captured a small detachment of forty-nine marines when they overwhelmed them and took control of their transport, the U.S. gunboat *Wake*, as they evacuated Tientsen in China on December 8. Several hundred miles due east across a vast portion of the Pacific Ocean, the Japanese gained their first major foothold when Guam fell in Micronesia. The cost was 400 American sailors' and 155 marines' lives. It would be many months before the United States gained the upper hand in the war.

The effect of the first day of war on Clark airfield crippled much of

5. Combat Begins

the U.S. air power. All but seven of the B-17s parked on the runway and about fifty-five of the seventy-two P-40s were completely destroyed. Nearly every truck sustained damage. Another casualty was the movie theater where *Gone with the Wind* was scheduled to be shown that night. It was demolished.

Nichols Air Base, about eight miles south of Manila, did not fare any better than Clark airfield. The majority of airplanes were destroyed, their parts strewn everywhere. Hangars were torn apart into confetti-like pieces. Barracks and buildings were crushed and burned. A straight line could not be followed more than a few yards before coming to a bomb crater. Wainwright sent orders for the 200th to be split into two antiaircraft regiments, the provisional Manila group and 200th, after the initial bombings halted. A problem existed in Manila. There was no coast artillery unit in place to defend Manila. Troops such as the machine gunners set up in the Sunken Gardens, that vast grassy area immediately outside the walled city of Intramuros known as the city within the city of Manila, were vulnerable to air strikes. Officers began selecting five hundred men for the new Provisional 200th Coast Artillery (AA) of Manila regiment that Colonel Harry M. Peck of Albuquerque would command. Colonel Memory H. Cain remained with the 200th as its executive officer.

The provisional Manila group, renamed the 515th Coast Artillery (Antiaircraft) regiment, mirrored the organization of the 200th except the 515th did not have an E battery. In these regiments, Batteries B, C, and D operated the three-inch antiaircraft guns. Battery A manned the searchlights. Batteries F, G, and H manned the 37-mm guns. Battery E in the 200th had the .50-caliber machine guns, and since the 515th lacked an E battery, the .50-caliber machine guns were equally dispersed throughout its other batteries.[18] Errett, Bill Meyers, Jesus Silva, Winston Shillito, and Bill Brown were among the five hundred troops selected from the 200th for the 515th.

The new 515th regiment, augmented by 175 men from the Philippine army, assembled at 8:30 p.m. the night of December 9, loaded themselves onto trucks, and covered one hundred miles of roads before reaching Manila and Ft. Santiago where they would receive newly arrived equipment from the reserves stored at Ft. Santiago. They made good time without interference from the enemy, arriving at a Manila baseball diamond at two in the morning where they spent the night. Before sunrise, they moved out, quickly threading their way through heavy Japanese fire directed at destroying key transit sites in an attempt to fracture the enemy into small groups, isolate them, and prevent them from moving their equipment. As they exited the developed landscape of the area around Manila, they entered thick jungles crammed from the canopy downward with trees, brush, plants, and vines. As Errett and the 515th pushed farther south, the density of trees thinned and intermingled with farmland.

The easier-to-travel open land could have been a relief were it not for Japanese snipers with mouths taped shut and literally tied to the treetops to avoid detection if they happened to be shot. As long as they remained gagged and lashed to the trees along with their rifles, they would not fall to the ground or make any sounds and had a greater chance of confusing their enemies and not betraying their whereabouts.[19] The snipers used rope to climb trees and secure themselves into position. They wore green cloth hoods and mosquito netting over their helmets and had with them a five-day supply of rations, water, quinine, first aid kit, gas mask, extra socks, a toothbrush, gloves, and chlorine to purify their water.[20] Once past the farmland, the company plunged into groves of thick, multitrunked banyan trees so dense that the bombs sometimes could not penetrate their umbrella-like canopy. The route had been dark the entire way. Lights were not used, and GI blankets had been tacked up over windows in the buildings the military occupied. Even the hospital, which had filled up with the wounded earlier in the day, had blacked-out windows. Basements of the larger hotels in Manila took on the overflow of casualties.

The Filipinos attached to the 515th were mostly farmers untrained in the realm of guns, strategy, and other military basics. Although untrained, they proved invaluable. They were issued two-wheeled carts and assigned to certain groups of Americans as support personnel. They filled carts with ammunition, gasoline, kerosene, and any other items needed by the gunners. When they were not hauling or fetching supplies, they dug emplacements and filled and stacked sandbags. In other units, Filipinos filled in as fresh troops, also largely untrained, when an American company pulled back after several days of fighting.

Errett's battery was moved southwest of Nichols airfield on December 16. The adrenaline from the day carried the 515th through the busy night. They uncrated, cleaned, and assembled guns and the other equipment throughout the night. When the 200th first arrived in the Philippines, all of their guns and equipment were ready to use. When they pried open the crates with crowbars at Ft. Santiago, they were confronted with odd shapes of thick black goop. Errett felt frustration building up in him. He wanted to put the weapons together fast. He wanted to be ready for another attack as quickly as possible. He did not know how long the job would take now. There seemed to be more gunk than equipment in the crates. The gunk was standard Cosmoline, a petroleum grease packed around the unassembled guns to protect the metal from salt corrosion. Errett's anxiety was well placed. It took them considerably longer to clean off the goop than to assemble the parts. Despite the labor-intensive work, Errett's was the first battery of the 515th in position with their new equipment and ready to shoot by mid-morning; other batteries were functional soon afterward. In all, they assembled twelve three-inch guns, twenty-three 37-mm guns, three directors and height finders, .50-caliber guns, and acquired vehicles to transport their equipment.[21] Their indefatigable effort paid off. Japanese attacks on the Manila docks resumed that morning and the 515th was able to send them away short four airplanes and crews. The Japanese became more cautious. The next day, they appeared but too high overhead to be within range of the 515th's guns. The men fired anyway even though futile. It was a spectacular show that the men felt demonstrated to the enemy the defiant stubbornness coursing through their veins.

As bombs dropped around Errett in the Philippines, a big snowstorm hit Santa Fe. When the bombs and snow stopped falling, news of Errett's situation reached his hometown. A kind of stupor blanketed the town. The Lujans and other families hung on every word coming in on the radio about the Philippines. Merle and her coworkers listened to the radio at work, as did people at most every office, home, and store. Jess received a letter from her aunt Abbie Nisbeth. She sent comforting words that Merle forwarded to Errett in a letter dated January 9 and also let Jess know that her seventy-year-old husband, John, "is cranky because they won't let him join the fight overseas. He was right where Errett is," referring to his World War I experience.

Five days after the first attack, the family heard that Ft. Stotsenburg had been bombed and severely damaged but no word on human casualties. The anxiety level in Jess escalated, and two days later, she turned the radio off, made a quick exit from her house, and walked to the Red Cross station in town where she commenced sewing clothes for the troops. She had volunteered the day before. Merle also went, adding first aid classes to her service there.

Two days later, Jess was provided a drop of relief. A missive from General Charlton with the National Guard in Santa Fe was sent to each family of the 200th informing them the soldiers were okay. Jess and Louis promptly wrote their son a letter on December 12 in which she tells him, "We have a Christmas tree that someone gave us but it just sits on the porch and Daddy just stares into space." She put the letter in front of Louis so he could add his thoughts. He penned, "I only regret that I am not there by your side fighting." Louis, at forty-nine, probably would not have been accepted into the army to engage in battle, but he truly wished he was there. He signed the letter, "your dad who is thinking of you and only you. L.G. Lujan." They reiterated several times they were "praying for you."

On December 9, more Japanese infantry landed on the north and west shores of the Luzon coast. With their boots on the ground in large numbers, it was only a matter of time before the many nonmilitary would come face-to-face with the invaders. Orders were given, and two hundred thousand civilians were evacuated. The evacuation was tricky. Manila's docks were assaulted, but most evacuees made it off the island due in large part to the steadfast defense put up by the 515th.

It is often cited that MacArthur commanded one hundred and twenty thousand troops in the Pacific theater when war broke out. Most in this number, however, were the Philippine army and not officially in MacArthur's army until December 19, 1941, when it was inducted into the American army along with General Bailio Valdes, the commanding officer. Major James Ivey, American military, served as headquarters commandant of the twelve thousand Filipino scouts.

Filipinos were a conglomerate of various ethnicities living among the islands. Filipino troops came from almost every group, and Errett befriended several. The broad, flat faces of the Igorots and their short powerful bodies were easily recognizable. They proved to be highly accomplished stealth fighters. They usually struck at night. They slipped their powerful mostly naked bodies through the jungle toward their prey using hand weapons or the occasional grenade. The ears and heads of the Japanese they killed were cut off and brought in to get rice from the Americans. There were also the Cagayanos from the lowlands in the north near Aparri and the Ilocanos who were broadly settled throughout northern Luzon. As is true today, many Filipinos were Christians, a faith that took root since the time the first Spanish settlers who arrived nearly four hundred years before World War II.

Another unmistakable feature of the Filipino soldier was his attire. Their uniform amounted to nothing more than blue trousers and some sort of short-sleeve shirt. They wore no leggings and usually lacked helmets. If they did don head gear, it was made of easily penetrated shellacked canvas or coconut pulp helmets. Most also lacked the U.S. standard issue mosquito nets, dog tags, and blankets. Errett saw the obvious disadvantage of their circumstances and statistics confirmed the concern. Proportionally, they suffered the highest number of casualties due to the lack of helmets, and most Filipino bodies were never identified. Those who were were often the few to whom dog tags were issued or the fewer who had fashioned their own from cut metal ammunition containers.

The Philippine Military Academy at Baguio had been training Filipino cadets as officers since 1935, but enrollment was low compared to the far superior numbers of well-trained and experienced Japanese soldiers under General Homma. Against such a force, the number of Filipino officers coming out of the academy was insignificant. What they accomplished, though, was extremely important.

5. Combat Begins

At the time, the U.S. military consisted of three hundred and sixty thousand of all ranks. When World War II was over, fifteen million had served. A contagious fervor swept hordes of young men between the ages of seventeen and twenty-five into the ranks of the military after the United States and Great Britain declared war on Japan. Japan immediately reciprocated with their declaration against the United States and Britain. Three days later, December 11, Germany issued a declaration of war on the United States.

From the first attack on Clark airfield through Christmas Eve, the troops were bombed every day at noon. Cloud cover often hampered early detection of enemy planes. At night, the skies were lit by flares and tracers. Occasionally, Japanese approaching southern Luzon were picked up by the ECR 268, a primitive precursor to the more proficient radar system developed later on in the war. What turned out to be more reliable than the ECR 268 was Private Gregorio Gachupin's, a Zia Pueblo Indian, and the native Filipinos' abilities to sense the direction of incoming enemy planes before most even heard their engines.[22]

Because they were often on the defensive, enemy shellings dictated the Allies' strategy. As a countermaneuver, they stationed themselves within the visual shelter of an adjacent banana grove with a sixty- to eighty-foot tapestry of tree canopy encircled by a sugar cane field.[23] In certain spots, the gnarled balete trees grew to one hundred twenty-five feet and reinforced the troops' obscurity under its thick, wide canopy. Visibility on the ground was also limited to no more than fifteen yards in the dense jungle. About one and a half miles distant from Ft. Stotsenburg through the banana grove was an abandoned hacienda. The troops converted it into their mess hall.

Shellings of Manila were meted out as regularly as on Clark airfield but with little damage to the troops. Errett considered the poor aim of the Japanese probably par for the course. This, he determined, gave him an advantage. He could more or less live by a schedule of his choosing. Sleep when tired, eat when hungry, and have plenty of time to ready his station for the predictable midday attack. Errett and others moved their emplacements only once during the first two weeks in the Manila camp. Other defenses such as the twenty-four artillery guns stretched across thirty miles to cover Subic Bay.

The 200th and 515th had more practice shooting live rounds in the first week of the war than they did during their entire seven months of training at Ft. Bliss. They learned fast in that first week and quickly devised techniques not taught in the standard training regime. It was easy to see that their P-40 pilots could outdive a Zero. They worked with their pilots to exploit this to their advantage. A P-40 pilot would dive for Manila Bay, pull up at the last minute, leaving the Zero to plunge into water or, at the very least, become an easy target for keen marksmen working the antiaircraft guns.[24]

Because ammunition was lacking for the defenders, certain rules of engagement were issued. The teams were limited to firing six rounds at any one plane per pass. This was often inadequate with regard to fine-tuning the settings of the height finder. Compounding the problem was a 30-percent malfunction rate in the guns due to the age of most of their ammunition.[25] Also, single Japanese piloted planes were not to be shot at unless they attacked first.

The Japanese had their own rules of engagement that sometimes worked against them. The Japanese had what the men described as tunnel vision when it came to flying missions. They habitually ignored potential targets they encountered if those targets were not explicitly included in their orders. Watching hostile planes pass up high-value targets on the ground left Errett scratching his head but thankful that they did.

From December 10 through 14, the Japanese landed troops at Vigan on the upper west coast of Luzon. They were unopposed. Within a couple of days, they had organized themselves, formed a strategy, and began pushing south toward the concentrated defensive lines of the allies. The day-to-day fighting merely slowed the Japanese advance. Setbacks for the allies were piling up. By December 12, the Japanese had gained ground in Vigan, San Fernando, and Lingayen. Japanese bombing raids were let loose on Olongapo, Clark airfield, and Batangas as more Japanese troops landed on the northern coast at Aparri. Nichols airfield sustained substantial damage from ninety-six bombers during a second air raid. In the meantime, since "it was against international law to use shotguns in battle,"[26] the Allied forces in the Philippines were turning in those weapons to central command.

A brief lull presented itself in mid–December. The wounded were moved to triage stations, and the troops rested from constantly moving their equipment to gain better defensive positions. Errett took a moment to send a cablegram home letting his family know for sure he was alive. They replied immediately through the Western Union Telegraph office and told him that mail service was suspended—something Errett already knew. Letters sent in December to him began coming back in the post with a red-inked stamping that read, RETURN TO SENDER SERVICE SUSPENDED. Ironically, the postal service reduced the price of an air mail stamp to 6 cents at this time. Merle also cabled Lilly to tell her they had heard from Errett. Errett was able one last time to cable home just before Christmas. It had the effect he wanted. It made his family's Christmas a little bit more bearable. To make herself more useful to the plight of soldiers,

5. Combat Begins

Merle signed up as a volunteer with the American Women's Voluntary Service just days after her twenty-fourth birthday in early January. Several such auxiliary organizations were operating, but this was the largest in the country. The women were trained to drive ambulances, fight fires, provide emergency medical aid, and attend to other tasks desperately needed during war. It was a civil defense strategy developed specifically to react to hostile invasions of the home front. Merle took three two-hour classes a week during her training.

6

Retreat to Bataan

Authorities in Washington believed early on that winning in the Philippines was not within the realm of possibility given available resources. There were small victories such as when Filipino fighters wiped out a Japanese force attempting a landing at Lingayen on the central west coast of Luzon. That victory and others were overcome simultaneously as three waves of Japanese bombers struck Nichols airfield killing seventy-five and wounding three hundred others. On the other side of the world, Hungary and Bulgaria declared war on the United States. Roosevelt was compelled to funnel the country's resources to the European theater because the odds against making headway in the Pacific were overwhelming and what was at risk in Europe was determined to be more important.

One brief glimmer of hope for the Allies in the Philippines shone temporarily for three days in mid–December when the Japanese were forced into a defensive position. They sustained extraordinary losses during a succession of fourteen air raids during this brief time. Every approach to land their planes was met with heavy artillery fire. In the end, a total of forty Japanese planes crashed into the sea. The shores, on these occasions, were well defended. The pilots swam toward the open sea in hopes of being picked up by their transports. Eight, however, had been sunk and the sea rescue failed. They died in the shark-infested waters off the Luzon coast.

On the nineteenth Cavite and Monte airfield at Mindanao were bombed. Word of the influx of Japanese troops and heavy fighting prompted the evacuation of Paracale, a mining town 125 miles southeast of Manila. Once the people were safely away, the tunnels were dynamited, allowing them to flood. In the fray of intense combat, troops in the Philippines were wholly unaware that Belgium had declared war on Japan.

Allied offensives at Vigan claimed another twenty-six Japanese airplanes and more at Aparri and Legaspi. The Japanese troops moving southward from Vigan, however, were still unimpeded, and as quickly as it seemed the United States had the upper hand, they lost it. The Japanese, with their far superior number of troops, successfully put in troops at Vigan, Aparri, and Davao by December 20. On the 22nd, General Homma's Fourteenth Army landed at Lingayen with an estimated forty-five thousand troops aboard at least one hundred vessels. The full-scale invasion of Luzon had begun, and the only obstacles the Japanese met were high seas and a heavy surf that interfered with their communications systems. U.S. submarines managed to sink a Japanese transport and destroyer, but the Japanese were undeterred. They responded by inflicting heavy bombing raids on Nichols and Zablan airfields and at Panay.

The war continued to deteriorate for the Allied forces in the Philippines. Mindanao (the southern-most large island), Luzon, and Cebu (lying between the two), received thorough bombings. Eighty Japanese transports landed at Lingayen, Luzon, on December 21 and disgorged eighty thousand Japanese army troops, the largest landing to date. Allied combat teams were loaded onto big red buses and headed north in hopes of repulsing the incoming Japanese. Without having a secure passage, the buses came under fire. Most did not reach their destination and became cut off by the advancing Japanese on the side roads.

Examples of some of the best tactics in defending the Philippines on land in December were at Damortis, off the Lingayen Gulf, and San Fabian. After the Japanese landed on the beaches of Lingayen, the Twenty-Sixth Cavalry, a Philippine scout unit, rode into the jungle squadron by squadron on their horses and mechanical conveyances, quickly set up defensive lines, and calmly waited for the enemy. The eight hundred scouts carefully aimed their semiautomatic M-1 rifles with deadly accuracy, nearly annihilating the Japanese force there but at a cost of one hundred and fifty of their men. Every pull of the trigger on an M-1 shot nine rounds.

Most of the M-1s were just out of the crates when the fighting began, and many were not destroyed before surrender. The Japanese preferred the single-action five-round Springfield rifles, so after taking the M-1s from the surrendering hordes, they disabled them.[1] Japanese vessels lined up from Vigan to San Fernando in the waters west of Luzon while the Twenty-Sixth Cavalry continued one withdrawal after another interspersed with discharging their weapons with chilling success. Scouts celebrated their victory over this relatively small piece of land as U.S. troops surrendered at Wake Island.

Advance Japanese patrols were spotted every now and again as they rode ahead on their bicycles through the jungle and through small villages. The seemingly tame scene belied what was in store for the Filipinos. As Japanese troops overwhelmed the countryside, they became crazed with power and acted in a frighteningly similar manner as they had in China. Violent atrocities against Filipino women and children became the norm.

The last step of War Plan Orange-3 was unavoidable. Written orders were issued to withdraw into the twenty-mile wide by twenty-five-mile long Bataan Peninsula beginning at 7:00 p.m. on Christmas Eve.[2] A couple of days before Christmas, the 515th relocated back to Clark airfield and stayed there until ordered to withdraw to Bataan. For protection, they set up at least one hundred yards away from transportation corridors. During their brief respite there, they saw a convoy rolling down the closest road about a hundred yards away. Some of the men in the 515th ran to the road in hopes that it was the reinforcements and supplies they believed would arrive. Their hopes shattered when they discovered it to be a Japanese convoy. They went undetected, cautiously made their way back to their positions, and packed up to head for the interior of the Bataan Peninsula where they would soon be embroiled in the first major U.S. land battle in World War II.

Steen found cases of candy bars in one stash measuring at least fifteen feet long and six feet wide while awaiting orders to move out. "I got me a case of Mounds and put it in my foxhole ... and covered it up with dirt."[3] Twenty other men were somewhat luckier on Christmas Day and enjoyed an eight-pound turkey, pork and beans, cheddar cheese, and a bottle of Scotch.[4]

When the time came to move out toward Bataan, the 515th did so as quietly as possible on Christmas Eve knowing that at least one convoy of Japanese lay somewhere ahead. The bombings seemed to have ceased for the night. As they carefully moved southward, they came around a bend in the road that opened up to a canyon view where glimmering lights on trees greeted their eyes. An orchard in the canyon bottom was lit up with millions of glow worms. It looked as if Christmas lights wrapped all the trees. "You could see every leaf and stem on every tree ... because they were so thick.... It was the most beautiful sight you ever saw,"[5] Steen recounted.

With that beautiful image still in their minds, the 515th arrived around 2:00 a.m. at their new emplacement about twenty miles north of Manila at an ice plant downstream from the Calumpit bridge that spans the Pampanga River. They were to protect the bridge from Japanese bombers. The withdrawal of troops, the flow of former Filipino military troops, and some of the twenty-six thousand civilian refugees stalled traffic at the main junction nine miles north of the Calumpit bridges, backing up foot and vehicle traffic in both directions for miles. Crossing the Pampanga via the Calumpit bridges was either by rail on one span or by a parallel road on another span.

On Christmas morning shortly after Errett's breakfast of half a grapefruit and oatmeal, nine Japanese bombers came in and circled the bridges, apparently formulating a plan of attack. Shortly afterward, they flew some distance away but remained visible in the distant sky for some time. Then

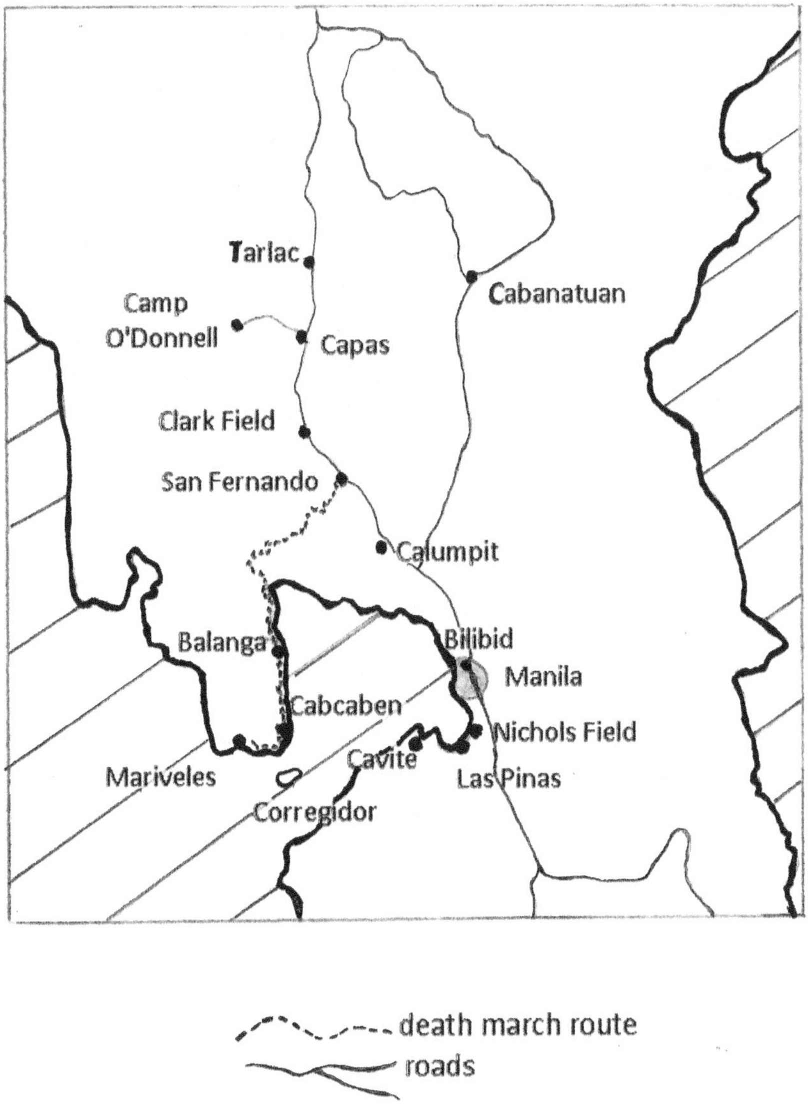

6. Retreat to Bataan

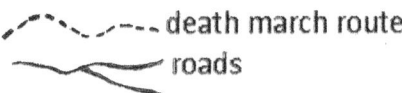

Southern Luzon, Philippines, showing key locations and roads as well as the route of the infamous death march.

they returned in groups of three flying low and straight, a perfect target for the 515th. Two of the first three bombers were shot out of the sky and all their bombs fell into the river. This altered the pilots' strategy and they came in one at a time, low but not straight so their bombs sort of flung out of the planes. None of the seven remaining planes' bombs hit the bridge and they left the area. It was not too very long before another nine Japanese bombers appeared. It was a rerun of the first group's inability to hit the bridge. This left a third and final group of nine planes to move in during the early afternoon hours. They, too, missed the bridge and lost three more planes.[6]

Japanese bombers keeping out of range of the American guns allowed throngs of exiting troops to retreat unmolested as they headed for the Calumpit bridges. The columns of foot soldiers and brightly colored orange-and-yellow buses were easy targets as they traveled south on the only road going into Bataan. Their worried faces often turned skyward, expecting the drilling sound of whistling bombs to pierce their eardrums at any moment. If the order had been issued to the Japanese pilots to attack the retreating columns, most vehicles, what supplies they had, equipment, and thousands of people would have been lost before the retreat to Bataan could be accomplished. While the 515th kept a steady and deadly fire on the Japanese bombers, anyone not shooting was busy transporting supplies from Clark airfield and Manila. Some doubted whether they could maintain the safety of the bridges and keep it intact long enough for everyone to cross.

On the night of December 27, Errett moved with his unit south into Bataan near Mt. Samat for one day and joined the center of the main battle position that crossed Bataan from the west coast of Manila Bay to the base of Mt. Natib. Here, the 515th did not fire their guns as only one enemy reconnaissance plane flew over at high altitude. This encampment was also low on food, so the men butchered the Twenty-Sixth Cavalry horses. The stew was tasty, but Errett, a horse lover, was saddened at their sacrifice.

The 515th left the next night, December 28, and continued their retreat south but stopped for another day in Pilar near the west central coast of Manila Bay. A slow reconnaissance torpedo plane flew over them there, too, but this time, it was low, so they loaded up and brought it down. As it swooshed the crew to their deaths, it passed close enough to clearly see the rear gunner. Much to their astonishment, the gunner was a Japanese admiral.[7] Pilar was another short stop. Errett and the 515th continued their southward retreat arriving the next day at Bataan airfield, their target destination, the night of December 29–30. The 200th set up less than a mile south at Cabcaben airfield when they came in the next night.

Withdrawing became very difficult in certain hot spots as the Japanese provided cover for their major Christmas Day landing. All day long, the Japanese poured into the islands. Forty more transports landed and one hundred more waited just offshore. They could land at any one of the seven beachheads on Luzon they controlled. The heaviest fighting

6. Retreat to Bataan

occurred at Lingayen, the main invasion site, and at Aparri, Vigan, and Legaspi. Atimonan, seventy-five miles from Manila, was hit especially hard. Japanese tanks churned out of Lingayen and drove twenty-five miles to Baguio, another village target. A total of fourteen inland towns were bombed. The American navy and artillery were strafed and bombed from the air while more and more Japanese troops, tanks, artillery, transports, and supplies came ashore. All the while, Allies inched their way toward Bataan at night. A column would withdraw slowly with their rear guard left behind to protect them. Just before dawn broke, the rear guard would move quickly to rejoin those whose backs they covered throughout the night. The movements were repeated nightly.

MacArthur was informed of the British surrender in Hong Kong on Christmas Day and hustled out of Manila. He darted his way to the battlefront between four waves of bombings on the capital. All nearby Allied troops followed suit. Manila had been declared an open city on Christmas Eve, the conventional process to indicate it was no longer a legitimate military target since only civilians remained. But the merciless killings of Filipinos continued for quite some time and could be seen from Corregidor. Schools, hospitals, and churches in Manila were demolished along with innocent people. Corregidor was given a wide berth until December 29, when the onlookers on that tiny tadpole-shaped island became primary targets of the Japanese. Droves of bombers and strafers attacked Corregidor with full force. Some of the raids lasted nearly three hours, and the pounding shook every inch of the island. The 200th was stationed within view of the spectacle. Twenty-seven troops were killed and eighty wounded from the attacks.

Part of the Allied strategy to prevent unnecessary deaths was to dismiss regular Filipino troops from duty in hopes that they could blend back into the local population. According to the plan, only Americans and the Philippine scouts would remain in service to provide a last-ditch defense. Many of the discharged Filipinos discovered, however, they had no homes to which they could return. They were either bombed into oblivion or occupied by the Japanese.

The retreat to Bataan airfield took Errett three days to complete but seemed like three weeks to him. Looming high above his position to the northwest were the Mariveles Mountains. Their new orders were to protect the three or four P-40s still flying in and out of Bataan airfield. Errett and other members of the 515th immediately began to dig foxholes. They worked through the night to establish their gun emplacements in the best strategic locations they could find to provide cover. At daybreak the next morning, three Japanese bombers in the lead of three others let loose on their positions. It was a bitter battle that spanned five days. The determination of the 515th and 200th seemed to match that of the Japanese pilots. None of the few remaining operational P-40s under their protective guns were damaged. Their combined perseverance and success boosted morale of other units when they realized that those antiaircraft gunnery teams made it nearly impossible for the Japanese pilots to get close enough to the retreating infantry to do damage.

Word spread after the first day of combat at Cabcaben airfield that Battery F had taken a beating since they had neither foxholes dug nor guns in position. Battery C defenses of the 200th were ready just in time, but the men sustained a loss that reverberated through their ranks. Photo Joe, a Japanese reconnaissance plane with dive bombing escorts, approached the battery's position. Errett braced himself as the details that happened at an adjacent gun were described. Staff Sergeant Francis VanBuskirk and others pulsed into action as the planes streamed in.[8] First Sergeant Richard Daly and Staff Sergeant Felipe Trejo were sitting outside the gun emplacement[9] on a mound of dirt excavated for a foxhole when the early morning attack came. Their team of gunners held nothing back in trying to down the plane. Their pile of 1930s shells came with one of two kinds of fuses—powder train fuses or mechanical fuses ignited by a timer. Both types were plagued with problems. Half were complete duds and never exploded. Others sported varying degrees of corrosion. The men learned quickly that when the red-and-yellow inserts fitted into the body of the three-inch rounds were faded, which were about five out of six, they usually did not explode, so they tended to use the ones with brass timers. The brass timing device could be manually adjusted to explode a certain number of seconds after leaving the gun. Corroded brass timers were extremely difficult to set.[10]

During the battery's assault on three Japanese bombers this day, a shell exploded from VanBuskirk's antiaircraft gun as it left the barrel. The muzzle burst riddled Trejo with shrapnel from behind. He was evacuated to the closest hospital but died two days later.[11] He was buried at Limay. He was the first and only Santa Fean in the 200th to be killed in combat, and it was the first of many losses to come for Errett. Felipe Trejo left behind a wife, Juanita Trejo, and several family members. It was believed by the witnesses at the time that Trejo had been hit by enemy shrapnel as he tumbled into the foxhole,[12] but Daly inspected the shell parts and found that the timer was stuck at "0" seconds, which caused the American shell to explode directly behind Trejo.[13]

The regiment's morale was dampened by other realities. The defenders were exhausted. Supplies of food, medicine, and ammunition were running dangerously low. Medical supplies were down to a simple field kit of compresses, bandages, and morphine in most areas. Perhaps one of the most regrettable blunders of MacArthur's command was to overlook moving the twelve-month food supply from the main quartermaster warehouse on the island of Cebu[14] and whatever remained at Ft. Stotsenburg to Bataan along with the troops. The civilian rice supply left at Cabanatuan was intentional as it was forbidden by law to move it out of the province. The result was devastating. The fighting men on Luzon were completely cut off from critical supplies and forced into an untenable situation.

A minor, albeit temporary, relief serendipitously presented itself around January 2 when the rice growing around Manila Bay ripened. The fields produced thirty thousand pounds of rice each day, which was equal to about half of the Americans' rice ration. The U.S. Army collected, processed, and consumed it by the middle of February. The twenty-five thousand pounds of bread produced each day for the troops ended two weeks later when the flour supply ran out.[15] A supply of rice and bread, however, is inadequate fuel for human beings to sustain their battle-worthy strength.

At 6:15 a.m. on New Year's Day 1942, and with Japanese ground troops firing at them, the last of the three American infantry divisions crossed the last of the Calumpit bridges, which were then blown to bits. Bridges were always high-value targets for the Japanese. If blown up soon enough, they could not be used by the enemy. On the other hand, if the enemy blew them up after they had crossed but before the Japanese ground troops could, it would delay their advance on the enemy. This conundrum led Japanese air crews on several occasions to not release their bombs near bridges. Everyone quickly learned to recognize when a pilot was really going to let his bombs fall. When bombers with bridges in their sights, or any target for that matter, made an approach, it was low, aggressive, and direct. Pilots simply monitoring those retreating flew high, but there were plenty of bombs and guns directed at those on land. The defenders were aggressive, too. Thirty-six Japanese planes were taken out of commission by the 515th and 200th antiaircraft regiments. This, no doubt, saved the lives of many of the troops making their way into Bataan.

In small continuously moving groups, people made their way into the peninsula where they could finally stop to catch their breath. The trek had been harrowing. Radios were turned on during the welcomed respite on January 5 only to hear one of the biggest lies of the war. Someone declared San Francisco had been destroyed. The fallacious chest-beating propaganda was followed up by a call for Americans to surrender. The Allies responded by moving deeper into Bataan toward their assigned locations using cogon grass and rice straw to camouflage their exact whereabouts. Other radio programs included the *Voice of Freedom* from which reports on the status of various battles in the Philippines and elsewhere in Southeast Asia were aired. Captain Carlos Romulo, the program newscaster, read updates three times daily. He began his first transmission with "People of the Philippines, you are listening to the *Voice of Freedom* from the battlefront of Bataan." By surrender day, the program had aired over three hundred times.[16]

Retreat into Bataan was successful despite the odds, but there was no time for a longer rest. The task at hand for the commanding officer was to select strategically important defensive locations on the peninsula and get the best combination of weaponry to those places. Brigadier General Parker had been given command of the Bataan defense force on December 25 as troops flowed into the peninsula. Parker was "in poor health, lacked the vigor needed to animate soldiers in a desperate situation, and never visited his front lines,"[17] making him a less effective leader than Wainwright, so the officers of the 515th were not quite sure what to expect.

With so few Allied planes to protect at Bataan airfield, the 515th was ordered to move to the front lines for a short time where the final crossing into Bataan via the Culo Bridge was happening. When they fired at planes, they drew return fire from Japanese ground troops about four to five hundred yards away. The 515th gun positions protecting the Culo Bridge were also identified and recorded during the day by a Japanese spotter plane. Errett and the others abandoned their positions during the night and set up elsewhere nearby before daylight. The 515th managed to stay one step ahead by moving each night, avoiding heavy damages or casualties. American troops blew up the Culo Bridge at two in the morning in early January.

Errett had a good look across the bay before returning to Bataan airfield. From his vantage point, he suspected things were not going well near Manila. The reality was worse than his fears. Within two days, Japanese ground forces were within twenty miles of Manila, Laguna was abandoned, and the roads and air were entirely under Japanese control. Japanese tanks and reinforcements rolled into the area from ships in staggering numbers. The 515th pulled out and headed south once again to Bataan airfield.

When the men first got to Bataan, they lined up every day to take a dose of quinine to stave off the effects of malarial mosquitoes. An officer looked on as each man swallowed the pill. Soon, the pills ran out and a bitter liquid form was administered. In one hand, the soldier held out his spoon, which was filled with his dose, and in the other was his canteen. It was imperative to down a liquid chaser after swallowing the quinine. Without a quick chaser or by taking a drink too slowly afterward, the medicine would come right back up. Powdered quinine replaced the liquid form as the former ran out. A prescribed amount of the powder was spooned onto a square of toilet tissue. The tissue was folded around the powder to form a pellet and the pellet sent down the gullet with a substantial gulp of water.[18]

A month of fighting, moving, hauling gear, and assisting the wounded took its toll on the men's uniforms. A time or two when they were near a stream, they were able to wash their clothes. They were quick about it, tearing open the package of lye-based soap, submerging the clothes in the stream, scouring the material with the soap cake, and finally, another dip in the stream to rinse. Once dry, the uniforms had a whole new look—the lye had bleached the tan khakis almost white.[19]

It was a noteworthy accomplishment protecting the eighty thousand troops (American and Filipino) and twenty-six thousand refugees while they made their way into the peninsula. Bottlenecks on the road were frequent. The MP trying to direct traffic and keep it moving received assistance from the 200th when they were ordered to help clear a badly clogged area on the road. They parked their guns and joined the MP in their task. The presence of the 200th guns, however, drew Japanese fire. Having wreaked havoc on their pilots, the Japanese began firing at these attractive stationary targets. The MP trying to keep people moving were quick to ask the 200th to move on so they could continue their job without the complication of having a bull's-eye in their midst.[20]

The selection of the Bataan Peninsula as the place for an inadequate number of defenders to hold off the enemy until reinforcements arrived was a pragmatic choice. Access to Manila Bay to the east could be guarded, a series of a half-dozen high peaks from three thousand to over four thousand feet high filled the interior giving some protection to the troops' backs, and having only two main roads into Bataan limited rapid access into the area. The Allies had gained the best defensive ground by retreating to Bataan. Along the way, they destroyed 184 bridges behind them and inflicted 2,000 Japanese troop casualties. The Filipino-American forces suffered 1,200 casualties. That number would increase considerably over the next three months.

7

Losing Ground

The Japanese dropped incendiary bombs, torching cane fields and rendering telephone lines inoperable as the insulation around the wires melted away. Allied orders and other communications were handwritten and sent via dispatch runners. The departure of the 515th from Manila left the city vulnerable. Japanese bombs had a more devastating effect with fewer operable antiaircraft artillery aimed their way and virtually no American planes to defend the island. American ships pulled out of Manila Bay to lessen their chances of getting hit. As they did, the marines and sailors unable to join their crewmates aboard cheered them on and then formed a new fighting battalion on land.

In two weeks, Homma's army gained footholds in four locations across Luzon.[1] They reached Manila on the second day of January[2] as Trejo futilely hung on to life and the U.S. Navy base at Cavite was evacuated. The Allied strategy employed desperate activities in hopes of keeping the Japanese at bay for as long as possible. Men entering Bataan were peeled away from their units, "dressed up in clean uniforms and run them up the road to make us think new troops had arrived!"[3] The charade was an attempt to bolster the resolve of American troops. The ruse could be sustained only so long, but in fact, a few real reinforcements in the form of American airmen reassigned to the infantry whose squadrons and communications had diminished significantly joined the soldiers. Unfortunately, these were very few and their lack of basic infantry training put them at a disadvantage. Some of the long-standing defenders on the ground felt they were somewhat of a liability, but these men had no alternative.

The Japanese resorted to their bag of tricks to fool the enemy, too. When they came across a dead Filipino in his uniform, they would strip his clothes off, put them on, and then try to get close enough to small groups of American soldiers to shoot before they were discovered. When the Japanese were routed, some would feign death to the point of letting maggots crawl on their faces. Others would pull a dead comrade on top of them to create a convincing scene.[4]

7. Losing Ground

The 200th and 515th maintained their positions around the airfields in the southern rear areas on Bataan and remained there for several weeks. Errett and every other soldier pondered ways to offset their food shortage as superiors imposed policies against cutting sugar cane from the local fields or killing carabao. The policy extended to a largely ignored ban on shooting at the enemy if these two food sources were likely to be collateral damage from shots fired. Errett considered the directive absurd. He liked rice, but like all of the others, his strength was sapped without protein and other nutrients. If he crossed paths with a potential meal walking on all fours, he was not going to let it walk away from his empty stomach. Filipinos aided the Americans by letting them know which indigenous animals were edible and which were not.

Saving a cane field at the expense of their lives was ludicrously self-defeating and irrelevant since the Japanese burned them as a matter of course to rid the battlefield of hiding places for their enemies. The Filipinos and Americans quickly discovered that the cane fields left unburned were traps. Although strewn with land mines, they were often the best route to safety when on the move. To mitigate the threat, a few carabao were routinely herded through the ten-foot stalks of cane to detonate and absorb the blast of the mines, clearing a pathway for the troops to use and possibly creating some edible collateral damage. If a carabao triggered a mine, the men had to act fast. Its meat could spoil in as little as thirty minutes, making it a meal for maggots rather than the starving troops.

Consequences for violating the ban on harming carabao and sugar cane fields were disseminated. Commanding officers were to personally account for failures to comply, a risk the frontline fighters were willing to take rather than move closer to starvation or lower their guns from the enemy. The slaughter of cattle, carabao, cats, monkeys, horses, and iguanas, along with their own mules and horses ensued to stave off their hunger while learning the subtleties of their cuisine. Shillito "ate cats, lizards, horses, and caribou [sic]. Caribou is tough."[5] "We had a little meat to go with our rice and salt. This meat had a sweetish taste. Later we found out we were eating General Wainwright's cavalry horses."[6]

Despite the extra protein, the overall condition of the defenders was bad and things got worse on January 5 when orders came to cut to half rations.[7] Within a few fleeting days, the men were cinching up their pants a belt notch or two tighter. They scrounged everywhere for food. Sometimes they came across edible stashes, but more often, they did not.

Gaunt khaki-clad Philippine scouts and American soldiers interspersed with what remained of the Filipino army established two parallel east-west, coast-to-coast defensive lines on Bataan. The northern-most line stretched westward from the north side of Abucay on the east coast. Looming up from the landscape and forming the center of the line were the twin peaks of Mt. Natib and Mt. Santa Rosa. At about the midsection of the peninsula and south of the Abucay line, another defensive line positioned itself between Orion on the east coast and Bagac on the west. In anticipation of a Japanese rush, American troops were given three days of extra rations that were to tide them over. As it turned out, the Japanese force was far stronger than expected.

Japanese artillery fire in the middle of the afternoon on January 9 marked the first assault on the Abucay line, the line of allied defenses stretching across the entrance to the Bataan Peninsula. Initial bombing was sparse since most of the thirty-six Japanese planes had been redirected to attack other island locations in the Pacific. Poor accuracy in the beginning on the part of the Japanese bombardiers allowed the Americans to push back in an impressive but short-lived effort. The Japanese took advantage of a weak spot in the line by shelling it for eight hours straight on January 11. The Japanese gained ground. On their fourth assault on the Abucay line, it faltered and finally cracked, enabling Japanese ground troops to penetrate. Two weeks later, the Filipino-American troops completed their withdrawal from the Abucay line.

Some Japanese maneuvers employed by their pilots were more distracting than threatening, including dropping delayed-action firecrackers at night. The purpose was twofold. First, it was hoped that the psychological effect of an enemy apparently at the rear as well as in front would soften the Allies' will. They also hoped the Allied muzzle flashes of return fire would betray the locations of their gun emplacements.

Filipino and American casualties mounted. A glut of bodies filled the trenches, some of which buried men alive who had flattened themselves in the bottom of the foxholes for protection. Some of those buried were able to crouch, form an air pocket, and hang on until they were dug out. Retreat at this point was chaotic. Droves moved erratically following networks of carabao and farmer trails cleared between stilted homes and cane fields. By the last week in January and nearly two weeks after the last of the extra rations were doled out, the whole of the Japanese army that was on Bataan had overrun the Abucay line and was now confronting the Orion line.

The Japanese controlled the northern half of the peninsula after fifteen days. They were poised to attack the southern half where the defenders had bunched up to secure the best possible defensive ground on the main island of Luzon. If the Japanese could see who they were up against, they might have laughed and planned nothing more elaborate than to stroll in and effortlessly finish the job. The Filipino and

American troops were weak with hunger. Malaria ravaged more than 70 percent of the men.[8] Only a fraction of the quinine needed to prevent or treat malaria was sporadically getting through aboard small civilian aircraft. Victims of the disease had increased. Chills violently shook their bodies one moment, then gave way to fevers swathing them in sweat. The cycle seemed interminable, often leaving the sick men too weak to even sit up. As if that was not enough, almost everyone had dysentery for which there was an inadequate supply of sulfathiazole pills to keep pace with the problem. Weight loss was rapid and dramatic. Marked ambulances that traveled in daylight became preferred bombing targets, but veiled by darkness, they went undetected. Tropical diseases were insinuating themselves into Errett's body and he felt acute pangs of hunger, but the effects were mild compared to the steady stream of medical evacuees passing through each night.

A thankful but eerie quiet settled over the Philippines during the second week of January 1942 after two weeks of constant battle in close proximity. One particular night was especially savage. The 200th and 515th knew the Japanese were closing in but were unsure from which direction they would come. They hunkered down and waited. That is all they could do. A group of machine gunners waiting behind an old barbed wire fence in the east sector of Bataan overlooking Manila Bay faced the same dilemma. They scrounged a few rusted tin cans, put a couple of pebbles in each, and hung them from the fence.[9] In the darkness just before dawn on January 14, a barely audible but distinct chorus of rattling tin cans sounded. Machine gun fire responded to the alarm without hesitation. The Japanese boldly escalated the fight with a full-out charge accompanied by great yelling. The shouts did nothing to stop the bullets, and the indistinct shapes running forward melted into the ground forming vague little hills as time passed.[10]

The growing heaps of bodies on the landscape did nothing to sway the charge. The faceless, yelling shapes in the night continued running forward into wave after wave of bullets. The scene was a nightmarish loop—leaping, lunging, falling shapes, over and over again. The futility of their foes unnerved the defenders. They yelled back thinking that might turn the Japanese away, but it did not. The dawn light revealed the sickening piles of dead and wounded, and still, more Japanese came scrambling unflinchingly up the heaps.[11] The Filipino and American troops were stunned and perplexed at the seeming indifference exhibited by the Japanese as they trod over their countrymen.[12]

The intensity of the assault made it impossible to get drinking water to the machine gunners. They improvised by drinking the water issued for the cooling jackets on their guns and replacing it with their urine. The drawbacks were twofold: their guns emitted quite a stench as the urine boiled off when fired and their thirst was only partially assuaged.[13] The attack ended just after sunrise. Small-arms fire and the constant sound of moans replaced machine gun fire. The early morning sun clearly defined the killing field between the defenders and the barbed wire fence. Several Americans lay dead or wounded, but indelibly horrific were the piles upon piles of Japanese bodies.

By the middle of January, the Americans were down to only two bombers. They could do little damage, but optimism sprouted among the troops every now and then from other aspects of the war. The men cheered when the *Voice of Freedom* reported that a U.S. submarine sank a seventeen-thousand-ton Japanese supply ship. Rumors also fueled hope, especially after the broadcast of MacArthur's help-is-on-its-way message from the Malinta Tunnel at Ft. Mills on Corregidor in mid–January. The message was based on a false promise from Washington, D.C., but buoyed the spirits of the downtrodden men for a time. MacArthur iterated the message with confidence. "Help is on its way …thousands of troops and hundreds of planes.… No further retreat is possible.… We have more troops on Bataan than the Japanese have thrown against us.… If we fight we will win/if we retreat we will be destroyed."[14] Thus assured, the allied forces on Bataan began a litany of what was coming their way, how they would put the expected reinforcements to good use, and the consequences to be suffered by the Japanese. It was not just idle talk. New Mexicans rebuilt the airstrips at the Cabcaben and Bataan airfields and guarded them so the expected arrival of Australian airplanes carrying supplies and men could land.

Understandably, the most frequent rumors whetting the appetite of the troops were those pertaining to the imminent arrival of food. Most of the cattle, mules, horses, carabao, and monkeys in the area had been killed for food. The men were tired, sick, and hungry, but if they just had enough food, they believed they could prevail over exhaustion and illness enough to take on the enemy. After all, the Japanese were lousy shots,[15] their grenades proved to have more bark than bite, they had recently halted their forward movement, and the last few battered American P-40s pilots had begun night missions inflicting some damage.

The heavy casualties among the ranks of the Japanese stalled their advance, but it did not slow their ships from landing. Not all beaches were an easy inroad, though. During the Battle of Quinauan, for instance, over nine hundred Japanese infantry were killed, which is almost double the Filipino-American losses. On the night of January 27, the Americans wielded a heavy blow to the Japanese in an air raid. There were two things going for them—a full moon and cloud cover. Seven P-40s took off and flew at low altitude just above the clouds from Bataan, over Corregidor, and on to Manila. The P-40 crews laid waste to a considerable number of Japanese planes, fuel, and oil and killed about three hundred Japanese soldiers without the enemy having a single opportunity to fire on them.[16]

The delusion of making a stand and gaining the upper hand was literally hammered out of their minds in late January when the Japanese returned to the tactic of daily bombings. Fast-flying Zeros and artillery shells wreaked havoc on temporary camps every two hours. Japanese ground troops pushed forward after each strike. The Filipino army in particular suffered heavy casualties during these raids. Many were lost in their freshly dug foxholes that were dug too close to barbed wire barricades and allowed the Japanese to toss hand grenades into foxholes without first crossing the barricades.[17]

Occasionally, the defenders gained a hundred yards or so after days of fighting, but the tactics meted out against them were at an increased level of gruesomeness. Errett heard a firsthand account of one such nasty incident later on when he was held in a Japanese prison camp. It happened in late January 1942 at Silaiim. A single tank from the 192nd tank battalion got out a little ahead of the others and drove over a land mine that forced its tracks off. The disabled tank was stranded. A group of American infantrymen set out to rescue the crew. What they found, they could not rescue. "The four-man crew had been doused with gasoline and burned."[18] The combined Battles of the Points and Pockets, which was a three-week offensive by the Americans on the west coast of Luzon, began January 23, during which the Allies repelled about 3,500 Japanese of which only 650 survived but in bad shape. It was the first major advance in two months of heavy fighting. A brief lull in the battle allowed men to comb debris to conduct their usual process of scavenging for food, usable weapons, and American cash.

Jess listened to her radio all day, changing the dial from one war newscast to the next even though the reports rarely varied. She felt the news about the Philippines on February 12 was particularly depressing. Days later, the news was even worse. British and Australian troops were some of the ninety thousand to be taken prisoner in the Far East by the Japanese Shanghai division in Singapore in February 1942, after a bitter jungle battle. It was the largest surrender in British history. General Arthur Percival surrendered on Sunday, February 15, after enduring several twenty- to thirty-mile retreats. The fall of Singapore was another impediment to relief reaching the defenders in the Philippines. Officially, the status of the Allied condition in the Pacific battle zones was reported as being worse than it had been before. A respite from the hard news was the February 21

Bing Crosby program dedicated to the soldiers fighting in the Philippines as requested by General MacArthur. Merle remarked in her letter to Errett of February 12, "When people speak of MacArthur's troops, they speak of them in the same way and the same reverence as they do of God." The Lujans listened to the program with more melancholy than enjoyment.

8

The Lull

The great hardships and losses punctuated by occasional victories put Allied morale on a seesaw. Combat rations continued to be held back from the Americans. In fact, a warning was passed around for each man to acknowledge by adding his signature. They were agreeing to turn in anyone eating C-rations and, if they did not, would face a court martial along with the offending soldier who was caught and his commanding officer.[1]

At this point, the Allied army was put on quarter rations. They were limited to two meals a day, which usually consisted of nothing more than a small serving of somewhat reddish unpolished rice studded with a paltry inclusion of brown rock salt and, occasionally, canned salmon or tuna. The lack of protein accelerated muscle loss and was accompanied by swollen legs, stomachs, and for some, arms. One of their two meals was served before dawn and the other after dark. To add the all-important salt to their diet, kitchen patrol boiled seawater each day to eke out four hundred pounds of salt, one quarter of what they needed. Sometimes their food was augmented by turnips plucked from the fields in Bataan. The last of the cavalry horses and pack mules from the Twenty-Sixth Cavalry were eaten by mid–March.

Chaplain Frederick Howden of Roswell, New Mexico, did his best to support, encourage, and provide solace to the men during these trying times. Errett watched as Howden slipped his tall, wiry frame through the 200th and 515th from battery to battery, talking some to the soldiers but mostly listening. After the war, when the men heard he had died in 1942 on New Year's Eve in Davao POW camp, there was a unified mourning for this fine man.[2] Errett hoped a friend was at his side when he took his last breath.

The situation, however, grew clearer each day. The odds were stacked squarely against Errett and the rest of the defenders. Supplies and reinforcements were not coming, and even if they were, they could not get in. A sense of abandonment exploded throughout the Americans in early February. Frank Hewlett, an embedded United Press International war correspondent, straightforwardly put their feelings into verse.

Battling Bastards

We're the battling bastards of Bataan
No mama, no papa, no Uncle Sam
No aunts, no uncles, no cousins, no nieces
No pills, no planes, no artillery pieces
And nobody gives a damn!
Nobody gives a damn!

They were not, however, the only ones lacking food. On February 6, the Japanese were temporarily cut off from their supplies and were unable to get out themselves. A dozen or so parcels of supplies were air dropped to them, but the Filipinos beat them to where they landed and scooped them up.[3] But yet, the Japanese were faring better than the Allies. They had sweet corned beef, sweet fried meats, rice, hard tack, and a few vegetables,[4] and, unlike the Allies, they had reinforcement and supplies on the way.

On February 8, General Masaharu Homma ordered his troops to fall back and rest until their reinforcements arrived. Periodic lulls in the fighting such as this allowed the defenders a much needed rest and, for some, spiritual relief. Chaplains improvised. A small folding table was set up as a makeshift altar and mass was held, putting at bay the feeling for some of being forsaken. The Japanese completed their withdrawal by the 12th, giving the Allies a somewhat extended respite and coinciding with the climax of the three-week Battle of the Points during which the Japanese made five landings. The toll of this battle was heavy. Seven hundred Americans were killed and two Japanese battalions of eighteen hundred men met the same fate. It also cleared the skies for an Allied drop but not of supplies and food. Instead, bundles of leaflets landed reassuring the troops that hundreds of planes and thousands of Allied troops were on their way to the Philippines. Japan also papered the Americans with their own propaganda, but the troops did not bother to read it; the sheets were more useful as toilet paper.[5]

In the midst of the withdrawal, a dog fight in the air over Bataan captured almost everyone's attention. In the end, the sixth and only Zero not shot down made its getaway and returned to Pilar airfield only to be shot down just before landing.[6] An incident on water also played out one moonless night when Japanese troops tried to reach Bataan by quietly rowing across Manila Bay on rafts. It was a gutsy attempt that ended badly. American searchlights lit up the bay and the big guns sank every raft.[7] The Filipino army supplemented by native Igorots using bolos had a coup of their own against the Japanese when they prevailed in a counterattack on the west flank of Bataan. The arrival of a large Japanese flotilla on March 3 was too enticing a target to pass up. Four P-40s took to the skies and managed to sink nearly forty thousand tons of ships along with their cargo.

8. The Lull

Meanwhile, the navy downed sixteen Japanese bombers. It was not without cost, however. Three of the P-40s crash landed on a too-short runway, leaving only one functioning P-40 at their disposal.[8] The event put a stop to the planes obtaining intelligence by day and smuggling quinine in at night, and the *Don Esteban* was sunk, thus ending the last meager deliveries of rice to the Philippines.

A short-lived euphoria weaving its way through the defenders during the lull was cut short when stunning news filtered through the troops—Singapore was in imminent danger of falling to the Japanese, prompting orders on March 11 from President Roosevelt to MacArthur to leave the Philippines. Word of his departure spread quickly. The troops knew it almost as soon as he read the orders.[9] He and his family departed the Philippines via PT boat. He left Ft. Mills on Corregidor where he had been since mid–January. MacArthur's departure affected the troops' morale.

MacArthur assigned General Wainwright command of Corregidor and General Edward P. King to replace Wainwright as commander of the Filipino-American forces on Bataan. Colonel Peck remained commander of Errett's regiment. King tallied the population he was given charge of. There were 79,000 soldiers, 6,000 civilian employees, and 20,000 refugees. Of the 79,000 soldiers, 11,796 were American, 8,270 were Filipino scouts, and 59,000 were in the Filipino army.[10]

Before the MacArthurs boarded their conveyance to Australia, the general penned a message that was copied and distributed to the troops. "I am leaving," he wrote, "but I shall return with thousands of men and hundreds of planes."[11] Each man was required to read it, initial it, and pass it on. MacArthur's departure to Australia was particularly demoralizing to the native troops. Almost everyone at this point harbored no hope of resupply, reinforcement, rescue, and ultimate victory. However, fresh U.S. troops were, in fact, arriving in the Pacific theater but in Australia and could do little to help the situation in the Philippines. A slight uptick in morale manifested a week later when MacArthur, newly appointed as the supreme commander of the southwest Pacific, gave his I-shall-return radio speech from Australia.

The disintegration of cohesive Allied units was apparent. Only the 200th and 515th regiments remained intact and active. Fortunately, a quiet settled in through the end of March, providing some relief. General Homma used the time to rest his troops, plan his next attacks, and request reinforcements for the endeavor. Thus far, he was the only commander in the Pacific under Tōjō who failed on several counts. His troop offensives on the west coast were repulsed. He failed to take Limay and failed to break the Orion-Bagac line. The Allied resistance on the west side delayed the arrival of Japanese reinforcements and left them in an untenable situation reeling from widespread malaria and dysentery among their troops[12] and over one thousand American navy prisoners to tend to.

By mid–March, the defenders' food supply dwindled to a meager pile amounting to no more than two more weeks on low rations. A plan was drawn up to alleviate the situation and send in food by way of submarine. In the end, the risk was too great as the Japanese simultaneously tightened up their blockade and warships effectively shelled three Philippine ports. The plan to get food in was aborted. The formidable blockade was not the only obstacle taking shape. P-40 reconnaissance flights confirmed a massive buildup of Japanese ground troops—the largest number of enemy troops to date. They were all pointed toward Bataan, and Japanese patrols increased.

Allied forces transferred most of the patients, doctors, and corpsmen at St. Scholastica in Manila to Bilibid Prison without incident during the lull. The wounded and ill in the field could only be accommodated in makeshift hospitals near headquarters. Patients hung listlessly in hammocks stretched between trees. A thousand new malarial patients arrived each day. Some were fortunate enough to have mosquito garb draped over them and even luckier to receive the last available doses of quinine to combat the relentless infectious disease.

According to Captain Jack Boyer, "January, February, and March saw our position deteriorate from bad to worse to serious."[13] The average American fighting to defend Bataan had lost 25 percent of his normal weight.[14] They did not have the same benefits of food and field hospitals that the sick and wounded had toward the end of the war when 96 percent of those patients survived. General King's definition of troop readiness required a man to walk one hundred yards without stopping while carrying his weapon and gear unassisted and be able to shoot accurately. About 15 percent of the troops met this standard.[15] The radios alone were the size of a bread box and none too light. Rest during daylight was the order of the day while each battery kept one sentry on watch.

Merle continued to write to Errett in hopes of something getting through. On February 28, she touchingly wrote, "I hope when this horrible thing is over we can make you forget it all. We read everything we can about MacArthur and his men. It makes my heart fill with pride and my eyes with tears to know you are one of them." She promised him a "good ole night on the town" with him. She backed her promise by purchasing Defense Bonds every month at $18.75 each, which is half of what she paid every year for taxes. She included well wishes, of course, saying she "prays for him every morning and every night." Their four-year-old cousin in California, Carol Jean, also included him in her nighttime prayers, she wrote, by whispering, "Dear God, bring Errett home." But Merle's letter of kind words and promise of a night out never reached him.

8. The Lull

Some tasks were pursued during quieter hours but were slow in completion due to the serious muscle waste resulting from the 2,500–3,000-calorie deficiency in their daily diet. New trench latrines were always needed. No matter how deep and narrow they were dug, the cesspits produced a tremendous stench and breeding ground for disease. If it was available, crude oil or a strong disinfectant was sprayed into trenches daily. At any rate, a single slit trench could not be used longer than six days. To close one, an oil-soaked burlap cloth was placed over the waste and the entire feature buried with the fill dirt set aside when it was first excavated. The men also set about repairing about thirty miles of burned telephone lines in an attempt to restore communications.

While troops kept a watchful eye on the calm front, twenty-six thousand refugees huddled to the rear of the Allies. Across the airwaves came Roosevelt's March fireside chat. The mood of the troops was sour, and those with time on their hands and inclined toward poetry wrote their sentiments in rhymes such as

> In Australia's fresh clime,
> He took out the time
> To send us a message of cheer.
> My heart, he began,
> Goes out to Bataan,
> But the rest of me's
> Staying right here.[16]

And this one sung to the tune of "The Battle Hymn of the Republic":

> Dougout Doug MacArthur lies a shakin' on the Rock
> Safe from all the bombers and from any sudden shock
> Dugout Doug is eating of the best food on Bataan
> And his troops go starving on.[17]

While these and other lyrics sprang up like spring flowers, Hewlett's "Battling Bastards" was the most often repeated and remains the unofficial slogan of the postwar organizations such as the American Defenders of Bataan and Corregidor.

In the third week of March, the Japanese began blanketing the Allied troops with messages. Empty beer cans with ribbons and an ultimatum attached peppered the area. The ultimatums, called surrender tickets, were addressed to Major General Wainwright and called for surrender by noon on March 22, 1942, or "we shall consider ourselves at liberty to take any action whatsoever."[18] The three-by-five-inch papers included instructions on how to surrender and a suggestion to sing and pray for peace. The men used them to bump up their supply of toilet paper. On occasion, the Japanese dropped food by parachute. Printed on the box containing the food was American Red Cross Earthquake Relief—Japan 1923. The Japanese spoke directly to the Filipinos in the front lines through loudspeakers in their own language urging them to surrender and, if they complied, were assured of good treatment and eventual return to their homes. The fight, they said, was "an American war and the Americans want the Filipinos to die instead of themselves."[19]

9

War News Stirs the Home Front

On December 7, Americans in the United States listened to the shocking news on their radios. Understandably, New Mexicans at home were paying more attention to attacks on the Philippines than those on Pearl Harbor. Their loved ones were in the Philippines. Louis and Merle were at work when the news of the Pearl Harbor attack came through. Jess and Claire were at home on Gildersleeve Street and did not move farther than five feet from the radio most of the day, navigating through the news with tear-filled eyes. For most families, that innocuous piece of furniture, the radio, had taken on an importance that could not be overstated.

A collective voice from Americans issued throughout the United States as publicity of the bitter fighting in the Far East came through the day after bombardment of the 200th. The idea of isolationism that had percolated through cities and towns for so long was quickly pushed aside as if it had never existed. People insisted the country fight back and waste no time in doing so.

The personal connection between New Mexico and the Philippines did not go unnoticed by others. Shuji Fujii, editor of the *Doho* Japanese American newspaper, sent Governor Miles of New Mexico a telegram. In it, Fujii vehemently condemned Japan's attack on "our democratic Americans" and informed the governor that he had wired President Roosevelt immediately after the attacks urging an immediate declaration of war against Japan.[1] Miles issued a proclamation the same day declaring a "full emergency to exist and urge that all citizens of this state cooperate to the fullest extent with municipal, county, state, and Federal governments, and in full harmony, strive in our common cause until our armed forces have time to exact just retribution from our treacherous, despicable, and infamous foe."[2]

The citizens of Santa Fe reacted, too, as the government encouraged meetings in communities. A series of civil defense meetings garnered widespread attendance. Everyone was anxious to do their part even if they were not yet quite sure what that role was. Meetings were seen as a way to dispel war hysteria, discourage witch-hunting, prevent mob spirit from prevailing, and allay fears, benefits direly needed since almost everyone tuned into the *March of Time* radio broadcast and listened intently as the attack, invasion, and battle in the Philippines was recounted in as much detail as the government allowed. Errett's family did their patriotic duty as Merle explained in a letter to her brother on March 13, "Daddy has been going out to the American Legion hut on Saturday nights and playing bingo—they give defense stamps and bonds. He has won about five dollars in stamps—which I hope buys a gun for you darling. I have six $18.75 bonds now. I buy one every month."

Jess received her letter from her aunt Abbie Nisbeth dated December 11, 1941. Abbie sent comforting words but also let her know that her husband, John, "was dying to be in it—said he wished they would put the age up to 70." She continued, "I suppose you know they extended it from 18 to 65." John was sixty-eight at the time.

There was a unified outpouring of support for the New Mexico national guardsmen who had been shipped to the Philippines three months earlier. Groups began buying Defense Bonds, collecting scrap metal, and volunteering their time toward the war effort. Leaders from powerful organizations formed the Council for Democracy to help unite the country against the enemy. Governor Miles joined all of the other forty-seven governors in signing a statement addressed to the president of the United States to answer the call to arms "grimly, dynamically, and victoriously" and assured Roosevelt of their "immediate and wholehearted support' and promise to share "that responsibility with you every step of the rough road." They went on to say that this "is everybody's war and in a world of treacherous, brutal, war-mad dictators yours is the task of leading us forward under God with the march of democracy to ultimate victory …that the nature of this crisis is such that it calls for a national unity even greater than is ordinarily achieved by free people in war time."[3]

The resolve of the people buoyed Roosevelt's outlook, but it brought about another set of problems. How would the United States fight a world war on two fronts on opposite sides of the globe when it was not at all certain they could be effective in even one? Louis Lujan talked almost every day about the war. He was a man of few words but felt no reservation in talking about his dislike for the war. Errett's sister Claire reminisced decades later that Louis could hardly wait for it to be over so his son and the other boys could come home. It was a prevailing feeling. Everyone wanted it to end. Errett's great-uncle John Nisbeth continued expressing his concern as he recounted to his wife his service during the Spanish-American War. "He has been right where you are now," wrote Merle on January 9.

In January 1942, Governor Miles initiated a campaign to help the USO surpass its goal of $32 million for food to be shipped to troops in the Pacific. He hoped they could reach $50 million. He issued a memorandum to all his departments suggesting that "at least one-half of one day's salary"[4] from each employee be donated. A collection box was set up in the state capitol building for donations. Santa Feans contributed generously, yet the aid could not get through to the men of the 200th and 515th. The supplies bought were years in reaching the starving, sick troops.

Although the first U.S. troops arrived in the British domain of Northern Ireland on January 26, 1942, it was not until February 23, 1942, that an official preliminary agreement between the United States and the United Kingdom to support each other with defensive articles, property, services, and information was drawn up and signed. The arrival of U.S. troops in England was perhaps the first public indication as to which war front the United States was going to support. The brunt of the decision was to be borne by the men in the Philippines.

With little news coming in on the situation in the Philippines, Governor Miles wrote Secretary of War Harry L. Stimson a letter inquiring on the well-being of the 200th Coast Artillery fighting in the Philippines. In late February, Stimson replied that nothing was known except information through official channels of those who had been reported dead or captured. Secretary Stimson's words to Governor Miles "that everything possible is being done to feed, supply, and protect our soldiers in the Philippines"[5] were true but rang hollow. A choice was made at the expense of the defenders of Bataan, and it left a bitter taste in the mouths of many including some Brits. They, too, had military forces fighting for their lives in the Far East. British and Australian troops were some of the first to be taken prisoner by the Japanese Shanghai division in Singapore on February 15, 1942.

The fact, unknown to almost everyone, was that Western European–held countries in the Far East were falling like dominoes, allowing Japan to position itself for an attack on Australia had it not been for the extended effort required of them in taking Bataan. While Timor fell, Wake crumbled, and as the Battle of the Java Sea raged, the dwindling, exhausted defenders of Bataan held on. The exhausted and starving men of the 200th and 515th were immediately acknowledged for their gallant defense through outstanding technical ability, courage, and devotion to duty against overwhelming numbers of hostile forces during which they defended Clark and Nichols airfields and portions of Manila and covered the retreat into the Bataan Peninsula enabling "the prolonged defense of Bataan."[6]

In the United States, Roosevelt issued Executive Order 9066 on February 21, 1942. It is one in a long litany of presidential decisions in World War II with lasting consequences. The order allows for the confinement of Japanese and those of Japanese descent living in the United States. Under this law, Secretary of War Henry Stimson was empowered to prescribe certain areas in the United States and its territories as military zones where any person or groups of people could be excluded for the duration of the war to safeguard the country. At the time, the United States, including its territories and possessions, had a population of 150,621,231. Among these, 113,874 were identified as noncitizens of Japanese descent. New Mexico's population was 531,818 and that included 186 Japanese of which 114 were citizens of the United States.[7] By the end of this embarrassing episode in our history, one person was found guilty of spying for Japan.

The conservative *San Francisco Chronicle* turned their opinion in support of President Roosevelt signing Executive Order 9066, saying, "We have to be tough even if civil rights do take a beating for a time."[8] If it was a mistake, Roosevelt insisted he was erring on the side of caution rather than risking the alternative exemplified to him early on when anti–Japanese attitudes in several neighborhoods reached a feverous pitch. Violence erupted in certain U.S. West Coast areas two weeks after Pearl Harbor was attacked despite efforts to ward against mob spirit and witch-hunting. A recently honorably discharged soldier of Japanese descent but born in the United States was stabbed to death in Los Angeles. Japanese in Gilroy, California, were attacked, and other incidents led to seven other deaths. Riots filled the streets of Berkeley and San Francisco, and several Japanese were killed.

To carry out the goals of Executive Order 9066, two newly formed agencies, the War Relocation Authority and the Wartime Civil Control Administration, were assigned the responsibility of formulating and carrying out a program for the planned relocation of persons evacuated from potential military areas. The entire West Coast was proclaimed such in early March 1942. The rationale given for the program was cited as twofold: in the event the West Coast would become a combat zone, for persons of Japanese ancestry, there would be "possible cause of turmoil and confusion which could seriously jeopardize military operations" and "military considerations cannot permit the risk of putting an unassimilated or partly assimilated people to an unpredictable test during an invasion by an army of their own race."[9] Henceforth, U.S. law now allowed for the forcible removal of Japanese from their homes and placement in relocation centers.

News of surrender in Bataan fueled other problems related to the

9. War News Stirs the Home Front 79

issue of the Japanese population in the United States. The notion was put forth to establish Japanese colonies on farmable land in the American west, similar to the Indian reservation system, for the purpose of containing the Japanese. New Mexico was touted as such a place. "We have read with alarm the tentative proposal to settle 60,000 American Japanese in the State of New Mexico."[10]

Plans were published by the National Reclamation Association to utilize Works Project Administration and Civilian Conservation Corps (CCC) camps to establish Japanese colonies in the west. These Works Project Administration and CCC labor camps had operated before the war in thwarting soil erosion problems in the west and trying to give the economy a boost during the Great Depression. The twenty-page outline explained the problem, described the proposed relocation program and areas, suggested work opportunities, and contained complete information on all phases of the program. The outline was sent to governors seeking sponsorships of Japanese colonies be established in their states.

Piles of letters protesting colonization besieged Governor Miles's office, but among them were two in favor of the idea. One of the two writers, Mr. John Wight of Los Angeles, went as far as to inquire of the secretary of state in Washington, D.C., about the possibility of "buying or leasing from 25,000 to 50,000 acres of private irrigated lands for colonizing purposes." The response informed him that "the Governor [Miles] has requested the Attorney General's office to use any and all legal means possible in opposition to any such colonization plans."[11]

The people's voices and sentiments in New Mexico were fiercely against the idea. To take control of the situation, Governor Miles quickly reiterated the attitude in New Mexico that New Mexicans were bitterly opposed to Japanese colonization in any form and cited economic, social, and political reasons for the opposition as well as the fact that more than two thousand New Mexico men were now prisoners of the Japanese.[12] Bitter opposition to a Japanese colony in New Mexico was an understatement. One letter to Governor Miles suggested that "planting Jap colonies over this country would be worse than filling our water supply with typhus germs."[13]

Reaction to the published National Reclamation Association plan was not supportive. Proposals to change the hot-button word "colonization" to "relocation center" and imposing tighter restrictions on the freedoms of the enlistees were made. With those changes in place, the roundup of certain people from military zones began. The grand total of Japanese evacuated from their homes and sent to relocation centers was about forty thousand *Issei* (Japanese-born immigrants to the United States and non-citizens) and seventy thousand *Nisei* (children born in the United States of the *Issei*) removed from their homes under Executive Order 9066,[14] and about five thousand of these were interned throughout the war.

In addition to the several relocation centers, the Federal Bureau of Investigation identified Japanese residing in the United States who were likely to carry out acts against the security of the country. They were placed in the Enemy Alien Program administered by the Department of Justice and put into high-security camps such as the Santa Fe Japanese Internment Camp. These camps received very little publicity and were established swiftly and quietly. The Federal Bureau of Investigation seized nearly twelve thousand enemy aliens during the first year America was at war. Over half were Japanese, the others were Germans, Italians, Hungarians, Romanians, and Bulgarians. Both Japanese and Germans were held in camps in New Mexico.

Federal government surveyors lost hardly a day after Roosevelt authorized internment camps for those of Japanese descent who were considered to be a danger to the homeland. The surveyors arrived in Santa Fe on a cold day in February to assess as secretly as possible retrofitting an abandoned CCC camp on the north side of the city into a high-security internment complex. The assessment was favorable, and the New Mexico State Prison Board, the landowners, granted the Immigration and Naturalization Service (INS) use of the eighty-acre prewar facility with the expectations that fourteen hundred Japanese enemy aliens would be held there.[15]

Modifications of the forty-two buildings in the CCC complex began March 3, 1942, the day after permission was granted to the INS to use the camp. The first group of 425 Japanese enemy aliens arrived by train on March 14, along with another 209 arriving thirteen days later and another 192 on April 29,[16] twenty days after Errett was ordered to surrender. Among the group was the Reverend Asataro Yamada from San Jose, California, and the father of Ruth Hashimoto. Ruth was sent to the University of Michigan to teach Japanese language to U.S. Army intelligence officers, and her mother was placed at a camp in Heart Mountain. Since the United States and Japan were still at war, her father remained confined until he became ill and moved to join his wife.[17] James Matsu wrote from his dormitory room at the University of New Mexico in Albuquerque that "last week thirty Japanese from Clovis were sent to Ft. Stanton to be interned."[18] However, other reports state that no people of Japanese ancestry living in New Mexico were confined or relocated. Nonetheless, it seems evident small groups of Japanese were already being taken into custody.

A small number of local residents were hired to work at the Japanese internment camp in Santa Fe. Jobs were difficult to come by, so even these few were welcome. In the first two months of 1942, Santa Fe suffered a net loss of seventy businesses. Prewar New Mexico had just begun to enjoy an economic benefit from the motor car tourism industry. In 1942, however, income from that industry dropped by one-third from the previous year and steadily declined until after the war.[19]

The first complaints from internees about the camp were received in May 1942. Although they had unlimited hot showers, traditional baths were lacking. Bathtubs were immediately installed. Although applications for repatriation were quickly processed and hearings held, the internees were dissatisfied with the time it took to learn the verdict of their hearings. But all in all, the inspectors found the men well treated and of high morale from the first inspection through to the last. The Spanish consul, who carried out inspections, reported the facility to be spotless.[20]

10

Surrendered

Antiaircraft units were highly coveted by Filipino-American soldiers, almost as valuable as food and perhaps worth their weight in gold. Toward the end of March, gunnery troops on the east flank of Bataan Peninsula were pressed into nighttime training shifts from six in the evening to midnight and from midnight to six in the morning just before the Japanese resumed their attacks. The 515th rejoined their brothers in the 200th, along with Battery A of the Second Coast Artillery to form the new Groupment A (AA) under the command of Colonel Sage on March 21, 1942. The new regiment engaged in little combat for lack of targets when Homma's offensive began the next day with artillery bombardments instead of planes.

The deadline stipulated in the Japanese demand for surrender came and went. Wainwright chose to ignore it even as 75 percent of his troops languished in a state of severe illness. Their situation was now more dire. American food rations were reduced once again, this time to one-fifth of a normal allotment. General Wainwright sent an assessment of the problem to his superiors. All food, including C-rations, would be exhausted by April 15.[1]

A serving of rice came with worms. The men decided to eat them, too, for the scant protein they promised. The few monkeys remaining in the area became a meal for dozens of hungry men. The soldiers were forced to expand their food harvesting to include crickets, the inside of the cabbage-tasting palm tree, and tree leaves. Mango leaves were steeped to make tea. Other foods scavenged included elephant ear leaves, some freshwater shrimp and fish obtained with grenades, wild hogs, skinny wild chickens which proved difficult to catch, birds, iguanas, snakes, worms, and grasshoppers.

Finally, the Japanese began what was to become their final advance. It was late March. They advanced on Bataan by way of the Pampanga River corridor blanketing a fifteen-hundred-yard-wide area in front of them as they went. Their aerial strategy changed. Before, they flew three to nine planes to an objective, bombed it, and returned. Now they were sending as

10. Surrendered

many as thirty-six planes on a mission, and despite Homma's directive to plan attacks with skill and detail, their targets appeared to be chosen literally on the fly.[2] The greater number of aircraft overhead made it easier to exact a toll. Dozens of Japanese planes were either shot down or seriously damaged by antiaircraft guns along with considerable numbers of transports and over a dozen warships. The losses caused the Japanese to pull back slightly, but a concerted effort against the Filipinos seemed to coalesce. Against the backdrop of the Mariveles slopes next to Bataan airfield, Japanese captured Filipinos, stabbed and shot them, tied their bodies to timbers using barbed wire, and dumped them into the water where the current would wash them ashore. The tactic was meant to scare the natives into surrendering.[3]

Japanese radio messages pulsed out as the drizzle of the rainy season commenced in early April. They promised those who would surrender immediate solace, salvation, and plenty of sex and steaks. The solicitation was followed up by a heavy, five-hour barrage of howitzer fire and mortar launches, bombs, incendiaries, and Zero strafings starting at ten in the morning on Good Friday, April 3, 1942. A short half-hour respite from 1:30 p.m. to 2:00 p.m. allowed pockets of Allied forces some semblance of regrouping. By 3:00 p.m., Japanese infantry and tanks advanced from the east and began an assault on the men heading for Corregidor and on Mt. Samat in areas where the defenders' weapons were installed. The couple of dozen white phosphorus bombs let loose on Bataan scorched the peninsula. The dust and smoke made it impossible for the soldiers to see anything farther than ten yards away. Telephone wires on the front lines were once again inoperable as the insulation around the wires melted off. Runners relayed and retrieved messages and orders from the rear to the front lines.[4] When the lines were operable, Taos Indians delivered messages over the wires in their native Tiwa language. It was the first use of Native American language in World War II and the precursor to the Navajo code talkers.[5] Neither language "code" was ever broken by the Japanese.

Action intensified on Saturday. The Japanese navy approached beaches near Bataan at dark early on the 4th. Three boats steamed southwesterly leaving a trail of smoke six thousand yards offshore to screen the movements of the other ships. The smoke moved ashore and pressed in around buildings and hunkered down groups of defenders. Through it, the men saw dull flashes. It was like watching a distant lightning storm until the bombs from the ships landed. The dull sparks were enough for the men on land to pin down a target and the advancing ships turned back, never getting closer to the shoreline than four thousand yards. As the ships retreated, their debris washed in—a couple of lifeboats, some life jackets, lots of smoke cans, and some unlucky Filipinos who had acted as spies, as

Mallonée suspected, for the Japanese. They were bound, bayoneted, and dumped overboard.⁶

The mid-morning light of Easter Sunday shone on a Japanese attack on Mt. Samat. By the end of the day, they controlled the point at its base. After five more days of heavy fighting, the Japanese crossed the peak and gained a commanding position against the Allies. The Mariveles Mountains between Mt. Samat and the southern tip of Bataan, where the intertwined jungle of trees and vines ended at either cliffs or boulder-strewn beaches, were the only geographical obstacles left facing the Japanese. The one area clearly out of their reach was the menacing rock-fortified stronghold of Corregidor that plagued Japanese gunboats.

Following orders, Wainwright planned an organized attack in response. The men, however, did not have the stamina or ammunition to carry it out. Errett was one of the 15 percent who could still walk one hundred yards and shoot his weapon without resting along the way. The payroll safe was buried in the jungle and the U.S. flag burned to keep them out of Japanese hands. Equipment was destroyed for the same reason. The 515th was ordered to Cabcaben for a last stand as infantry rather than antiaircraft personnel. They traveled against the push of refugees and retreating soldiers. Battery C, Errett's battery, arrived on a ridge above Bataan airfield at four in the morning on April 6.⁷ They had relocated from the farthest north position where they had been continually harassed by fifteen Japanese bombers in a short period. In spite of this, Battery C managed to fire on every enemy plane.

Their spirits were buoyed somewhat at that vantage point as they watched two U.S. gunboats from Corregidor lob artillery shells at Japanese ships precluding their ability to get within range of land troops on Bataan. The USS *Mindanao* and *Oahu* scored when they sank four Japanese boats off the east coast of Bataan. Allied onlookers peered around their antiaircraft guns, cheering each craft as it slowly disappeared into a watery grave. A closer look to his immediate surroundings doused Errett's elation. It was obvious that his life, all of their lives, were probably at the end of the line. It was only a matter of time now and crossing over that line would bring either death or capture. Others were just as aware.

Oddly enough, the general retreat to Bataan boosted morale. They saw it as their last chance to fight and hold or lose. They were not going to give up prematurely; they were going to fight and this included the indefatigable Filipino scouts that Errett so admired. They shouted over and over, "*Petay si la!*"—"They shall die!"⁸ The retreating soldiers occasionally tried fishing with dynamite, but usually, the fish sank due to their burst floats. Instead, the quartermaster corps established a fishery at Lamao, paying local fishermen who brought in their nightly catch. Very soon, twelve thousand pounds of fish each night was coming in, but the venture was short-lived as the Japanese began killing locals they discovered on the water at night.[9]

The Allied retreat and Japanese envelopment of the island made getting mail in or out almost impossible. The last the Lujans heard from Errett was his cable just before Christmas. Word spread quickly through Santa Fe, however, that many of the Albuquerque families seventy miles south received letters on March 30. This spawned another writing campaign by the Lujan family. Mostly, it was news about the family—Uncle Alfonso married Josephine, Merle was making $140 a month at the state attorney general's office, which was almost three times her brother's pay, and Errett's first bunkmate's, Jack Rogers's, wife was living with them.

Meanwhile, Errett's composure deflated during a particularly unfortunate episode. While his battery was defending Cabcaben airfield, a faulty fuse detonated a three-inch shell just as it cleared the muzzle. Several scouts and two American officers were killed and two others wounded. The incident put Battery C out of action for several days.[10] The lines broke and entire batteries, even regiments, began to surrender even though there was no order to do so. The sick seemed to be the most vulnerable now as hospitals and pharmacies were mercilessly bombed. Officers organized burial details under the protective cover of darkness. The dark made it difficult to identify the dead, and on occasion, the identification tag put on a body by the officers was handed back by the supposed corpse. The muffled monotonous scrapes of shovels through dirt were the only sounds that penetrated the dark.

What was to become the last issue of food to the Americans came on April 7. Like some others, Errett's regiment received one bag of rice and seven jars of mustard to share among the lot of them. That was everything edible within reach of the 200th and 515th. Others lucky enough to receive food had no more than one tablespoon of condensed milk and three tablespoons of rice per man for breakfast. The lunch menu was expanded by one can each of tomatoes and corned beef shared by five.[11] As Errett swallowed the last morsel of his breakfast at seven in the morning, enemy bombing resumed, interfering with American troops trying to establish defensive lines. The Japanese bombers' accuracy was poor but improved later in the day when their bombs hit within two hundred yards of their intended targets.

On this final full day of battle on Bataan, no men were held in reserve. All defenders who were physically capable fought. Most were trying to function on one hour of sleep over the past harrowing fifty-four hours, barely any food, and many were down to their last canteen of water. As they straggled through the bombed-out, charred wasteland that had been a lush jungle not so long ago, they kept a sharp eye opened for the mixed cogon grass and bamboo stands, signs of possible water. Sometimes they were lucky, found water, and drank their fill although mud and sand came with it. At other times, the undrinkable water was contaminated with gasoline.[12]

Most of the 200th regiment moved in behind Bataan airfield and set up their guns. Some of the regiment were assigned the task of retrieving water from Mariveles. Provided with three cans of food each, they set out only to discover the Japanese were at their destination before they were. Swarms of Americans, Filipino army troops, and civilians retreated. The dead, wounded, and exhausted choked ditches along roads as the numbers of those who simply could not go any farther increased. The road itself bore a steady stream of vehicles moving south, three abreast. Only a handful of American tanks headed for the front lines to effect whatever defense they could; however, without infantry to back them up, they were largely useless. The east road was particularly bad. Complicating the problem was the lack of medical stations. No one knew where the wounded could be taken for treatment, mostly because those areas had yet to be set up.

Late in the afternoon, American troops encountered six enemy tanks rolling toward them, precipitating another retreat mostly carried out after sunset. By the end of the day, the last regiment west of Mt. Samat was destroyed and the Japanese gained considerable ground. One of the last fire fights of the day was between two low-flying Japanese bombers taking aim at U.S. teams trying to blow up the last of the bridges and the American gunners protecting them. The bridge was successfully destroyed as well as one bomber when a shell clipped its wing causing it to crash.[13]

Everyone not already to the most southern part of Bataan was ordered to retreat there after sundown on the 7th. They moved cautiously into the ink-black darkness by each soldier holding on to the one in front of him in order not to become separated. The leader of one such line of retreating men walked directly into a bivouac of sleeping Japanese soldiers around three the next morning. The Americans proceeded through with grenades in hand, pins pulled, and ready to toss if any awoke. Miraculously, none did. It was only later in the wee hours of the morning that they discovered most of the grenades lacked powder.[14]

Large units needing to retreat further and who had no or little food were disassembled into groups of three and four men and, with no more than four clips of ammunition per soldier, were ordered to move south as best they could on their own. They were instructed to join any larger unit they might happen to meet along the way.[15] Engineers also retreating under the cover of darkness carried out work orders along their route. They felled trees, turned over disabled vehicles across trails, and stacked

10. Surrendered

anything else they could put across trails to slow down the Japanese advance. Word was passed down for the troops to try to get to Corregidor via the shore near Mariveles if at all possible.[16] Most could not make their way to the coast due to the glut of Japanese troops in the area. A few who did make it around the Japanese to the shore missed the few boats going out. They attempted to swim to Corregidor, but the shark-infested waters brutally ended their crossing.[17] The last boat to Corregidor left at daybreak on April 9.[18]

Throughout the day on the 8th, Japanese pilots continued to heavily bomb the roads. Official word was being transmitted by telephone, radio, and runners that General King had determined their situation on Bataan was hopeless and it was senseless to risk the men's lives in a battle that could not be won. He had decided to surrender the troops.

As the USS *Conopus* was scuttled, the men of the 200th and 515th received news that had apparently taken some time to be processed and reach them. They were now officially recognized as two separate brigades, a situation that had existed for months now. The 200th, 515th, and Philippine Provisional Coast Artillery Brigade (the scouts) were the only units in Corps II holding defensive lines at midnight April 8–9.[19] They were dug in and stubbornly refused to give up any ground. Roads were jammed with people coming back from the front lines. The exodus to Mariveles was one of chaos. The odds were clearly against the defenders. They were facing over 250,000 Japanese on Luzon and 43,000 more on Mindanao. Fighting had been going on for 124 days. The top generals had hoped they could hold out through the end of May, but that was impossible. From the day the war began to the day of surrender, the fighting men were forsaken, deprived, harassed, hampered, threatened, and stymied. Decisions mostly rendered by the U.S. government and its military created dire conditions. They had minimal food, medicine, clothing, and ammunition.

At 5:45 p.m. on April 8, the 200th and 515th began their last deployment as MP directed the retreat along the roads. Just before moving out, Errett heard yelping in the distance similar to that of pup coyotes he heard back home in the middle of the night. He discovered the sound emanated from the advancing Japanese when they stumbled across a body. The Americans had intentionally repositioned the dead along the road and trail sides in hopes of creating a makeshift alarm. Only minutes from the time Errett began walking, the familiar yelping telegraphed the Japanese advancing and they were surprisingly close. The American batteries stopped, aimed, and shot through the darkness in the direction of the sound. How much damage this did was uncertain, but it helped keep Errett focused.

General King sent orders to Brigadier General Sage that any of the six antiaircraft guns that could not be modified in short order for use as infantry weapons were to be destroyed at 7:00 p.m. and the antiaircraft units converted to infantrymen. The orders were carried out. By dusk, the 515th was formed into a line that started on the edge of a canyon descended into it following a trail above the Cabcaben airfield about eight miles east of Mariveles. The 200th were in place by 9:00 p.m. on the other side of the road. They would provide cover for the retreating troops. They tensely waited. The minutes seemed to tick by in concert with the erratic rhythm of war surrounding them. At half past nine, the ground shook violently. Startled men girded themselves, their eyes darting side to side, searching for the source. Then they realized they were in the midst of an earthquake. The epicenter of the 7.4 magnitude earthquake was west of the island of Mindanao and about 125 miles southwest of Bataan. Trucks swayed, causing their springs to let out ungodly squeaks. Loose items were tumbling in every direction, adding to the chaos and destruction of the area. "Even God doesn't want the Japs to have Bataan,"[20] Gilewitch thought as the shaking ground began to still.

Ultimately, the battle was lost due to starvation, disease, lack of ammunition in the face of an overwhelming number of Japanese troops, and the inability of the U.S. military to send reinforcements. An agonized General King sent the surrender order out to the troops in Bataan without talking it over with General Wainwright on Corregidor. The order was to surrender on April 9, exactly seventy-eight years to the day after General Robert E. Lee's army surrendered to General Ulysses S. Grant. They were instructed to turn themselves in to the nearest Japanese unit. King knew they would fight to the last if asked to but thought it useless to sacrifice so many good men. They were in a no-win situation. All defensive lines on the Bataan Peninsula had collapsed. He ordered depots, equipment, and warehouses destroyed at midnight.

There were six times more Filipino fighters than Americans, and Sage knew that that number of prisoners would overwhelm the Japanese resources. Filipino fighters had already been relieved of duty a few weeks earlier; many had left seeking safety. Filipinos could blend into the community, not a viable option for the Americans. The last organized unit of Bataan defenders to surrender was the forty-eight-hour-old infantry unit Group A of the Philippine Provisional Coast Artillery Brigade (Antiaircraft) under the command of Sage.[21]

Some men were sullen, others were angry, most were frightened, and all were weary, but they went about their business of rendering useless anything that would benefit the Japanese. Under the dark sky of a moonless night, the men got about their task. Ammunition dumps exploded for an hour, creating large fire clouds that lit up the war-torn jungle. They

10. Surrendered

rendered radios, vehicles, and other equipment useless. Their tasks were bookended in the dark by aftershocks of the earthquake, one around 1:00 a.m. and another an hour or so before dawn. As if Mother Nature were attempting to help the Americans, the second aftershock destroyed a stockpile of ammunition that they had not had time to blow up.

At around five in the morning on April 9, the 515th and 200th could hear Japanese tanks rumbling below them in the canyon from their position above in an irrigation ditch. They had not yet received word about the surrender. Eventually, the surrender order from King filtered down to officers, to their underlings, to the end person in the ditch, and up the line of crouched men. They quietly went into rapid motion to rid themselves of weapons after disabling them and grabbed a stash of combat rations they found near a hospital just before Japanese troops made their appearance. VanBuskirk vividly remembers his last meal as a free man: "I shared a gallon of ketchup with some other guy."[22]

It did not take long for the new prisoners to witness the first killing of an American just outside the fence at Cabcaben airfield. One marine was being forced to dig a hole. When it was an adequate size for a grave, he was ordered to stop. The marine threw down the shovel and flicked his lit cigarette in a Japanese soldier's face. He was shot instantly before the cigarette hit the ground and "his body slumped down into the fresh hole. The guard just turned and walked away."[23]

It was the end of the fighting. The Japanese expected intact units to surrender. Instead, they slowly appeared in small groups of men from unrelated units totaling an astonishing thirty-seven thousand troops and far more later. The scenario was a little different for the 515th and 200th, though, since they remained intact and anchored to their last defensive position at Cabcaben when dawn came on April 9. They had been the first to fire on the Japanese in the Philippines and were the last to fire in Bataan. In their last position, they endured shelling from their own forces who were answering the volleys of the Japanese. The men from Santa Fe totaled around two hundred. The Santa Feans in the 515th tallied thirty-five confirmed airplane hits and the 200th had fifty-one.[24] They were also the closest to the Japanese as they advanced to take charge of the surrendered Americans. In the end, fewer than two hundred of the eighteen hundred men of the 515th and 200th died in battle, but only half came home alive.

The Japanese searched the new prisoners, confiscating belts, pens, jewelry, money, and sometimes footwear from those walking in to surrender. As Errett's turn to be searched approached, his captors' interest waned. Then he noticed they seemed unsure as to what to do next. The imperial soldiers ambled among their captives puzzling over new circumstances. Their stature compared to the taller Americans gave the impression of shorter pawns moving across the squares of a chessboard surrounded by the larger pieces.

Later in the afternoon, the Japanese began assembling three to four hundred POWs in the immediate area of Cabcaben airfield on a hill overlooking one side of the runways. They then moved their field artillery into position just below the POWs and commenced firing on Corregidor. Not to be daunted, Corregidor returned fire, propelling one shell in the direction of the American POWs. The men scattered as best they could. The explosive whistled overhead and landed where moments ago they had been standing. Fortunately, it happened to be a dud, the one time the men were relieved about problems with their ammunition. No one was hurt, and the men regrouped only to be confronted with a shocking display of things to come when a kerfuffle broke out next to them.

A senior Japanese officer paced over to one of his subordinates and tersely called him to attention. What happened next was something none of the men had ever witnessed. The officer beat the living daylights out of the soldier. The prisoners were shocked, but it would happen again and again before their ordeal was over. The official status of the surrendering Americans and Filipinos gave the Japanese considerable latitude in their harsh treatment. To negotiate a complete surrender on Bataan, they insisted that all prisoners taken in would be treated as war criminals until all had surrendered. Once that had happened, though, the Japanese officers announced that they had not signed the Geneva accords regarding POW treatment although they pledged in February 1942, through the Swiss government, to abide by its provisions with respect to the treatment of POWs.

Bataan and Corregidor (which fell a month later) were the last Allied strongholds in Southeast Asia to fall to the Japanese. Many Filipinos either could not or would not leave the battlefield and return home. Filipinos surrendering numbered five times more than Americans. The eighteen hundred men who had arrived in the Philippines as the 200th Coast Artillery (Antiaircraft) regiment had few losses, but that was about to change. Disgust and contempt seethed through the Japanese for warriors who surrendered. To surrender would be a crime against Japan and the emperor himself. To die for the emperor meant the highest and most honorable sacrifice one could achieve and almost none shied away from that honor.

The protracted defense of the Philippine islands had pushed the Japanese six months behind schedule in their plans to invade Australia by acquiring control of various Pacific islands. Their plans had to be completely revised. In fact, it is argued that the attack on Australia was thwarted by the defenders of the Philippines. The delay also allowed General MacArthur to mount an offensive. Both sides were gearing up for more than they had yet endured.

11

In Enemy Hands

The Japanese officers looked over their enemy as they prepared to march Errett and the others from Cabcaben to the train station at San Fernando fifty-four miles north. Those further southwest around Mariveles had a distance of sixty-five miles to trek. The Japanese high command was expecting only about twenty-five thousand POWs to care for, not twice as many as would soon straggle in. The Japanese were bewildered as they surveyed the prisoners. How could these men in such terrible condition have resisted for so long?

The question gave rise to alarm. Were others hiding, waiting in ambush? Most could not understand the other's language. They pulled several POWs aside and attempted to beat the information from them, but the technique was ineffective since they possessed no knowledge of who was hiding, who was surrendering, or how many troops they had. Word spread quickly that the Japanese were taking Americans prisoner and killing the Filipino men. Filipinos were trying their best to run, hide, and escape capture.

All the while, more and more American troops were arriving to turn themselves over to the mercy of the Japanese. The Japanese were dealing with two problems at once—the enemy firing on them from Corregidor and rounding up the Americans on Bataan. A rattle of trucks joined the din of artillery and shouting as a convoy rolled in. The trucks jerked to a halt about the same time Japanese reinforcements picked up from the train depot in San Fernando disgorged from the back ends. They stopped where most of the 515th and 200th were gathered. Hastily, about 375 men from the glut of POWs were culled and herded into the trucks to be taken to Camp O'Donnell.[1] Errett was not one of them but glad to see some of his buddies were. Those POWs arriving by truck were responsible for getting Camp O'Donnell, the first of several prison camps Errett would be in, ready for the prisoners following on foot. These lucky few transported by trucks arrived at Camp O'Donnell at dawn the following morning. Civilian POWs were kept separate from the military and usually taken to their respective prison camps by vehicle.

In a cloud of dust from the departing trucks and through a series of gestures, grunts, and rifle prodding, Errett was told to raise his arms and clasp his hands behind his neck along with the others. Talking among the prisoners was not allowed and was met with a rifle butt to the head. Some GIs tossed their helmets so they could not be used as scrap metal to further the Japanese war effort. Those without helmets had their heads cratered when the butt end of a rifle came their way for whatever reason. One hundred POWs at a time were lined up in rows four across, twenty-five men to a column, and prodded forward by rifled bayonets.

The first of the marchers to reach Camp O'Donnell made the trek in three days, the last who traveled the entire sixty-five-mile route arrived ten days later. Many did not survive the ordeal. Errett began his march against the looming backdrop of the Mariveles Mountains. Many POWs found the daily temperature rise close to unbearable. Even under better circumstances, it would have been arduous. Marchers, trucks, and tanks churned billowing clouds of choking dust into the air. The guards marching with POWs donned surgical masks to prevent inhaling the powder-fine dust filling the air. The POWs marched day and night with minimal stops for rest.

Japanese truck drivers plowed through the throng indiscriminately, running over marchers and then steered to the other side of the road to run through marchers there. Their passengers wielded rifle butts against POW heads, splitting many wide open along the way. Bodies were run over time and again along the route, some pulverized into nothing more than stains in the dust, unrecognizable as anything that once had life. The weakest prisoners had an advantage if they were placed in the middle two columns where POWs either side of them could aid them if they stumbled, but once down, it was usually a death sentence for anyone down or trying to help.

Errett witnessed various tortures that grew aggressively more deadly as the miles clicked away. Initially, guards abruptly cut marchers and then beat them. When a beaten man slumped to the ground, he was frisked for trinkets that the guard might fancy. If none were found, the man was repeatedly kicked. The beatings became more vicious as time passed. If the POW could not stand up, he was skewered several times with a bayonet. But having POWs die so quickly became unsatisfying. Instead of causing immediate death, the POW was rolled onto his back and run through only once in the gut and various body parts sliced away. This extended the time it took to die and was more painful. It became a game for the Japanese, eliciting pleasure from the guards. They pointed, laughed, and mimicked their writhing victims.

In short order, Errett discovered that anything Japanese found on a

POW meant instant death and other items were lumped into the contraband category. One poor soul had a cigarette lighter with "made in Japan" stamped on it. One guard stood aside the man, his rifle pointing at his chest. The other guard drew his sword from the scabbard, swung, and lopped off one arm. Without hesitating, he raised it again and severed the other arm before the man fell to the ground. Then he was stabbed repeatedly while Japanese soldiers laughed. The goal of this game was to sever both arms before the body hit the ground. "From the number of armless corpses already on both sides of the road," reflected Gilewitch, "this must have happened numerous times."[2]

It was considered a capital offense if a prisoner was found with Japanese money. It was assumed, and probably correctly, that the money had been taken from a dead Japanese soldier. Robbing the dead often elicited a beheading. Armless corpses, headless bodies, and dead prisoners propped alongside the road with their penises shoved in their mouths lined the route along with the numerous lifeless bodies that were run over by vehicles. The spectacle wrenched the stomachs of the prisoners. The treatment inspired some to endure the march and reach camp. For others, it was a reason to give up or give in—to just die or do something to be killed to get it over with.

Fresh and rested replacements for the Japanese were constant along the entire route. It seemed that the ones being relieved briefed their replacements about the sadistic pleasures they had devised in torturing the prisoners. And although the dehydrated marchers had no water, the guards did. They stood among the prisoners, raised their canteens to their lips, sipped slowly, let some water dribble down their chins, smacked their lips, and broke out in laughter.[3] In all, the marchers passed a dozen or so artesian wells along the way, lifesaving water gurgling from the spigots the prisoners were not allowed to access. Desperation pushed some to try to fill cupped hands held shakily underneath the pipe. It amounted to just one more reason to be killed, bayoneted during day and shot during the night. Others simply died from the lack of water. Dying for a drink was a literal reality.

The march proceeded at an irregular pace. Sometimes it was almost a run, sometimes a fast walk, and sometimes a slow dragging step. Abrupt changes in the pace caused the very weak to collapse, producing more targets to slay. The guards then ordered the adjacent prisoners to drag the body to the side of the road.

Some prisoners were waylaid briefly in a fifteen-acre field. Surprisingly, some of the POWs had managed to procure food. The more fortunate among the fifteen hundred prisoners who still had money on them were able to buy some food from Filipinos to stave off the hunger. A joint of sugar cane fetched one dollar as did a turnip. A canteen of rice could be had for twenty dollars, but the money eventually lost value and was replaced mostly by cigarettes.[4]

The columns of prisoners sometimes walked through the night, but the usual first overnight stop was the village of Balanga, nineteen miles from Cabcaben and a normal distance for American infantry in good condition.[5] Colonel Tashimitsu was assigned by Homma to move POWs from Mariveles and assemble them at Balanga.[6] Upon arrival there, Errett was searched and then stuffed into an outside compound for the night with hundreds of others. The cool night was a welcome relief from the scorching days. A good rest was mostly unattainable, though. Clouds of mosquitoes swarmed over Errett; however, the insects had trouble penetrating the mud, blood, and scabs that cocooned him. It was the constant buzzing, hunger, thirst, and aches that made sleep elusive.

Through sign language, guards had promised food would be provided to the weak and starving men. That promise would not be fulfilled for at least five days or longer for some. Some relief came when the marchers neared a village and Filipinos appeared roadside clutching an assortment of food. They began tossing it to the POWs. When seen by a guard, they were bashed in the face, chest, head, stomach, or wherever they could deliver their best hit. Not to be dissuaded, the Filipinos continued but more cautiously. The prisoners felt disgust, anger, and helplessness when young Filipino boys were sent reeling or babies were skewered out of their mother's arms with a bayonet. The bravery and compassion they demonstrated was heartening beyond words to the POWs.

Major General Yashikanda Kawane assumed responsibility of the POWs at Balanga and was charged with getting them to Camp O'Donnell,[7] previously used as a Philippine army training facility. His method was more benevolent compared to what the prisoners had experienced thus far. Some were moved to the San Fernando train depot directly from Balanga by truck the next day, and during the ride, they were provided with food—one rice ball. Those who marched the long distance, however, far outnumbered those driven in by truck. Those who made the longer journey by foot were waylaid one to three nights at San Fernando.

The comings and goings of prisoners at San Fernando was erratic. Strings of tired prisoners had their first view of the camp from a short distance away. It was a huge area with a large wooden building in the center enclosed by a high fence sporting barbed wire on top. Countless Japanese patrolled just outside the fence. It was a modified cock-fighting arena. The exhausted prisoners sat inside on the ground and were given the first food they had since surrender—a cup of cooked rice, one in the morning and one in the evening. Within a couple of days, the compound was crammed with POWs. New arrivals were funneled in by pushing and clubbing the men while constantly shouting. The longer the stay, the worse conditions became, but at least they were not walking.

Movement from San Fernando to the train depot was sporadic. Guards used long poles to jab men into groups and force them from the compound when the time came to continue toward Camp O'Donnell. They were still weak and had no idea where they were going or how they would survive the day. The Japanese guards flanked either side of the column of prisoners at regularly spaced intervals. These guards had considerably more control over themselves than those in the preceding days. There was no shouting, no torture, and no killings, and a POW could assist another without punishment.

It was a mercifully short walk to the depot where they were brought to an abrupt stop, then inched forward ever so slowly to the edge of the tracks aside the waiting boxcars. Relief was momentary before evaporating. Clubs came out and rained down on their heads and shoulders, the standard procedure for separating and moving the men. Using these tactics, groups of one hundred were put into each scorching wooden boxcar that reasonably held half that number. They were packed so tightly that they could not sit, could not turn around, could not move. The door slammed shut making it difficult to merely breathe.

Concentrating on breathing held every person's attention. Some slipped into unconsciousness but were held upright by the crunch of bodies around them. Some of those slipped beyond unconsciousness into death. The three- to four-hour train ride ended in Capas. The prisoners' eyes were shut when the doors rolled open. Only after fresh air swathed them and they managed some deep breaths did they realize the train had stopped. Ramps were thrown up to the doorways, and gaunt, dazed marchers stumble out. Those who were simply being held up by the mass of other bodies around them slumped to the floor. Those who got out were lined up next to the tracks.[8]

The fresh air somewhat revived the men, and they found it easier than it had been in days to walk. They had only a few blocks to go to reach the town of Capas proper where the Filipino women had laid out an abundance of food for them. There were rows of ready-to-go meals—bananas, mangoes, chicken, pork, and rice wrapped in banana leaves. The Japanese guards lined up the POWs in front of the food, paused, and then marched them away with nothing. Undeterred, the Filipino women tossed as much as they could to the POWs.[9] The thought of the food left behind made the nearly ten-mile walk to O'Donnell seem longer for the men. Filipino villagers living near Camp O'Donnell were allowed to give other groups of POWs food and water, which they did, even though they were in dire straits themselves, living in barrios decimated by poverty and combat.

Many more groups of marchers, however, were still being subjected to ruthless treatment. Some cargo trains transporting POWs from San Fernando to Capas stopped midway at Clark airfield. After making their way down the ramp, they were put in a secure area and told to lay out all their belongings. Seven men of the estimated six hundred, five of whom were from the original 200th, were pulled aside for having Japanese artifacts. They were marched away and never heard of again. It was later learned that they were executed.[10]

It was at Clark airfield during this time that the POWs' paths crossed with a Filipino they had known before the war. He was of rare character among his countrymen in that he had been allied with the Japanese while he held a prewar job at the post exchange at Clark. No longer needed as a spy, his new position was that of interpreter, and the message smugly relayed to the POWs was "Things are going to be plenty tough for you. We hate Americans and don't care if all of you die."[11] His new posting was Camp O'Donnell.

Errett's death march ordeal spanned ten days of exhaustion, hunger, dehydration, sleep deprivation, near suffocation, and abuse. Most of those from the 515th and 200th arrived at O'Donnell by April 19. Errett was relieved to see so many from his unit as he marched through the gate. They readied the camp for the incoming marchers, doing the best they could with what they had. Their priority was to purify water using iodine to make it drinkable for the thirsty arrivals. After hours in the hot sun, the over-aged, arrogant, shorts-clad Japanese commandant, Captain Yoshio Tsuneyoshi, also known as Baggy Pants, yelled a speech to the arriving prisoners from atop a box to improve his stature. He was short at about five feet three, bowlegged, sported a little Hitler mustache, and wore baggy shorts, a white sport shirt draped with medals, and riding boots with spurs. His interpreter translated a thirty-minute boast of Japanese superiority and how they would fight for one hundred years, if necessary, to win the war. He made it clear that their status was as captives and not prisoners, and therefore, the Japanese could do anything they wished to them. Errett witnessed men falling dead during the welcoming address as it continued without pause or recognition of collapsing men. Tsuneyoshi then sat and ate lunch in front of the starving prisoners.

Those who made the death march shared their experiences with those who did not. It was the first they had heard of the atrocities, yet there were many more to come and no one would escape them. They sat stunned, in disbelief, as they listened to the sickening accounts of dismemberments, clubbings, shootings, beheadings, beatings, flayings, and stabbings and those who were driven over so many times that they simply became a discolored part of the road. Some had calculated hearing one gunshot every half mile walked.[12]

12

Wrestling with Defeat Stateside

News of defeat in the Philippines quickly reached Santa Fe. Families dug nickels from their pockets and purses to read the bad news in the *Santa Fe New Mexican*. Two editions were printed on April 9, 1942, the day after the surrender date in the United States—a regular paper and an extra printing done on pink paper. The glum headline was in three-inch bold letters: "BATAAN CRUMPLES." The bleak news spread over four pages with headings such as "Doubt if Many Can Get Away," "Bulk of Defenders Army Lost," "First Corps Makes Gallant Counter Attack but Fails," "Troops Completely Spent," "Fighting New Mexico Regiment Somewhere on Luzon at Finish of Gallant Defense," and "Charlton [New Mexico adjutant general] Confident of Boys' Courage." In one, it was reported that 336,853 Allied troops were in the Philippines when it collapsed. Other articles appealed to the civilian war effort: "You Have Wanted to Help—Be Ready for the Minute Man," where citizens were alerted that in Santa Fe, volunteers would conduct a door-to-door campaign on the next Tuesday and Wednesday asking for war bond pledges or collecting stamps, all proceeds to aid our military.

People did not stray far from their living room and kitchen radios. Two blocks east of the plaza in downtown Santa Fe, KVSF radio station sent out news broadcasts from seven in the morning to eleven at night. The morning tandem broadcasts were *The Press* and the *American Red Cross Program* followed by William Winter and the news in mid-afternoon. The news and news of the world closed out the night. All in all, it was a combined amount of time just slightly over an hour in duration. After nine fifteen at night, after the last news aired, families were left to wonder and worry in their homes until broadcasts resumed the following morning.

President Franklin Roosevelt punctuated the regular programming with his own messages. In them, he chose words to bolster people's resolve most of the time, but as much as he would like to, he could not shroud the dire circumstances. Listeners' hearts sank when he compared the battle at the Alamo to that of Bataan.¹ Was that the awful fate of our troops in the Philippines? Was everyone lost?

New Mexico governor John E. Miles did his utmost to prop up the people's courage through a series of proclamations after the fall of Bataan. His first was a day of prayer in New Mexico asking for the "spiritual aid of the Almighty in the strenuous and difficult days ahead," as it was "entirely fitting that we beseech the blessing of God for those who may be in prison camps and for those who are still fighting the battle of survival. With God's help we will hasten the day when the defenders of the Philippines can return to their families and homes and carry on again their civilian lives in peace and security."²

Santa Fe mayor Manuel Lujan, Sr., no relation to Errett, immediately called for a meeting to confer with all civic organizations regarding the role of the Santa Fe Council of National Defense with regard to the war effort. The strategy ultimately agreed on was to pool resources through donations of money, supplies for care packages, scrap rubber, and metal, just as other cities and farming communities were doing throughout the country. People were encouraged to purchase war bonds. Rationing of critical items such as gasoline was ubiquitous.

The U.S. military went to work to redress the assault on U.S. troops in the Pacific soon after the bombing of Pearl Harbor. Project Tokyo was to be a retaliatory air strike against the Japanese homeland. Its primary purpose was twofold: boost morale among the U.S. citizenry and impede Japan's progress across the Pacific Ocean. General Hideki Tōjō was aware that U.S. Navy bombers' range was limited to about three hundred miles to effect a strike and return. With no known U.S. air base within that range, Tōjō was not concerned about an attack on Japanese soil.

Project Tokyo planned to circumvent this limitation. Its success depended on modifying medium-range bombers to allow them to take off from navy aircraft carriers with a payload of bombs. The only airplane that could be transformed thus was the army's B-25 Mitchell. Lieutenant Colonel James Doolittle was tasked with assembling and training pilots. He vaguely outlined a risky mission to prospective pilots with undisclosed targets. Starting immediately and in complete secrecy, pilots underwent extensive training in Florida. They would have less than a month to perfect a way to get the heavily laden Mitchells airborne from terrestrial runways modified to simulate the length of an aircraft carrier.

Momentum for the operation was strong. Within several weeks, the USS *Enterprise*, USS *Hornet*, and their escorts met in the Pacific to carry out the mission. One of the sailors on the *Hornet* sighted a Japanese picket boat, the *Nitto Maru*, when they were about six hundred miles from Japan.

12. Wrestling with Defeat Stateside

Had the Japanese on board the vessel detected the Americans? Had they sent a message forward? The logical conclusion was that if the Americans had seen the small boat, their giant ships could easily be seen. The USS *Nashville* was ordered to attack, and as a safety precaution, Doolittle and his pilots were ordered to ready for evacuation from the *Hornet*. The *Nitto* raised a white flag nearly thirty minutes after they had been hit. American boats sped toward it, but it sank just as they approached. Eleven Japanese sailors were rescued. They discovered, when interrogating the crew, their captain had shot himself and the location of the American ships and planes had been radioed out, so Vice Admiral Halsey ordered the attack to commence on the cities of Tokyo, Yokosuka, Yokohama, Kobe, and Nagoya in Japan's main island of Honshu.[3] It was only nine days after the men on Bataan were surrendered. The B-25s were at the very maximum range in simply reaching their target, much less returning.

In the early morning of April 18, 1942, and with the B-25 bellies filled with bombs, the pilots eagerly set out on their mission despite the less-than-ideal circumstances. They reached Tokyo and the other target cities without incident. Whistling bombs plummeted toward Japanese soil. For the most part, the physical damage was minor. The Japanese carrier *Ryuho* in dry dock at Yokosuka was hardest hit. The real coup was the psychological devastation rendered by the attack. The Japanese were at a loss in comprehending how the United States had pulled off an attack on their capital.

Low on fuel, Doolittle's squadron headed to wherever they could make it but looking for a friendly air base. All but one of the B-25 bomber pilots were forced to bail out. Eleven crews ditched their planes over China while three crash-landed there. The Japanese meted out severe reprisals on the Chinese in Chekiang Province who assisted or were perceived to have assisted the downed crews, resulting in the killing of an estimated two hundred and fifty thousand Chinese civilians. The one pilot who landed safely did so in Vladivostok, Russia, where the crew was held along with their transport for a short term. In all, eight crew members were taken prisoner by the Japanese, of which half died during captivity. Sixteen B-25 Mitchells were lost.

Admiral Yamamoto regarded the raid as a "mortifying personal defeat."[4] With deflated morale, he expanded the defensive perimeter beyond its resources to do so and initiated the planning stage for an attack on Midway. The United States, in the meantime, sent troops to the European theater, and by late April, the newspapers in Santa Fe were touting the Americans' success in driving back the Germans and announcing the benefit of buying the newly issued government savings bonds.

Despite the end of the battle on the Bataan Peninsula, angst in New

Mexico escalated. Responding to an inquiry from Governor Miles, the War Department replied that "with the fall of Corregidor we must assume that the officers and men of the 200th Coast Artillery are prisoners of war," and when an official list is "received, it will be made public." Attached to the letter was a list of 106 men of the 200th who were evacuated to Corregidor before the fall of Bataan.[5] Errett was not among them. One event buoyed the outlook of the War Department. The Japanese code had been broken, revealing their plans to attack Midway.

The adjutant general of the United States reported a slightly different update to Jess. They expected a list of POWs from Japan transmitted through Geneva soon. Until then, the men not yet reported to be under Japanese control would be listed as missing in action. But as soon as Errett's name shows up officially as a prisoner, the Lujans would be notified. If no news of Errett comes from the Japanese for twelve months, the War Department will reevaluate Errett's pay and allowances, and any questions regarding continuation of benefits were to be directed to the American Red Cross.[6]

Under regulations developed pursuant to Executive Order 9066, orders for Japanese and those of Japanese descent to be removed from Sacramento, California, came in May as Japan was holding over one thousand U.S. Navy personnel as prisoners. Part of Roosevelt's internment strategy was to have Japanese people to trade for American POWs. Facilities for internees in the Japanese internment camp in Santa Fe included a staffed hospital, several barracks with iron cots, a softball diamond, croquet sets, a library with both English and Japanese material, horseshoe tossing area, radios, censored in- and out-mail service, a canteen, a bakery, a recreation hall, a kitchen for preparing Japanese cuisine, a hothouse to grow vegetables, a twenty-acre garden, a laundry, and several other service buildings. Although the internees favored playing softball above all recreational activities, others such as watching movies, performing dramas, competing in judo and Ping-Pong tournaments, orchestral performances, and conducting science classes had dedicated followings.[7] The detainees cooked their own meals, were allowed unlimited visitors, and practiced their own religions whether it be Christianity, Buddhism, or Shinto.[8]

Around July 1, 1942, a fire broke out and destroyed the internees' and officers' mess halls and several other buildings. Five weeks later, in September, all of the Japanese were evacuated and the camp was temporarily closed.[9] After attending to some paperwork and cleaning out the camp, it was vacated except for a couple of caretakers. The camp remained dormant through most of the winter.

With the fate of the 200th unknown, a desire to pay tribute to them grew among New Mexicans. A committee of Santa Feans came up with a

12. Wrestling with Defeat Stateside

solution that involved moving the 200th's regimental marker from Logan Heights at Ft. Bliss to the state capitol grounds in Santa Fe. A solemn dedication ceremony followed on May 28, 1942, after the marker was moved. New Mexico adjutant general Charlton said the marker was "the most intimate thing we could find to maintain a link with the regiment."[10] *Life* magazine's July 7, 1942, issue covering the event included a photograph of Governor Miles and General Charlton. No matter how artistically rough the marker, New Mexicans loved it being installed on the capitol grounds.

The war effort stateside generated other large-scale government projects. Santa Fe was selected as the site for one of several hospitals to be constructed to take care of injured veterans returning stateside. Construction of Bruns Army Hospital on the south side of town began mid–1943 and received its first patient shortly thereafter. Shortly afterward, Errett's father, Louis, was employed at Bruns as a storekeeper. He became good friends with his boss, a colonel, who kept Louis updated with any news he heard about the POW situation in Japan. Louis's previous job at the New Mexico State Penitentiary made news around the same time when 241 inmates sent a petition to Governor Miles requesting release "to serve in active duty on condition that when released from the army we will report to New Mexico authorities for such disposition of the remainder of our sentences as they deem fit to impose."[11] Louis knew many of these men well. He had ordered special hand-crafted leather belts and wallets from some. Their products were top notch, and he was impressed by their willingness to fight in the war. But they were, after all, convicts, and how much trust could one put in such a person, especially if your life depended on them? The job at Bruns was better. Other families in town knew nothing about POWs in the Far East, so it was a relief to Louis to have a conduit through hospital personnel regarding news even though nothing specific about Errett or his location ever came through.[12]

13

A Parade of Death at Camp O'Donnell

Between April 12 and 24, 1942, between fifty thousand and sixty thousand POWs arrived at the fifty-acre Camp O'Donnell. The Capas road through the camp split the Americans from the Filipino POWs. Years later, the death tally for this camp through January 1943 was determined to be more than fifteen hundred Americans and twenty-five thousand Filipinos.[1] As POWs straggled into O'Donnell, Australians in Timor were rescued from that Japanese-occupied Pacific island in the Malay Archipelago. Camp O'Donnell was originally built to house twelve thousand Filipino prewar troops. One water faucet was designated for prisoner use. Sometimes men had to stand in line two days to get water.[2]

The scene intimidated the prisoners as they entered O'Donnell. Large buildings made of bamboo and thatched roofs included tall, imposing guard towers all around. A high barbed wire fence enclosed the prisoners' area, and there were thousands of prisoners. Errett saw most sitting or lying down; only a few could stand. There were 8,675 American survivors immediately after marchers reached O'Donnell. Within six weeks, one out of every six of them died of malaria—an estimated 1,450 prisoners.[3] Malaria victims suffered two to three hours of chills, which was then replaced by fever for two to three hours and followed by profuse sweating for two to four more hours. Then the poor soul might sleep a little only to repeat the cycle the next day.[4] Other prominent diseases included scurvy, wet beriberi and the considerably more painful dry beriberi. It was here that Errett learned from General King himself, with tears in his eyes, that the surrender was his call and his responsibility alone.

Some death march prisoners were held in camps north of Luzon after the march. There was an underground network of people in civilian camps and Filipino priests who smuggled news, food, supplies, and money to those prisoners. Two months previously in February 1942, the Japanese had taken into custody hundreds of British and Australian POWs from

13. A Parade of Death at Camp O'Donnell

Shanghai. Soon afterward, on February 20, the Japanese enacted Regulation #8, which stated in part, "3 yen per month from prisoner of war pay was to be set aside for POW daily necessities."[5] None of the Americans at Camp O'Donnell ever heard of or were provided amenities using this allotment.

After being searched, one wool American blanket was issued to each POW. Two American officers had what was considered contraband. One was executed for having Japanese money in his pockets.[6] The confined men's barrack assignments followed grouping by their unit, such as infantry, air corps, antiaircraft artillery, and so forth, then rank. Their first morning began with roll call at formation to ensure accountability. They gathered and counted off although accuracy proved difficult since so many were dying each day. Their first two meals were small and non-nourishing. Breakfast was lugao and dinner comprised of soup made from sweet potato greens with a little bit of rice.

Errett's fifty-foot-long open-ended barracks was constructed of bamboo poles held together by rattan strips. Cogon grass fronds were layered on top for roofs, and woven bamboo shutters hung as flaps covering windows in the grass-made sides. The structures provided no protection against flies and mosquitoes. The huts stood two stories high and about eight feet off the ground. A middle aisle ran the length of the hut. Two bays of sleeping cots, one above the other, were on each side. The lower bay was about two and a half feet off the floor and about four and a half feet long. Split bamboo formed the decking of the few cots available. Upon arrival, many barracks sported unfinished roofs and only a few cots.

A few of the prisoners managed to grab and hold on to C-rations before the march began. Those were the lucky few who had something to eat for a few days after arriving at O'Donnell. Since the Japanese were not prepared for the vast number of prisoners they held, meals from them were scarce. To cope, 135 dogs were killed and fed to the thousands of POWs at O'Donnell.[7] Over the course of time at O'Donnell, notes, money, and medicine were smuggled in in hollowed-out fruit and mislabeled medicines. Money and medicine were exchanged for meager portions of rotten fish, vegetables, camotes, cornmeal, coconut milk, corn soup, canned food, coconut brittle candy, rice, ginger tea, and white radishes, which Errett could never in his life eat again. This was all, of course, a black market activity. Malnutrition was rampant and led to neurotic pain, numb hands and feet, eye aches, blurred sight, double vision, raised and red skin spots that dried, then scaled, then bled, lip sores, swollen tongues, anemia, headaches, toothaches, and incontinence.

The near dead were put into the Zero Ward, one of the largest buildings in camp and thus named indicating an infinitesimal chance of survival. Those in the Zero Ward had so low a chance of survival that the Japanese never assigned them a POW number. It was separated from the "healthy" prisoner barracks by an open field and low barbed wire fence. No Japanese personnel were assigned to treat prisoners in Zero Ward, and it was off limits to other prisoners. Those lying awaiting death in the hospital at O'Donnell were in St. Peter's Ward.

Once a prisoner died, he was moved to the Double Zero Ward, the morgue, near the hospital. Errett noticed that those who lost their will to live died first and they happened to be, for the most part, the bigger guys. Bodies were tossed through wide windows and door openings into the building. The bodies piled high in contorted positions with limbs jutting out from the heap and stiffening in place. In a short time, Double Zero Ward contained a three-foot solid pile of bodies extending from end to end and side to side.[8]

By necessity, burial details were the only detail initially formed. Nonetheless, the workers could not keep up with the number of dead stacking up. The detail was put to work on the first day men arrived from the march. They made stretchers from a blanket and two poles. They were forced to straighten the contorted bodies by snapping outstretched arms and legs into place and forcibly uncurl rigid bodies before placing them on the stretchers.[9] Prisoners hoisted the stretchers at the front and back ends of the poles and rested the weight on their shoulders. With their loads in place, the detail waited for the Japanese guard to bark out a guttural order to walk. Most could not bear to look at their unrecognizable and usually naked cargo. The remainder of the prisoners watched the parade of death leave the compound every day, loudly counting the tally as each body was carried through the gate. At the end, either a high-spirited shout arose if the count was less than the day before or a pitiful feeble moan if it was more. With so many dead, blankets soon ran out and woven bamboo shutters from the barracks were removed to put into use.[10]

As horrific as this was, the Filipino side of the fence was far worse. Burial details could not begin to match the pace of five hundred dying per day in their section. Many bodies were simply left in the barracks as stacking them for burial was an unattainable feat. Filipinos carried their dead to assigned burial grounds in hammocks, but they were often too weak to lift the load, so they were dragged. Those whom they did bury were in shallow graves, and dogs constantly dug up the remains overnight.[11] The stench was tremendous.

After a few weeks, additional work details to collect wood, bring in water, rebuild bridges, repair roads, fix ventilation systems, and work in the kitchen were formed. Many of the details included American officers.

These men were mostly sent to Ft. Stotsenburg, Clark airfield, and other places close by on Luzon to repair the battle-damaged infrastructure. The Calumpit bridge was one of the high-priority repairs for the work details. When completed, a Filipino band was brought in for opening ceremonies. Much to the delight of the POWs and confusion of the Japanese, they played *God Bless America* for one of their selections.[12]

Prisoners on details outside the camp were more fortunate than their turnip-eating comrades left behind. Filipinos along their route to and from their work destinations would surreptitiously hand some of the luckier POWs food.[13] It was about this time that a small consolation of building a cross was granted to the prisoners. Each prisoner was given one bag of cement for its construction. In a more guarded way, Australians observed Anzac Day (April 25), British prisoners sang their national anthem in their heads, and several American POWs kept U.S. flags hidden from the Japanese.[14] The POWs were made to recognize with respect Hirohito's forty-first birthday on April 29 as the Japanese celebrated the occasion.

On May 6, 1942, Allied combatants on Corregidor surrendered, the last holdout in the Philippines. General Wainwright telegrammed a message to President Roosevelt that said, "With broken heart and head bowed in sadness but not in shame, I report ...that today I must arrange terms for the surrender of the fortified islands of Manila Bay.... Please say to the nation that my troops and I have accomplished all that is humanly possible and that we have upheld the best traditions of the United States and its Army.... With profound regrets and with continued pride in my gallant troops, I go to meet the Japanese Commander."[15] They had held on to Corregidor for twenty-seven days after the fall of Bataan. Many POWs from Corregidor were spared Camp O'Donnell and instead ferried to Manila and marched to Bilibid Prison in front of Sunday crowds as an exhibit.[16]

Sweeping changes came in the following days. Unbeknownst to the prisoners and the Japanese, Admiral Nimitz and General MacArthur split the Pacific theater into two commands. On May 10, senior POW officers at O'Donnell were moved to Tarlac, just west of Cabanatuan.[17] On May 14, the fifty-year-old Tsuneyoshi was relieved of command at O'Donnell. Lieutenant Colonel Shigeji Mori replaced him. One of his first acts was establishment of a plethora of rules for POWs based on orders from Heideki Tōjō. Among them, roll calls were to be twice daily, no smoking in barracks, a fire brigade will respond to fires, no food for those who do not work, one must follow a schedule to go to the toilet, all POWs must salute all Japanese soldiers, and ten-man squads would be designated—if one escapes or attempts to, the others in the squad were to be shot. Squad members referred to themselves as blood brothers.

The list of maladies at O'Donnell grew to include night blindness, tunnel vision, and jaundice, but the Japanese faced problems of their own and their brothers in arms were on the verge of heavy losses at the Battle of Midway after two days of fighting beginning on June 4. After the smoke cleared, the Japanese found they had lost four aircraft carriers, one destroyer, a heavy cruiser, three hundred planes, and about twenty-five hundred men.

An announcement was made at Camp O'Donnell on June 2: All POWs were to be moved, including some twenty thousand Filipinos who were not yet paroled. A contingent of five hundred POWs, including Errett, were held back at Camp O'Donnell to work as caretakers and on burial details and were the last to reach the new camp. Tōjō met with all POW camp commanders on June 25, 1942, in Tokyo, to lay out a plan to use POW labor for Japan's benefit. Japanese men were constantly being called up due to the enormous losses in troops, causing a depletion of workers on the home front. Tōjō stated that "the labor and skills of POW should be utilized to the development of industries." The official position of the POW Management Bureau directed that "the Army [Japanese] will take responsibility for control and supply but the POW camp facilities with the exception of repairs …will be the responsibility …of the companies which use POW."[18] The Japanese government would soon move to make this happen.

On the last day in June 1942, Errett was summoned to the Camp O'Donnell hospital area. He would be leaving tomorrow, he was told. His buddy Bill Brown, who was among the one hundred patients allowed in the hospital for treatment,[19] had not been transported yet. Some POWs from the duty side were allowed to visit the hospital area if they had a relative or, more often, they bribed the guard.[20] Errett managed rather easily to slip in to see Bill since he had been summoned to the hospital area. He scoured the cots, finally finding Bill. He was disheartened beyond words. It was clear that Bill had little chance of survival. Bill seemed to know this, too, and passed his ring to Errett asking him to return it to his mother when he made it back. Without hesitation, Errett vowed to do just that. He could not fathom the grief she would bear losing her only other child. Errett pocketed the ring and slowly returned to his group trying to understand the magnitude of the situation for the seven thousand POWs at O'Donnell who were still alive out of the original twelve thousand American defenders.[21] If deaths continued at the current pace, all would perish by May 1943.[22]

Conditions at O'Donnell were extremely bad for POWs. The Japanese response to the situation was to relocate the American prisoners to Cabanatuan and parole Filipinos once they took an oath of loyalty to Japan. The night sky poured rain throughout the dark hours. The Philippine islands' rainy season started at 9:00 p.m. on May 22, twenty-two days later than usual. This rainy season, which ended in December, brought the usual eighty inches of rain. With the rainy season finally here, they could wash what clothes they had with water running off eaves and rinse their bodies.

14

Life at Cabanatuan and Bilibid Prison

On July 1, all prisoners in the hospital were ordered outside and into formation. Errett helped carry those who could not walk in blanket slings, including Bill Brown. Bodies of their dead comrades were ordered to be loaded on the trucks along with the patients. Several of these on this last exodus from Camp O'Donnell died and probably were not tallied among the 1,462 Americans and 20,000 Filipinos who died at O'Donnell.[1] Bill Brown miraculously survived the journey to Cabanatuan. Errett and other prisoners able to walk made their way to what would be an eight-hour train ride packed in boxcars. During the trip men struggled to breathe, were hungry, needed water, passed out, and died. Most had diarrhea and those lucky enough to be near a door hung their backsides out to relieve themselves.

From the depot at Tarlac, they marched until late afternoon to arrive at Cabanatuan where they were herded through its large gate. No Japanese followed them inside. Those in the best of health were assigned to live in the duty area. A barbed wire fence separated it from the hospital area. Here, the Zero Ward was for the dead and Ward One for the near dead.[2]

By July 5, no POWs were left at Camp O'Donnell. The hundred-acre Cabanatuan camp was the Philippine army prewar camp located near the foothills of Sierra Madre. It was and continued as the main POW camp in the Philippine islands until near the end of the war. Sick POWs at Bilibid who recovered were transferred to Cabanatuan. Barrack roofs were made of cogon grass. To make the roof thatch, the one-inch-wide leaves are piled on top of one another, tied at one end, and laid across the roof beams. Large woven nipa palms formed the walls. Floors were wide-space bamboo slats to allow air circulation to cool the temperature. Each barrack housed roughly one hundred men and had a center hallway with sleeping bays about eighteen inches off the floor on either side. Unfortunately, they housed a worse bedbug infestation than anywhere else the POWs would

14. Life at Cabanatuan and Bilibid Prison

sleep. Basically, there were three camps. Camp 1 housed all but the POWs captured at Corregidor and had the largest number of POWs in the Orient. Camp 2 was in the center and housed the Japanese. The POWs from Corregidor were placed for a brief time in Camp 3 of Cabanatuan, which had ample water and fair conditions. The men from Corregidor were the healthiest of the lot.[3]

The camp was enclosed by a high barbed wire fence. Guard towers with spotlights were interspaced outside the fence. American soldiers were required to serve as guards inside the fence at night. If a POW escaped, the guards on that watch were to be executed by firing squad.[4] POWs arriving from O'Donnell were put on the west side of Cabanatuan Prison Camp[5] and quarantined for two weeks.[6] None, Errett included, thought conditions could be worse than at O'Donnell.

Lieutenant Colonel Shigeji Mori from O'Donnell moved to Cabanatuan as camp commander. Under his leadership, tortures such as being nailed shut in a wooden box with small air holes in which POWs usually died in two or three days, being stripped and hands tied behind the back, then hung by their hands dislocating shoulders, being hung by hands and clubbed to death, flesh burned with cigarette lighters, filling POWs' guts with faucet water, then jumping on their bellies until dead, beheadings, execution by rifle fire, pulling fingernails out, pushing bamboo slivers under nails, cutting fingers off usually to get rings, and making them kneel with five-gallon water buckets on their heads were common.

Guards were usually given nicknames. The cruelest were Liver Lips, Greaseball, Speedo, Long John Silver, Big and Little Speedo, Cyclops, Air Raid (a particularly ruthless guard), Smiling Boy (because he always smiled while beating men unconscious), and Donald Duck (who walked and talked like the cartoon character). Their shouting and yelling was constant. Among the kinder guards were Corporal Nishiyama, Whisky Pete, and Mickey Mouse, who felt his nickname was flattering.

Mori was given an immediate directive to stop dysentery. Each prisoner was to kill a minimum of fifty flies per day to counter the problem. To incentivize the prisoners, one heaping spoonful of extra rice would be given to those who brought in a full tin can of dead flies. An officer gave out the collection tins, collected full ones, and issued the extra rice. The reduction in the fly population was astounding, but only time would tell if the campaign could be sustained.

Men in the hospital were unrecognizable. Ninety unconscious men were put in the hospital upon arrival from O'Donnell. All had a skeletal appearance and a ghastly, sickly yellowish pallor and had hordes of these green, buzzing blowflies going in and out of their open mouths and their noses and over their wide-open eyes. In Ward One, the inmates could only be identified by their dog tags because of their disfiguration. The tags, either oval or round and about the size of a quarter, had a small hole near the edge to thread in the narrow strip of cloth tape so they could be hung around the neck. The men all died within four days.[7]

Scores of maggots competed with the flies at Cabanatuan for access to the festering, rotting sores on the wasting bodies. These men lay mostly naked on a dirt floor in a building with no openings other than doorways. The ends of the buildings were walled in. It was the perfect breeding ground for prolonged illnesses. In June, 487 died at Cabanatuan. That number rose to 801 in July.[8]

Initial accounts underestimated POW deaths in July in all of the Philippines to be 786. Nonetheles, thirty percent of the sick died during this month.[9] One of those deaths, Bill Brown, hit Errett hard and the helplessness he felt lasted his lifetime. The dying was not over, but it receded. The tally for August was 287.[10] The improvement was the result of the influx of the first eleven-pound parcels of Red Cross supplies that may have come in as part of a prisoner exchange transaction that involved diplomats and included food, clothing, and medicines.[11] Quinine and antitoxins reached Cabanatuan in August.[12] Quinine relieved the malarial symptoms rather quickly and was administered by the American doctors in the hospital. Also, the Japanese began inoculating POWs for dysentery, pellagra, typhus, cholera, and smallpox. Not wanting to interrupt work details, injections were given in the chest muscle so that arms were not too sore to work.

News of the first U.S. naval offensive at Guadacanal in the Pacific that began on August 7, 1942, reached the POW officers via radio later that month. The news also reached Santa Fe and prompted the Lujan family to pen letters to Errett, but they did not leave the States for Japan until eight months later.

The hospital doctors were POWs themselves. They improvised to save the sick. The most severely ill weighed somewhere between ninety and a hundred pounds after their short time as prisoners. The doctors made their own needles, thread, and saws from scrap metal, wire, wood, rags, and anything found lying around in the barbed wire enclosure. Rotten flesh was stripped off leg bones, the bones sawed off, and the sparse remaining flesh stretched over the exposed bone and sewn in place. Metal tubes fashioned by doctors were hammered into swollen bellies to drain pools of putrid fluids from stomachs. Long purplish intestines hanging from anuses were cut with raw ends sewn shut. These and other procedures were done without anesthesia or medication of any kind.[13]

The skin of those with beriberi stretched from fluid puddling underneath. Sometimes the skin burst from the pressure and then the flesh started rotting. It seemed everyone had malaria at one point and each

14. Life at Cabanatuan and Bilibid Prison

so afflicted suffered through the chills, fever, and sweat cycles. Five hundred POWs died of dysentery the first month the POWs were at Cabanatuan. Diphtheria was an epidemic, but other diseases such as pellagra and scurvy passed through the men. Most of the sick became intolerant of sunlight in their eyes. Stomach worms sometimes found their way out through the nose.[14] In September 1942, once quinine was dispensed for treating dysentery, beriberi became the most prevalent disease among the POWs.

The prisoners who could muster any strength at all did what they could to not be admitted to the hospital. That spelled doom. One morning, Winston Shillito became ill and had to be held up to count off for roll call. He knew he couldn't let himself get worse, so he forced himself to walk around buildings, holding on to them for two or three days until he was able to stand alone.[15] Errett practiced the physical therapy of walking around to avoid the hospital. Part of the walking was from Japanese drills moving the POWs from point A to point B, four abreast in two parallel columns. The Japanese began their day by bowing east toward the sun and then northwest toward Japan. At 9:00 a.m., POWs had to bow to a post representing the emperor of Japan.[16]

As it was at Camp O'Donnell, grave digging details formed as soon as POWs arrived at Cabanatuan. They dug each burial pit to the prescribed size of six feet deep, six feet long, and six feet wide.[17] Every morning at four, bodies were hauled to the grave site using window shutters as litters. Into each pit twenty-four bodies were stuffed in starting with eight bodies on the bottom, eight in the middle, and eight on top with their heads to the east, in the direction of the rising sun out of respect for Japan's national symbol. Men from the 200th on burial detail moved corpses into graves dug the day before at a rate of about thirty-two a day.[18] Graveside services, however, were not permitted in the first several months. The sermons of other religious services had to be approved beforehand, and Japanese interpreters usually attended them.[19]

Ironically, the hundreds and hundreds of deaths led to a reduction of the POWs' overcrowding and made available the lice-infested filthy clothes of the dead. Delousing of all clothes, blankets, and rags continued by putting them in a large vat that was placed into a searing-hot oven. Also, some POWs shaved their heads to rid themselves of whatever lice still clung to them. While this effectively worked against the lice problem, the men were not allowed to wear head coverings, so the ones on work details who had shaved their hair developed blistering and bleeding sores on their heads.[20]

Stench in camps was constant. Errett had to use the latrine often and it was anything but pleasant. He sloshed through the maggot- and fly-infested scum around latrines that were mere slit trenches. Excrement from POWs who could not hold it back on their way to the trenches formed the built-up scum.

Errett discovered an improvement at Cabanatuan over O'Donnell. Cabanatuan had mess halls, which Camp O'Donnell did not. The POWs were fed on a more regular basis and the food was a little better. He enjoyed a little more solid food such as hotcakes until he learned that diesel oil and tooth powder were ingredients of choice when cooking oil and rice flour ran low. The mess hall cooks depended on the one-hundred-man wood detail[21] daily to harvest fuel, often mahogany, for the cooking fires.[22] The Japanese paid POWs in cigarettes for live cobras, a delicacy for them to eat.

POWs worked a cassava field. Cassava is a shrub whose long, thick, spreading root is ground up, made into a loaf, and baked. Tapioca is the beady starch from the cassava root. POWs planted budded cassava stems in the fields along with corn, beans, squash, onions, compotes, gourds, okra, eggplant, and several types of greens. The crops raised were supposedly sold in the local market with the money used to benefit prisoners in some unknown way, at least from the prisoners' perspectives.[23] Camotes, a type of sweet potato, and radishes rejected from the market vendors were given to POWs to eat.[24]

Accountability of POWs' presence was a high priority at Cabanatuan, initially without relying on dire consequences if a POW could not be found. The first attempt to escape changed that with the horrific implementation of blood brother groups at Cabanatuan. One day, a group of Japanese soldiers barged into the POW compound and rousted everyone to the outside. Those unable to comply by their own power were carried out by other POWs. Errett looked to the top of a small knoll and saw three naked, bruised, and bloody POWs struggling to stand. Their hands were tied behind their backs and big signs hung from their necks: "THE FOLLY OF ESCAPE."

All POWs were forced to watch the scene unfold. A guard with a long sword went into a series of loud grunts, shouts, and exaggerated gestures. Then he smoothly drew his sword from the scabbard. "He repeatedly thrust it towards the tied up POWs. When he became silent a scholarly looking guard shouted out a translation in broken English. It boiled down to do not try to escape or you will be killed. Then each of the would-be escapees was tied to a pole between the Duty Area and hospital using barbed wire. The guard with the long sword flayed each prisoner, one after another, until they looked like ground meat. Soon after this a poster was nailed to a gate support. The killer of the three slain POWs took out his sword and worked himself into another frenzy looking like a chimpanzee. The translator then began. 'Escape impossible,' he paused, 'and ten men will be shot to death for every prisoner attempting to escape.'" The

14. Life at Cabanatuan and Bilibid Prison

translator was made to repeat this over and over by the sword-swinging guard. Then he stabbed at the post, and they marched out of the POW compound. Later that day, the officers in the camp made a census of prisoners, which was used to make groups of ten dubbed blood brothers. If someone from the group escaped or tried to escape, all would be put to death. The officers were given a choice to create the groups themselves or the Japanese would randomly kill nine prisoners for every infraction. Officers agreed that at least this way, the others in a group would at least have a chance to talk the other out of trying to escape. Within each group, men became close watchers of the others, checking on them, counting, and staying close as best they could to each other. They even slept packed side by side to feel if anyone got up at night. If they did so to use the latrine, all went. New lists were made each morning of those in the duty area since many died during the night.[25]

Despite the risk, two POWs tried to escape and twenty were executed. This second demonstration of consequences seemed to quell further attempts for a while. A couple of attempts made later were dealt with without the mass killings of their brothers. Instead, those caught were severely beaten, paraded around the barracks, then tied outside where they were intermittently beaten by passing guards over several hours, and left there. The next day, they were dead and carried away by the burial detail. After this, the poster on the gate disappeared. Thieves pointed out to the guards by informers were clubbed into unconsciousness, then relieved of the stolen items. After this episode, the POWs objected and said they would take care of these matters themselves. Lo and behold, a small building was designated as the POWs' jail to use for offenders. Trials for stealing were held, and those found guilty were put in the jail. Guards for jail were selected from POWs.[26]

When the Japanese at Cabanatuan decided to add a stemmed weed to portions of rice to add more food to the diet, it killed many POWs. Most POWs were unable to chew it given the condition of their gums and teeth. When swallowed without chewing it well, it often stuck in their throats and they choked to death. The POWs called this blight in their food whistle weed. Water at Cabanatuan was rationed and everyone was constantly thirsty. Baths were occasional, but one could not get clean without using a rough stone with the water to scrape off the thick grunge that had built up layer by layer over the weeks.[27] Errett still had his boots, but many were not as lucky. Making shoes became quite an industry for the POWs. They scavenged small pieces of wood and scraped them smooth and more or less level with jagged stones. Old shoes were cut into strips and tacked onto wood with short pieces of wire hammered through the leather and wood.[28]

In August, the POWs were required to complete registration cards containing their name, rank, abilities, and skills. Once the cards were turned in, the Japanese camp commanders declared their captives to be POWs and thus eligible to be paid for their labor,[29] but still no word was released concerning Errett's fate. In a desperate attempt to learn something, anything, about her brother, Merle contacted Lucy Wilson, an army nurse who had assisted the surgeons on Bataan in the final days. Did she see or talk to Errett? Did anyone she know mention his name or unit? Could she shed any light on his condition? Miss Wilson replied with what she knew, what it was like there, and why there was good reason to assume Errett was still okay, although probably a prisoner.[30] Her response both frustrated and gave hope to the Lujans.

Just as conditions started to improve via the incentive programs, a rash of blindness broke out in the hospital area. The outbreak swelled attendance of morning mass held in secret. Warnings went out to attendees to say responses/prayers to themselves so as not to draw attention. The POW medical officers distributed vitamin A tablets called caramels. They had come in Red Cross boxes and the Japanese hated the taste, so they were willing to pass them on to the POWs. The prisoners agreed they tasted bad, but the afflicted regained their eyesight.[31] Results of having just a little nourishment were miraculous. When given vitamins or foods with vitamins, bloated limbs returned to normal, skin ulcers and lesions healed, and vision improved. More important, it renewed the POWs' wills to live.

Communications between regular guards and POWs at Cabanatuan was a sort of charades using motions and sign language and intermittent clubbing. POW officers refused to work, citing the terms of the Geneva Convention and stuck to that regardless of beatings and tortures. They did, however, agree to be overseers of large work details to spare Japanese guards' cruelty toward the POWs.[32] Workers at Cabanatuan received one-third more rice than nonlabor POWs.[33]

Kitchen work included splitting wood and supplying it to the cooks as they made rice in a fifty-gallon cauldron sitting atop sheet metal above the flames. Lifting the cauldron required two and sometimes three men when it was full. Those working in the kitchen took whatever opportunity they could to steal food, mostly rice, by putting a few handfuls through their pants pockets where an opening led to a bag hanging from the bottom of the pocket. One of Mori's new projects to aid the POWs was the farm, a three-hundred-acre plot where radishes were grown. Errett so hated the radishes that he never ate another one once he was liberated. He could sometimes buy fruit on the black market. Salted fish was given to POWs twice a week. While recovering in the hospital, VanBuskirk stashed a small supply of brown sugar smuggled in by Mike Chavez and it came in handy as he lay sick in the hospital.[34] Fruit was sometimes bought on the black market. POWs usually had to stand in line five to six hours to fill a canteen with water.[35] Radios were smuggled in and used. The most sought-after news was about the progress of the war. To protect other POWs, only a few officers knew of the radios at Cabanatuan.[36]

Second Lieutenant Colonel Mori was relieved from duty at Cabanatuan and replaced by Major Iwanaka at the onset of September. In the few days that followed, POWs in the best health were selected to begin transport to Japan where they would work for companies that were urgently petitioning the military for prisoner labor.[37] Eventually, 127 POW labor camps for civilian companies were established on home soil and 169 others established in Japanese-occupied territories. Errett was among the early departures and had high hopes of having better accommodations, food, and medical facilities elsewhere. After all, over five thousand POWs had already died in the hands of the Japanese since their surrender. Could he be any worse off? He left Cabanatuan on September 26 with hundreds of others following each other in staggered groups toward Bilibid Prison in Manila. Eventually, only those too sick to make the journey remained at Cabanatuan; they numbered 511 POWs.

While at Bilibib, there was no opportunity to use the radio for news. The radio parts had been divided among the men and they did not end up together. Even if they were in close quarters to each other, it was far too risky at Bilibib to attempt using it.

An event that went unnoticed was when a Japanese airplane launched from a submarine off the Oregon coast flew inland over the southern part of the state and dropped several incendiary bombs in forested land on September 9, 1942. Other similar bombs made their way to the U.S. West Coast by another method—attached to unguided, free-floating, hydrogen-filled paper balloons. In fact, thousands of these were launched from Japan and traveled six thousand miles in the jet stream to the United States. Five landed on Gearhart Mountain.

An unlucky turn of fate led Elsye, wife of the newly established Pastor Archie Mitchell in Bly, Oregon, and five children, four boys and one girl from his church Sunday school class, to find them. They were on a fishing trip on May 5, 1945. As the group looked around for a good fishing spot, the pastor parked the car. Someone in the group must have handled or kicked one of the unexploded bombs. It exploded killing all six. Archie raced over to the explosion as flying debris had just settled down around the three-foot-wide crater. His wife was on fire. He put the flames out with his bare hands and then she died. Two of the children were siblings and Elsye was five months pregnant. Military investigators and local police were on the scene before the afternoon ended. They found four other unexploded bombs and the balloon that carried them from Japan. The U.S. military had found these balloons stateside before and immediately recognized them, but no deaths were related to them. These six people were the first and only deaths in the continental United States from these weapons.[38]

15

Entering Japan

A large percentage of the Japanese male population was serving in the military. They had been in battle beginning with China for longer than American forces had defended the Philippines. Japan needed manpower for its homeland industries in order to win. They looked to the three hundred and twenty thousand Allied prisoners to fill this need.

They started by reclassifying and moving Allied prisoners out of Cabanatuan and eventually on to China, Japan, and Korea. Planning the relocation of prisoners to Japan was initiated in October 1942 with 6,000 POWs pulled from Cabanatuan as the Japanese started to lose their foothold after Midway. Moving their new workforce to labor camps where they were to be "employees"[1] of Japanese companies producing materials, equipment, transportation systems, and energy to support their military goals followed the planning phase. They of course wanted the healthiest of the prisoners. Unfortunately, some of the healthiest were in considerably poor shape.

Volunteers were requested without being told where they might be sent to work, although some volunteers were selected by the Japanese to reach the work quota the companies needed. American officers had the responsibility of creating a list of those who volunteered. From this cadre, a few thousand were selected and more would follow throughout most of the war. The prisoners considered their choices of staying with what they knew or being taken to unknown places for unspecified work. Would they be treated and cared for better by Japanese companies in the homeland where they would be closer to resources needed to survive? They would definitely be able to escape the tropical diseases that ravaged the Philippines. On the other hand, they had no way of knowing if they would be given adequate shelter and clothing to withstand the cold climate in Japan and they would be in the enemy's homeland. Would they be found or rescued sooner if they stayed in the Philippines, a nonhostile country? Errett felt that wherever he might be sent could not be worse than either of the prison camps he had already been in, so he volunteered and was among the first groups selected to be shipped out. Those POWs who left found living conditions in Japan for some were somewhat better although inconsistently so, that the physical work for all was extraordinarily demanding, and many Japanese guards were notoriously cruel.

The next step involved getting the prisoners moved out of Cabanatuan via train. Their first stop before the Manila docks was the derelict three-story concrete Bilibid civilian prison built by the Spanish in 1865 in the city center. The building was in the process of being renovated when war broke out ten months earlier. It lacked a roof, doors, and windows. What did remain in functioning order was the ten-foot-high concrete wall encircling the main compound with a high-voltage wire snaking around the top. The only comforting aspect was the well-kept lawn in the yard.

As the column of prisoners Errett was in entered the prison yard on October 26, they were separated by rank. Officers were directed to the first floor and the enlisted men to the second. As the U.S. president's eyes and ears while she toured military hospitals in the South Pacific, Eleanor Roosevelt reported to her husband, "I feel one hundred years apart and as if I am moving in a different and unattached world."[2] Bilibid and other places where allies were incarcerated were far worse than anything she saw on that trip or could probably imagine.

Errett was with the nearly three thousand prisoners walking from Bilibid to the Manila docks one mile away on November 6, 1942, in what the Japanese termed a victory parade. The prisoners, most of whom were clad in tattered remnants of uniforms, were marched through the streets, bayonets poking them along the way. Some POWs who arrived directly from Cabanatuan via boxcars had been given blue denim jumpers and trousers. The parade guards laughed as they hazed and harassed the men. The Filipinos were in shock and stone faced. A few locals offered food to passing captives. Errett saw a young teenage boy toss an orange to a fellow prisoner ahead of him. A Japanese guard bayoneted the boy who instantly crumpled to the ground dead. The murderer smilingly claimed the fruit.

Errett was ever so glad to leave his eleven-day incarceration at Bilibid behind. The next day, they were provided with their first proper meal since December 1941, which was a thankful improvement for Errett compared to the one or two rice balls a day since his surrender, and given water for bathing, which was Errett's first bath in seven months. With those domestic issues attended to, Errett was culled into a group of about fifteen hundred POWs and marched to Pier 7[3] where two freighters awaited them—the *Nagato Maru* and the *Umeda Maru*.[4] The Allied officers organized the prisoners slated for sailing on the *Nagato Maru* into groups of one hundred and then combined them to make three more or less equal groups, one for each hold, and numbering between three hundred and five

15. Entering Japan

hundred POWs per group. Errett, it appeared, was to be going aboard that ship. At one point on the route to the pier, his relief mixed with a swell of pride as he passed a Filipino band playing "God Bless America."[5] Hearing the tune refocused his thoughts to Bill's ring hidden away in his pocket. The band strengthened his resolve to get home and personally hand the ring to Bill's mother, just as he had promised Bill he would do.

Errett marched on board the *Nagato* by way of its wooden gangplank with his group of roughly four hundred fellow prisoners, past the ship's four lifeboats, and descended five flights of stairs at the edge of the twelve-by-twelve-foot hatch opening and into his group's respective hold below. His transport ship was a far cry from the USS *President Pierce* that had brought him to the Philippines a little over a year before. The *Nagato* was part of the Yaifuku Maru #1 Class ships, or Kawasaki standard stock streamer boats. About forty other boats were in this class and all built between 1917 and 1920. Their average gross tonnage was nearly six thousand tons with a maximum speed of about fourteen knots. Most were around 385 feet long, but the *Nagato* was considerably smaller. Many Japanese transport ships were sequentially named *Nagato Maru*. Even the flagship from which Admiral Isoruko Yamamato orchestrated the attack on Pearl Harbor was named *Nagato. Maru*, Errett learned, is the name for a ship of a small size. This *Nagato Maru* was surplus junk from either the United States or Great Britain and sold to Japan in the mid–1930s as scrap metal. It had three holds below deck that had been mostly used to transport horses. In all, sixty-nine similar ships transported Allied POWs to work camps during the war.

One American officer was appointed to be in charge of each of the three groups. Errett's group was led by Captain Walter C. Hewitt from Minnesota. Ten other New Mexico boys were aboard the *Nagato* with Errett—Mike Chavez from Deming, Tom Foy from Central, Raymond Chavez from Gallup, Joe Duncan from Silver City, William Richardson from McDonald, Joel Rogers from Bayard, Wayne Wasson from Regina, Jake Smith, Jr., from Clovis, Frank Wilson from Española, and Charles Gavord from Deming. Just before weighing anchor, another thousand or so men clambered on deck[6] and made their way to the decks just above the POWs who heard their footfalls.

The new arrivals were Japanese veterans fresh from the war and heading home, making the total count on board almost equal between Japanese and their enemies. The ship pushed off on November 7, 1942, at around 11:00 a.m. and was escorted by eleven others in the convoy, including one destroyer with most of the POWs stuffed in the holds five stories down. As they passed Corregidor shortly after leaving Manila Bay, a Japanese orderly threw out a basket of trash that had a wreath of flowers and an

American flag among the debris. Only a few Americans saw this, but word spread quickly and their sense of defeat grew.[7]

Errett found himself in a hold with scrap iron and truck body parts piled in the center leaving insufficient open space for the men, so they scaled the heaps and sat uncomfortably atop them. Another hold also contained piles of scrap metal, and the third, the lowest deck below these two, reeked of horse urine and dung left behind by the previous cargo. Two tiers of wooden shelving, sleeping bunks were attached to the walls around the perimeter of the hold, but with so many men sardined in, no one could lie down.[8] The bunks accommodated about three hundred sitting men, leaving the others the space in the center.

Errett stood waiting his turn to sit. Small cliques of men looking out for one another formed more or less naturally. If a buddy's knees buckled, his mates would catch him and either ease him down or hold him up in a standing position if there was no room for him to sit.

Each prisoner, six at a time, was initially allowed briefly on deck each day to smoke or use one of the three squat toilets hanging off the side of the ship.[9] A small number managed to find an out-of-the-way corner on deck to sleep at night. Sometimes the relief of sleeping in the sea air instead of the sweltering holds backfired when drenching rains came. That happened on the first night out when the men on deck were soaked, bone cold, shivering, and could not dry out for two days. They were in a much colder climate as it was and the rain made it even worse. Another passenger aboard was a monkey the Japanese had brought on. It was leashed and tethered to a certain place on deck. The monkey apparently was not the sea-going type. It threw up the whole trip. Most of the prisoners were seasick by the third day.

A honey bucket, or portable toilet, was in each hold. It was passed around as needed, but for many men, their bowels let loose where they stood before the bucket reached them or it filled up quickly. Captain Hewitt appointed two twelve-man details, one to empty the honey bucket up top and the other to retrieve the men's food. The honey bucket detail worked constantly toting the bucket up the hold steps, across the deck, and to the side where they turned the bucket upside down and the slop fell away.[10]

Their first morning at sea, the prisoners were served breakfast at ten consisting of rice and soybean soup. At three in the afternoon, they were given rice and fish left over from the meals provided to the Japanese crew and soldiers.[11] A schedule of two meals a day continued throughout the voyage but was usually a tablespoon of water and a small cup of rice.[12]

Unbearable heat built up in the enclosed holds and men were collapsing with heat exhaustion, not to mention the putrid stench permeating the air from men with dysentery and seasickness, which was most of them. POW officers pleaded for better conditions. They repeatedly asked the Japanese for more deck time, more food in their meals, and more honey pots. The complaints and the foul smells emanating from the holds produced a couple of changes. First, the number of prisoners allowed on deck at a time was raised to sixty. Second, they inserted air funnels into each hold. It helped somewhat, but men were still dropping like rag dolls.[13]

Guards usually sat on gunny sacks next to the hatch openings. Their location created a problem for the prisoners. As prisoners passed the guards on their way to and from the deck, crabs and lice running every which way off the guards infected the prisoners. The vermin were so plentiful that they fell into the holds, too. There was no escaping them. Adding to the insect problem were tropical ulcers and prickly heat rashes that quickly became infected. Very few prisoners escaped these skin maladies.[14]

Once, Errett noticed the guard had left his post on the gunny sack. He climbed up and carefully surveyed the situation. No guard. He bent his torso onto the deck and drew in a deep breath. Never mind the lice, I need air, he thought. It turned out that the lice and crabs were the least of his problems when the guard returned. To make his prisoner go back down, he flipped his rifle off his shoulder, raised it vertically, and pounded the butt on Errett's lower back. Pain shot through his entire body. His feet slipped sideways on the step, but he did not fall off. Some buddies managed to help him down, but there was nothing that could be done for the crack in his vertebra.

It was not possible to identify the unmarked *Nagato Maru* as a POW transport and it became a target of an American submarine. The sixty prisoners on deck at the time were rushed below. Air funnels were yanked out and the hatch sealed. Everything went dark in the holds as the Japanese nailed thick canvas covers over the hatch openings. The Japanese unloaded depth charges and the prisoners felt the ship shake. Torpedoes hurtled toward the transport ship. The engagement lasted two hours. A short time later, a relatively calm sea reemerged, the canvas was removed, and funnels reinserted.[15] They were lucky, but Errett never learned how the submarine fared. Twenty-four other hell ships were sunk by Allied attacks on unmarked vessels such as the *Nagato Maru*.

Casualties during the voyage to Japan slowly mounted in each of the holds. Bodies were brought up in the mornings and tossed overboard like the garbage the Japanese thought of them as. Burial at sea stopped when the *Nagato Maru* neared the Japanese shoreline. At that point, the bodies were stuffed into gunny sacks and put in a pile to be dealt with later. They did not want bodies to wash ashore and spread diseases to their homeland.[16]

Finally on November 10, land came into view. The *Nagato Maru* was piloted into the port of Takao at the mouth of the hundred-mile-wide Formosa Strait that separates the island of Formosa, known today as Taiwan, from the mainland. About two hundred other freighters were docked in the port and they buzzed with activity night and day. Up until this point in the voyage, blackouts were required but not in Formosa. The docks were brightly lit at night. Formosa was given its name by the Portuguese, meaning beautiful. The prisoners, as much as they would have liked to go ashore on this beautiful land, were only allowed on deck twelve at a time while anchored. Topside, they learned that the second day they were in port, five more ships carrying Allied prisoners came in. One of the ships carried British and Australian prisoners.[17]

On the afternoon of November 15, the crew ordered all POWs below deck, and at eight in the morning, the *Nagato Maru* slipped away from the Takao port with Moji, Japan, set as their final stop via water. Dead POWs tossed overboard on this leg of the journey were weighted down so that American submarines could not trace the ship's route. Five days later, they stopped at an island, possibly Hoko, being used as a quarantine station before ships were allowed to proceed into Moji[18] much as Nova Scotia was used when Errett's ancestors came to the New World escaping the potato famine in Ireland in the mid–1800s. On the 25th, the *Nagato* pulled into Moji.[19]

Errett recorded this recollection of his experience in a small journal he obtained in early May 1943, as arriving in Moji on the 23rd. The dates he entered do not correspond with what others reported. Errett's discrepancy is understandable given the lapse of time before he wrote it down and his deteriorated condition from dysentery, malnutrition, and back pain during the voyage. His arrival date at his new prison camp, however, jibes with other accounts of prisoners traveling with him.

The city of Moji is on the western tip of Honshu, the main island of Japan, and forty miles south of the village of Nagato, obviously a popular name in Japan. Errett immediately faced new challenges. The temperature was freezing or at least near to it because frost covered all he could see. They had traveled from the tropics to a very cold climate wearing less-than-adequate clothing. The men were ordered topside, even the infirm. If they could not walk themselves, they were helped to the deck. The only ones not required on deck were the ten who lay dead on the floors in the holds. Adding them to those who perished en route brought the total death count to twenty-seven for the nineteen-day voyage from Manila, a miraculously low number given their hardships. Errett comforted his unease with knowing his family could depend on the allowance due him and mailed to them. He was, of course, unaware that the War Department was reexamining allotments and determined there was a lack of evidence of dependency of the Lujan family on Errett's military income.

Once on deck, the men were lined up. Processing the prisoners took several hours. First, glass rods were used to probe them for rectal samples. Then they were hosed down with icy water, then sprayed with a disinfectant to delice their bodies. They stood for hours in the freezing cold, dripping wet, and with an icy breeze blowing. Before disembarking, they were ordered to count off into three groups of about four hundred to five hundred in each and left the ship in their respective groups.[20] As Errett walked away, he noticed about 150 POWs still on deck too weak and sick to move. Many had collapsed, all were left there, and none were seen or heard from again.[21] Errett believed the death toll for the trip just increased exponentially.

A closer inspection of each prisoner began once they were ashore. Those watching the first to go through it realized that their belongings, such as they were, were either stamped as "authorized" or taken away for whatever reason. Cigarettes, the most common possession of the men, were limited in the number allowed before being taxed. Those men with more than two packs dispersed the excess among others in their group with the promised payment of one cigarette for their assistance in getting them through the bizarre customs routine.[22] Then they were issued one set of new clothes in a size not necessarily fitting to the recipient, but that did not matter much as the material was so thin that there was no possible way it would keep them warm even if it fit properly.

From the docks, the men walked one mile to an open lot near the train depot. A welfare organization began handing out boxed meals. Errett opened the lid of his and saw a cup of rice in the center, pickled white daikons in the corners, cheese, one small raw minnow-sized fish, a slice of orange, and a kelp roll.[23] It was not the Thanksgiving dinner of home, but it was far better than what he had had as a prisoner up until now. Before he could begin eating, his group was on the move again, headed for the train a short distance away to be loaded into third-class passenger trains to take them to Osaka. As he approached the train, he noticed that not all of his fellow prisoners received food. Pangs of guilt were assuaged, though, when he saw that those who did not get food in the lot were being handed a new, white, clean cardboard box containing flavored rice, fish, daikon, half an apple, and a cardboard cup of flavored water.[24] Errett unwrapped the paper napkin from around the chopsticks, tossed them aside, and began eating.

Upon reaching Osaka, three large groups of POWs of over four hundred in each were put on different pathways to their respective new homes. One group marched to a steel mill in Yodogawa, another was sent by train to a camp near the coastal village of Tanagawa outside Osaka to carve a dry dock out of the bay, and the third to Osaka's industrial complex at Umbeda to load and unload freight trains.[25] Errett's group of fewer than one hundred was sent to Tokyo Camp #3-B in the village of Mitsushima, meaning "three islands,"[26] on the banks of a major river. He completed his last 275 miles of the trek on November 26, 1942, Thanksgiving Day. He called the camp by the name he heard most often, Mitsushima, but better known locally as Hiraoka.

16

Settling into Camp at Mitsushima as a POW

All the nine other POWs from New Mexico who came across on the *Nagato Maru* were with Errett except Tom Foy. He was on his way to a different prison camp. The jostling passenger train from Moji carrying Errett eased alongside the depot in Mitsushima, at about seventeen hundred feet in elevation and overlooking the camp some seven hundred feet below. Errett and the remaining eighty-four POWs stepped down from the train, formed a line several abreast, and paced their way downhill from the mostly dark village toward their brightly lit camp on the eastern bank of the Tenryū River just south of its confluence with the Toyama River. The shroud of night mostly obscured the steep and rugged mountains lining this valley in the southern tip of Nagano Prefecture.

Under better circumstances, Errett and the others could have walked the distance in about eight minutes—that is, if it weren't freezing and the POWs were healthy. At least half were severely undernourished, sporting swollen limbs and bellies (beriberi symptoms) or scabbed lips, split tongues, and swollen throats (scurvy victims), or all of the above maladies. Almost all battled some degree of dysentery. The trek this Thanksgiving night took longer.

They limped toward the heavily guarded main gate on the south side of the facility about thirty minutes after leaving the train station. Errett could see two other gates with fewer guards. The front gates in the ten-foot wooden fence stood opened. Nails studded the top of the fence. Errett walked inside under the glaring gaze of the guards. All were drawn to attention in a clearing amid the ten or so buildings, some finished and some not. Errett looked around to assess the situation. Of the three barracks, only one was finished. Each was to house one hundred and twenty POWs, a clear sign that more POWs were expected.

The men were made to stand erect an interminable amount of time. Errett was in better shape than at least half of the men. He caught glimpses

Four main islands of Japan. Errett's transport from the Philippines, the *Nagato Maru*, landed at Moji. He was then sent to Mitsushima POW camp on Honshu where he was imprisoned for nearly seventeen months before being transferred to Kanose POW camp where he was kept for eighteen months before liberation.

of several who were extremely ill, barely holding on, and looking as if they would crumple to the ground any minute. His insides wilted, but he managed to keep a firm stance. Finally, Errett saw movement among the guards as they began searching the POWs for any contraband in their possession. The thing about these searches, they had come to realize, is that an item of contraband one day may be okay to have the next day. One of the guards approached Errett and began his search. He emptied his pockets,

16. Settling into Camp at Mitsushima as a POW

turning them inside out. The only thing he would have fought to keep was Bill Brown's ring and he hoped to God he had it safely hidden. The guard was not impressed with his meager belongings and moved to the next prisoner. The ring was safe for now, and he again whispered his vow to Bill to get the ring to his mother.

Just when he wondered if he could stay upright any longer, Captain Sukeo Nakajima, the camp commandant, strutted out of a building Errett presumed was his office and stepped forthrightly onto a box placed before the prisoners to improve his height while he addressed his new inmates. He spoke no English, but his ferocity needed no translation. His interpreter, Kunio Yoshizawa, translated the commandant's tirade into English with what seemed an attack on the language itself. The prisoners got the gist of it, though. "Americans and Japanese are eternal enemies.... We will fight you and win if it takes one hundred years.... Any attempt at escape and you will be shot"[1] and so on.

Errett did not feel better or worse about what he was hearing. He had heard it all many times before. Roll call, or *tenko*, would be a minimum of twice daily just before they left for work at around 6:30 a.m. and again at night around seven just before they retired. With the search over, the POWs began to relax but were quickly called back to attention. They stood as stiffly as possible for another long stretch of time. Errett held on but still worried about others' abilities to continue standing in the cold night. At last, this first group of POWs in Mitsushima camp was assigned to their quarters—not the completed barracks but one of the other unfinished ones.

At first glance, Errett thought it would be good enough to sleep in for the few hours of night remaining. Each of the three barracks, when completed, would be identical. Errett dragged his tired body into the 180' × 20' one-story frame building built up to fourteen feet at the eaves[2] while most POWs made their way to one of two wooden latrines marked water closet where thirty men at a time in each could straddle the slit trench to do their business.[3] They were newly dug and unused and did not yet have the stench, flies, scum, and maggots they were to harbor in the weeks, months, and years ahead.

Errett did not really care what bunk space he chose. All were obviously inadequate. He clutched the four threadbare blankets issued[4] him and took in the place. A double row of platforms attached to the walls served as bunks. He climbed one of the twelve ladders angled against the upper platform and lay down to claim his six-foot length. He could see a fair amount of light through the quarter-inch wood-slatted walls. The lower bunk platform, about six feet below his, was only a foot and a half above the floor. He covered himself with his four see-through blankets, although he doubted they would keep him warm. He looked overhead at the ceiling only to see light coming through the bark-like shingles eight feet above.[5]

It was not very long until the sounds in Errett's ears of slow scuffling feet moving across the dirt floor ceased as the POWs crumpled into unclaimed bunks. He rightly predicted his new home would not be warm. When approved in advance, they were told, fires could be lit between five and eight in the evening to heat the space in the three-by-three-foot firepits in each third of the room.[6] More often than not, though, fires were not allowed even though night temperatures often fell far below freezing in the winter.[7] He could see there was no wood to burn tonight. The firepits were the only designated smoking areas in camp. The Japanese displayed an inordinate fear of structural fires, perhaps from problems encountered with their customary paper and wood homes.

The thought of a smoke appealed to Errett, but he was just too tired. He was mighty thankful this day was over but completely unaware, of course, that he would spend the next sixteen months here, witness a host of atrocities inflicted on others, and be cruelly beaten himself many times. The treatment meted out by guards at Mitsushima resulted in the hanging of several of them after their postwar trials. He curled up in his space hoping the layers of grass matting topped with a tightly woven mat would give some relief from the cold, although he doubted it would. He nodded off to sleep thinking of home as two bare light bulbs dangling from the ceiling beamed brightly.

The Santa Fe Japanese internment camp reopened in February 1943 after being expanded to accommodate two thousand people and employ around ninety civilians. Within six weeks, just over five hundred Japanese were interned there.[8] It was a stark contrast to Errett's camp at Mitsushima. The spacious wooden CCC barracks, complete with screen doors, windows, and latrines inside, housed most of the men while others lived in sixteen-by-sixteen-foot plywood huts, four men to each hut. They slept on mattresses held off the floor by iron cots. They had the freedom to form a limited self-government, put forth grievances, and receive clean towels and sheets weekly, as well as access to unlimited hot showers. They could receive visitors, order or grow whatever food they chose, practice whatever religion they wanted, play softball, see movies, put on plays, hold concerts, play croquet or horseshoes, listen to the radio, regularly receive and send censored mail, and hold Ping-Pong and judo tournaments. The facility included a Japanese kitchen, laundry, mess hall, bathhouse, a twenty-acre garden, beer hall, golf course, library, soccer field, small hospital, and recreation hall. They were also provided with clothing. Errett fell asleep unaware of this or any other developments in the United States.

16. Settling into Camp at Mitsushima as a POW

Reveille woke Errett at 5:30 a.m., just as the yelling camp commandant had indicated. Errett learned, however, that fluctuations in set schedules often occurred. The next few days largely involved close order drills shouted out in Japanese.[9] In his spare time, Errett was figuring out where things were and what he might be in for at his new home. They were there to work, but he did not know much about that yet. His meals were much the same in these first two days as they would be most of his stay here—a mix of barley, rice, and millet made into something like a soup that sometimes had vegetables and, less often, meat or fish. American POW cooks prepared all the food in the cook house, a separate building. When the food was ready, buckets were loaded up and brought to the barracks. The most fair-minded and honest POWs were elected by their respective one-third section of the barracks to haul and equally dispense portions to the POWs. They served a six-month term.[10] On Errett's second night in camp, he and others were served their first dinner inside the barracks. Some POWs sat at the tables, but most, like Errett, sat on the floor with Mike, Ray, William, Joel, Joe, Charlie, Jake, Frank, and Wayne, the boys from New Mexico, and ate.

Water for drinking, washing clothes, washing faces, and cooking was pumped from a thirty-foot well alongside the river to a covered twelve-spigot washstand in the center of camp. The in-flow pipes often froze during the winter making it necessary for POWs to haul water up from the river. The showers and communal bath were not yet built but would be hooked into the well water line with just as inefficient pipes and insulation as the ones feeding the washstand. Water from the Tenryū was not potable. It was boiled, fifteen gallons at a time, before consuming to rid it of contamination acquired from the village of Mitsushima and the nearby Korean (of approximately 3,500 people at its peak) and Chinese (about 880 prisoners at its peak) POW camps along the Tenryū. The Korean camp was the closest,[11] and many of those POWs had their families with them, but camp conditions for them were a lot worse than Errett's. They did not want to make friends with the American POWs, and the feeling was reciprocated.

Two days after Errett arrived, 190 British POWs via the *Tofuku Maru* arrived at Mitsushima at 10:30 p.m. Errett watched as the camp commandant shouted out the same welcoming he had endured while noticing the Brits were in much better shape than the Americans. Next, they were made to sign a pledge not to try escaping.[12] They were divided into two groups, and each was assigned to one of the two unoccupied billets. This larger group of British POWs had far more officers than the two in the American group and included a few civilians like the ever cheerful Brit Pinky Fulford-Williams.[13] Their home countries were Singapore, Java, Malaysia,

Scotland, Australia, and Great Britain. The overall roster of 20,200 POWs in Japanese prison camps tallied 13,250 in the Philippines, 2,900 in Japan, 1,650 in China, 1,200 in Manchuria, 450 in Malaya, 250 in Celebes, 200 in Burma, 150 in Formosa, and 150 on Wake Island.[14] These numbers, however, do not include the roughly 66,000 Filipino POWs taken by the Japanese (most of whom were allowed to return home shortly after their surrender) and 14,000 civilians. By the time the camps closed at the end of the war, one-fifth of the POWs who entered Mitsushima would be dead.

Eight to twelve guards assisted Captain Nakajima at any given time. Nakajima himself was often away from camp, leaving one of his sergeants to run things. Sakamoto was the camp medical sergeant. The POWs sized up the guards quickly and labeled them with descriptive nicknames. The interpreter's (Corporal Yoshizawa) English made little sense, so Errett called him Mush Mouth to reflect his ineptitude. Others were Pasty Face, Smiling Sergeant (Shoidisan), Big Glass Eye (Sadaharu Hiramatsu, a large man by Japanese standards with one glass eye), Little Glass Eye (Tatsuo Tsuchiya, who lost his right eye in battle in the Philippines and was small in stature), One Arm (Nishino), The Punk (Tamotsu Kimura), Scar Face (Matsuzaki), Speedo, The Bird (Watanabe), Buick (Takeo Kirishita, because he wore that emblem on his cap), and The Snake. A few other guards worked at Mitsushima but did not garner nicknames or notorious reputations among the POWs. For a while, the nicknames proved useful as code names when the POWs wanted to speak more freely or warn someone about one of the guards, but eventually, the guards caught on. Buick and The Snake were a sadistic pair and, together, nicknamed The Gruesome Twosome, but the one Errett harbored the most hatred for was Little Glass Eye, the camp supply sergeant, and he had many run-ins with this cruel little man. Little Glass Eye was the only guard Errett was determined to kill.

Soon rumors about starting work reached Errett. Preparations to get prisoners ready began a few days after the British POWs arrived. Each was handed a scrap of white cloth about six inches high and eight inches wide. Written in black on each piece of fabric was a different number. Errett looked at his scrap of cloth with its nearly five-inch-high numbers. His was number 55. Next, sewing needles were distributed along with spools of thread, one for each group of men.

"Sew this on back" is one thing Errett figured out Mush Mouth said in his crippled English. More was said, but it required piecing together an interpretation by the POWs. After a little discussion, they figured out the directions. They were to sew the cloth on the center back of their jackets if they had one or, otherwise, their shirts and they had a limited amount of time to do it. All needles and spools were to be turned in at the end of their

16. Settling into Camp at Mitsushima as a POW

allotted time. If anyone did not get the job done, they would be punished. If anyone took more time than allowed, they would be punished. If needles and thread were not turned in, they would be punished.

A POW in Errett's group passed him the needle and thread. He had never sewn anything in his life but couldn't care less how it looked when he finished. He simply wanted to get it done and he did. Days later, POW numbers on smaller strips of cloth were distributed during *tenko*. This time, the number "55" was on the right and his name and number in Japanese written on the left. As instructed, Errett sewed this ID tag on his front-left shirt pocket again in a timed manner and with the same threats given if orders were not followed. By now, Errett knew how to say his prisoner number in Japanese—*go-jū-go*. Some situations make one a fast learner. Now when they had *tenko*, the guards could know if one POW was in another's place in formation. There were severe penalties if the POWs were not in their proper place or did not properly say their number in Japanese. They had started roll call over several times since their first *tenko*, and some POWs were knocked about for messing up. With all their tags sewn on, the guards could keep better track of them and they could be put to work outside the camp.

Errett's name (in Japanese) and POW #55 given to him at Mitsushima. He sewed it on his jacket with five or so snippets of very thin black yarn.

The Japanese POW Management Bureau established ground rules for the seventy-nine Japanese companies using their slave labor. The Japanese army would control and supply a POW labor force and be responsible for repairs at the camp, but establishing the camps was the responsibility of the companies who were to use the POWs. At Mitsushima, the Kumagai Engineering Company was also responsible for procuring food for the POW meals for their workers who were there to finish building the concrete gravity hydroelectric Hiraoka Dam across the narrow headwaters of the Tenryū River. Construction had begun in 1938, but progress halted when Japan invaded China. When ultimately finished in 1951, it would measure 203 feet high by 846 feet long and function longer than Errett would live.

The work schedule at the dam site was the same for everyone, ten consecutive days from 7:00 a.m. to 5:30 p.m. The POWs were to use any day off to clean their barracks and wash their clothes. Work would be called off only if there was inclement weather, which meant sustained torrential rainfall. Specific jobs at the dam fell into one of three main categories: dig out thirty-foot-diameter penstock tunnels to the power station, collect aggregate (sand and rock) and move bags of concrete from the village below to the warehouse near the top of the dam, or mix concrete. Errett received his primary assignment—mixing water, concrete, and aggregate in a wheelbarrow at the dam site one mile from camp. Other POWs loaded cable car buckets with bags of cement at the bottom of the dam, unloaded them up top into wheelbarrows, spun the bucket around so it could go back down, and wheeled the bags to the warehouse where another team stacked them as high as possible. The POW teams charged with relocating the aggregate moved sand and gravel from dump sites to the bottom of the dam again using wheelbarrows.

Igarashi was the Japanese civilian in charge of dam construction and primarily the cement stockpile, making sure enough raw materials were on hand to keep work on the dam constantly moving forward.[15] Oiwa oversaw the blacksmith shop, Iwatia was in charge of the general laborers, and Kamijo the machine shop.[16] Three Japanese civilian procurement officers working for the company lived at the prison camp. Their jobs were to acquire food for the POWs working on the dam.

Errett marched off to his first day of work with his group of about forty POWs and a few of the camp guards. Civilian guards hired by the company monitored the POWs and their work onsite. Usually, three camp guards escorted Errett and his work group of cement mixers to the dam. The Kumagai civilian guards dressed in dark blue clothes, split-toed black sneakers, small blue peaked caps, had whistles to blow for help, and carried the familiar large oak clubs shaped as swords. Most were former military

16. Settling into Camp at Mitsushima as a POW 133

personnel and had no reservations about using their clubs to encourage work. They seemed to be of a different mindset and often clashed with the personnel without military backgrounds. A cruel gesture often used by the civilian guards was to wave postcards in the faces of the POWs while at work to taunt them into working harder.[17] Errett would love to send a message home but would much rather receive one.

17

The Worst Winter

As Christmas neared, Errett's longing for home intensified. Most of the American POWs had no socks but were marched out to work, nonetheless. It was bad enough to be called out of the barracks at 5:30 a.m. in the dark each morning, but they usually stood around until 6:15 a.m. before *tenko*. POWs were still dying, and many—40 percent of the British and 55 percent of the Americans—were very ill, mostly with beriberi and dysentery, spawning an every-man-for-himself attitude. The Japanese conducted a health inspection on December 8, identifying over one hundred as ill.[1] After supper, they were put in Barracks #1, now called the Medical Ward. Those labeled as afflicted with the highly contagious disease of diphtheria were assigned to a small building behind the Medical Ward to be isolated but not necessarily treated. Not even the sickest POWs were taken to the hospital in Matsumoto,[2] 145 miles away by train. It would be a six-hour train ride with a one-hour stop along the way for those few who would make the trip later.

One American POW was sent to the hospital for an appendectomy.[3] Since he was to get medical attention in a hospital, he would probably fare as well as or better than Joe Quintero who, in September 1943 while being transported to Niigata, Japan, by ship, survived an operation by an onboard American doctor who had only a razor blade, forks, and spoons from mess kits, and no anesthesia. Joe lived in Albuquerque, New Mexico, after the war.[4]

Errett wished Bill Brown had made it this far. Here, he could have had hospital care or any substantive medical care for that matter. But who knows. One of the POWs from Mitsushima at the Matsumoto hospital died shortly after arriving, and soon afterward, four others followed. The sick in camp had it worse than the others. The commandant ordered them to receive less food because they did not work. Prisoners with dysentery were summoned outside, often in snow, to stand at attention to receive medication. Anyone needing to use the latrine at night had to completely dress first,[5] which was convenient in the winter when they usually slept with their clothes on, but it was different during warm nights. Many with diarrhea did not make it to the slit trench before soiling their clothes.

The other thing Errett longed for was a warm bath, but that did not look likely any time soon. By early December, the water buckets had a one-inch-thick layer of ice in the mornings and the pipes froze. To help with warding off the cold, the Japanese issued cotton long johns and a twin-size sheet to each POW.[6] It helped but very little. Then, tantamount to a Christmas miracle, Mush Mouth informed the POWs they would be allowed to write one postcard and one letter home once every four months beginning on Christmas, three days away.[7]

Christmas finally came but not the package sent by the Lujan family that included the wristwatch. Nonetheless, Errett was treated to his best day to date as a prisoner, which is not saying much. The guards issued him ten cigarettes, which he signed for, and blank postcards. The pipes had thawed and the prisoners filled a twenty-by-ten-foot concrete box with three feet of heated water at three in the afternoon. Anticipation seemed to tickle him all over during the entire three and a half hours it was in use. Suddenly, the excitement building in his daydream crashed into a black hole of nothingness when the guards shut it down and ordered it drained at 6:30 p.m. Only about a hundred men bathed.[8] Not letting the missed opportunity get him down, Errett joined the nostalgic crowd standing around a yule log burning outside. Carols were sung as Errett watched some of the men dance. *Tenko* was delayed until 8:00 p.m., and then Christmas festivities ended. Errett headed silently back to his bunk feeling better than he had in a very long time. The day had lifted his spirits.

Errett found the next day astonishingly good, too. Every POW received two oranges and four issues of the *Japan Times Advertiser* from earlier in the month. His spirits soared even higher when he read about the Allied attacks in North Africa and the scuttling of the French fleet. As much as he wanted to, Errett hesitated in writing out his postcard. Two hundred were handed in, but only eighty made it past the camp interpreter. That was the first hurdle. Scores of American POWs of various officer ranks worked in Tokyo assisting with the censoring of tens of thousands of incoming and outgoing mail. Over the next few days, about three hundred Red Cross parcels were delivered and unpacked. Word spread like wildfire listing the mouth-watering contents: cookies, gelatin, margarine, bacon, marmalade, chocolate bars, and so on. These, Mush Mouth announced, would be put in the store where the POWs could purchase them at a later date.[9]

One of the men in his barracks could not wait. He broke in to steal some of the new supplies, was caught, and was put in the guard house with no bedding and wearing only a thin shirt and pants. The temperatures dropped below freezing at night, but the punishment stood. A couple of days later, another POW in his barracks broke a window in the cook house. Errett did not know if it was intentional or accidental, not that it mattered to the Japanese. He and every other POW in that barracks paid the price. Each was punched by the guards and their supper withheld for a time until Captain Hewitt successfully intervened.[10] Errett could take one punch okay, but it sure made him mad. And on that note, 1942 ended.

New Year's Day 1943 was a holiday in Japan, much to Errett's delight. It started with *tenko* at 7:00 a.m. A guard barked orders to the men. Little by little, Errett came to understand most orders, but this one had him stumped. He stared at the guard's icy breath hanging in the air as if he might glean some clue from it. He knew from experience that not obeying would be cause for punishment, usually a punch to the gut or a whack on the back with a wooden club swung like a baseball bat. All at once, there was movement around him. He knew what to do then. He mimicked the others. He pivoted, raised both arms above his head in excruciating pain from his hellship injury, and yelled banzai three times. Later, he asked one of the officers what the devil it was all about. It was a salute to Emperor Hirohito on this special holiday.[11]

Then the good news came. Baths would be had by all today, and everyone received five cigarettes.[12] After the officers, the enlisted men lined up. Errett got in just in time before it cooled. It was not luxurious, but it was delightful. He sank in and truly thought he had never felt anything quite so good. He relished this first bath since arriving. The Japanese established a bathing schedule of about once a month, but the water was not always warm and it was definitely dirty before even half bathed.

The surprises did not end there. All 255 POWs were given one Red Cross box each that came from England. Errett rummaged through his and found a veritable feast of tins of meat paste, condensed milk, jam, pudding, tomatoes, vegetables, and cookies along with margarine, bacon, creamed rice, cheese, sugar, a chocolate bar, and a bar of soap.[13] It was a fabulous Christmas present, just one week late.

Later in the month, Japanese newspapers began listing names of some of the prisoners.[14] It took until March 6, though, for fifty-two names of boys from New Mexico to be printed in the local *Santa Fe New Mexican*. Errett's was not among them. Jess was despondent. This feeling was not unique to Jess or families of other Allied troops. The Japanese psyche was faltering, too, beginning with their loss in Guadalcanal on February 9, 1943. The Solomon Islands were invaded on the tails of this victory. It was the first marine assault of World War II. Ironically, the marines had trained in Chesapeake Bay on Solomon Islands.[15] Although Japanese defeats were not made public in Japan, bits of information crept slowly through their homeland. The war seemed to be turning in favor of their enemies. Rumors soon arose about their shattered jewel, as their country was referred to, and the pain from losing so many Japanese men was unavoidable. The Japanese people suffered, too, with poorly made clothes, shoes, and socks, not enough food, pots, or pans, and no protein in their diets. Conditions in the cities were worse than in rural Japan.

The roller coaster of mood swings among the guards was inexplicable to Errett. One day, Errett was given tube socks for the price of eight sen a pair, and the next day, the POWs were ordered to slap each other for fifteen minutes because the washstand pipes froze. One night, Errett and the others were given extra rice with their dinner along with vitamin tablets. Some even got shoes! Then without warning, rations were cut in half. This "good cop, bad cop" routine was no playacting. The derangement seemed a permanent feature of their personas.

One very cold morning soon afterward, all POWs were ordered outside and told to take off all their clothes. In single file, they were sent to the medical staff where they were weighed and inoculated for dysentery in the right breast. Errett supposed the injection might help, but it seemed to him not to be their biggest problem. A Japanese corpsman pointed randomly to ten British, ten American, ten Chinese, and ten Indian POWs and ordered them forward. All stood at attention while their legs were measured and the information recorded. Errett wondered what on earth that could be all about when he saw Nakajima stride toward them to inspect their barracks. He prayed his bunk and shelved clothes would pass. It was tricky since he had to fold his clothes into identically sized squares with a flat, thin piece of wood inside each and stacked on the shelf above his sleeping area.[16] Errett walked with his group inside the barracks. This time the inspector had no problem with his things.

Before leaving the barracks, Yoshizawa shouted another directive to them: Make a list of belongings as well as items they most needed and hand it in.[17] Any place else, he thought, I'd think they cared about our well-being, but Errett knew better. What they needed and asked for over and over never appeared. Most of the POWs were just wisps of malnourished men in great pain trying to stand at attention. One of the sickest was put in the Medical Ward and taken to the hospital.[18] Luckily, he returned in better health on February 9, but the death rate at camp was still climbing. Three men, Private Ray Chavez from Errett's regiment, Private Robert Teas, and Sergeant Kenneth Hunter, died over the next few days. The loss of Ray hit Errett hard.

Pay was distributed at the end of January to some of the POWs, and they were allowed to buy up to two packages of sweets at 11 cents each.[19] An additional method of payment was a diligence coupon earned by a POW if he showed exceptional effort at his work. Errett was unlucky and did not get paid and had yet to earn one but soon realized that those with diligence slips were allowed more freedom to purchase things.

Straggling in from work one day in mid–January, Errett was surprised to see a stove installed in his barracks with one pail of coal. The officers' barracks were allowed to light the stove for four hours in the evening, and men in the other two barracks could light theirs for two hours in the morning before work.[20] In early February, they were authorized to buy charcoal for fires at 2.50 yen a basket.[21] The guard quickly dashed Errett's hope for a warmer night when he added that the morning time before work was the only time allowed to have a fire. Two months later, all of Errett's hope to be warm at night plummeted when the guards yanked every stove out of the barracks.[22] After all, they reasoned, the temperature had risen to a little above freezing.

Morale was abating. The POW officers considered what they could do. If the men could get word on their mail, it would help. Errett surely wanted to know. The officers inquired only to discover that no incoming mail was available for distribution and the outgoing postcards turned in were still in camp. Instead, bundles of about two sheets of toilet paper were offered to the POWs at 11 cents a bundle.[23] Most refused the offer. Errett considered it an empty gesture. It seemed just as pointless to use his money that way as it did to buy the sour oranges recently proffered. Stealing from the Red Cross parcels increased. Those caught were put in the guard room for twenty days. The guards' moods changed inversely as that of the prisoners sank lower. Their captors carried on almost maniacally at night in monthly celebrations.

Despite the harsh conditions, construction of the dam was proceeding. By late February 1943, the Japanese civilian engineer updated the progress in what they envisioned to be a three-year project. Although the main dam construction had not yet begun, the Tenryū was now running through a diversion channel, the coffer dam was nearly complete, and dredging for the main structure had begun. The coffer dam consisted of log frames threaded on rods, filled with rocks, and faced with a one-yard thickness of concrete on the upstream side. Tunneling to the turbines in the powerhouse on the other side of the hill about five hundred feet from the dam site was mostly done by Koreans removing blasted materials by hand and carrying the debris away on their backs.[24] Once a section was cleared, it was Errett's job, along with other POWs', to line the tunnel with cement.

Before the end of February, the Japanese issued tangerines and stationery with instructions to the POWs for writing letters home. Only five hundred letters from the group would be allowed. Errett took his two blank sheets. He could write on one side only. He could have only five words per line. He could have no more than twenty-five letters per line. His entire letter could not exceed a hundred words, and he had to make an exact copy onto the second sheet for the commandant's files.[25] The task was not easy, and only a few men handed letters over to the interpreter before March. Errett was not one of them.

Mid–March 1943 had a few surprises and a flurry of changes for Errett. First, the Japanese decided to reassign many of the POWs to new billets in what seemed an attempt to have each barracks house a mix of Americans, British, and Singaporean Technical Corps prisoners. As soon as they settled into the new arrangement, morning *tenko* occurred inside huts, and a new work schedule was imposed. Morning *tenko* at five-thirty was followed by breakfast, then a work parade at six-thirty, off to work at seven, and lunch at eleven-thirty followed by another work parade at one in the afternoon. Errett stopped work, marched back to camp, stood for evening *tenko* at a quarter after five, and then ate supper.[26] Afterward, he wandered into the kitchen only to find that the rice he just consumed had been cooked in the old pot they had been boiling diarrhea-soiled clothes in.[27] He did not need anything like this to make him feel sicker than he already was.

One week later, the Japanese issued changes. Reveille at 5:00 a.m., eat breakfast, *tenko* at 5:50 a.m. at the main gate, start work at 6:00 a.m., quit work at 5:00 p.m., dinner fifteen minutes later, and finish with evening *tenko* at 7:00 p.m. Schedule changes were becoming frequent, but odd changes came, too. One of the more perplexing was a suggestion to wrap a sheet around them for work instead of wearing clothes. The consensus among the Japanese was that the clothes were too bulky, they would get hot, and work would slow. Wear a sheet! Errett was stymied about how that could make them work faster. He and 166 other POWs ignored the suggestion. Apparently, it was more than a suggestion. Mush Mouth spent their entire lunchtime slapping each one of them for noncompliance.[28]

On March 18, he learned it was a Japanese holiday, so no work. This was unexpected since the last holiday was just eight days prior when the POWs were made to parade around and salute Tokyo in celebration of Japan's defeat of the Russian fleet sometime in the past.[29] Then a guard approached each POW individually and handed over something. When Errett's turn came, he put his hand out and, much to his amazement, realized he was getting paid one yen for every day worked on the dam the first two months of the year less the ninety sen withheld to help pay for food and clothes received.[30] According to the pay scale announced when Errett was at Cabanatuan, officers, noncommissioned officers, and privates were to be paid somewhat equivalent to the Japanese military pay scale. Using that, Captains Hewitt and Faulkner were to earn 220 yen per month, but they found it did not work that way at Mitsushima. Instead, Errett, Captain Hewitt, Captain Faulkner, and all POWs in Mitsushima were paid the same except no officers received pay this day. With this, on his first payday, Errett bought ten cigarettes and enjoyed smoking a few that night.

Being paid came with requirements, and Errett did as he was told and recorded all of his paydays and purchases in a small ledger. Oftentimes, the Japanese counted the money he had and compared it to his ledger, making sure the tally balanced. If it did not, they would punish him for making illegal purchases. Some guards would sell items such as dried squid, peanuts, canned milk, canned peaches, and quinine to the POWs. Implicating a guard in the black market carried a heavier punishment than just having a ledger that did not balance, so the guards were fairly safe. Errett opened his ledger and entered his pay on the first page. On the inside cover, he wrote his name and rank. Before putting his pencil away, he was called in to complete yet another form. One of the POWs with the best command of Japanese asked Errett the questions and then interpreted them for Mush Mouth who wrote them down: What level of school have you completed? What branch of the military are you in? What special skills do you have?[31] and a host of other questions.

Incongruous with the drizzly weather in late March, the guards ran about the camp giddy. Their attitudes seemed a little better, too. Errett soon discovered what the commotion was all about. A high-ranking officer, the second in command of all POWs, was to visit the camp tomorrow. POWs with raincoats, which were not many, were ordered outside to clean up the grounds. All others worked inside to make the place as perfect as could be. The visiting major arrived at 10:00 a.m., performed a rapid inspection of all barracks and a few outbuildings, then left.[32] There must have been some mention by the major about being prepared for a fire. The POWs were put through five fire drills over the next three days. Each lasted about three hours, one longer. The guards must have been impressed because there was a lot less slapping, more cigarettes handed out, and all were issued a bar of soap, toilet paper, and tooth powder. The former Japanese military working for the company were not as amiable. They were being called up for duty in the Solomon Islands along with some of the guards.[33]

Over the course of this first winter in Japan, every day seemed pretty much the same to Errett. Reveille, followed by *tenko*, followed by breakfast often dished out by Nakajima, then off to work from before dawn to after dusk. And he was constantly hungry. Several wintery days of dreadful weather with heavy rains and snow greeted him through the season. He was anxious for spring to thaw him out. Errett was used to the cold

17. The Worst Winter

snowy winters of his Santa Fe home nestled into the tail end of the Rocky Mountains at an elevation of seven thousand feet. Although the Mitsushima camp sat roughly at fifteen hundred feet elevation, its winters were far more brutal because Errett lacked adequate shelter and heat for the below-freezing night temperatures. The only thing that did not seem to freeze was the Tenryū River. Errett could not sleep due to the cold. As it turned out, he suffered the worst conditions as a POW during this first winter in Mitsushima.

Work was called off on account of weather six days in February and March and the ground was usually covered in ice. In one storm, six inches of snow accumulated. This caused all sorts of other problems, too. The Japanese guards laughed when the POWs carrying Private Roger Derr's body uphill to the crematory slipped on the ice. They laughed even harder when the private's body rolled out of his coffin.[34] Then there were the fire drills called either before or after work hours, which meant in the dark. Errett joined the bucket line passing river water to the bathhouse uphill until the bathtub was filled. Once back in the barracks, coughing filled the otherwise quiet night.

In the April 19, 1943, edition of the *Santa Fe New Mexican*, a headline blazed across the page like fire to Jess's eyes: "All but Half Dozen of Santa Fe Battery Survives." She had already read it many times today but could not stop. "Errett Lujan, son of Mr. and Mrs. L G Lujan, Taos and Chimayo Roads" and a very long list of other Santa Feans were confirmed POWs of the Japanese. Errett had no way of knowing that his family had finally received word he was alive. If he had, his entire being would have been buoyed, and he would have immensely enjoyed the night's entertainment. He brightened momentarily when twelve letters for POWs mailed seven months ago arrived at Mitsushima even though none were for him. In fact, none of the recipients were or had been at Mitsushima.

A heavy rain delayed morning *tenko* slightly on April 29. At 7:00 a.m., Errett stood at attention in his spot, called out *go-jū-go* at the appropriate time, and then remained in place. More orders followed. They were told to bow to Emperor Hirohito; it was, after all, his birthday. Whether it was to show respect or something else, twenty-four Japanese bombers flew overhead. It was the largest group yet since their arrival. The deteriorating mood of the POWs was palpable. Errett's attempts to resurrect his optimism felt like a weightlifter's snap-and-jerk lift of a three-hundred-pound barbell. His dour mood waned somewhat after work when he was issued a Red Cross tin of corned beef and just under one pound of slightly dried pears.

Of the twelve thousand American defenders, about half died in the first six months after they surrendered.[35] Errett thought about Bill Brown and the other thirty-eight men from his regiment who died before he left the Philippines. The fate of the other New Mexicans of the 200th and 515th not at Mitsushima would remain a mystery to him until his return to New Mexico. Forty-four POWs at Mitsushima perished by the end of April 1943, this first winter. Errett did not know all of them, but he carefully wrote the names of seventeen of these poor souls in his thirty-nine-page diary Nakajima issued to POWs along with pencils for the purpose of journaling according to the rules of camp censorship. Errett acquired a second, smaller one he kept hidden in the wall next to his bunk:

> Technical Sergeant Gusta R. Krause, died 1–28–1943
> Technical Sergeant Arthur J. Burke, died 12–14–1942
> Staff Sergeant Asa A. Jackson, died 4–15–1943
> Sergeant Kenneth Hunter, died 2–14–1943
> Sergeant Francis B. Sherwood, died 2–11–1943
> Sergeant James A. Vitelli, died 2–9–1943
> Corporal Gerald M. Simpson, died 3–28–1943
> Private Roger D. Derr, died 2–6–1943
> Private Winfred D. Hayes, died 4–22–1943
> Private Clarence Hendrickson, died 2–21–1943
> Private Albert H. Roberts, died 3–1–1943
> Private Alfred G. Smith, died 3–3–1943
> Private Robert G. Teas, died 2–16–1943
> Private Garth Ginther, died 3–5–1943
> and two of the ten at Mitsushima from the 200th/515th Coast Artillery:
> First Sergeant J. [Jake] M. Smith, died 12–21–1942
> Private Raymond Chavez, died 2–16–1943

All seventeen were American except Hendrickson, who was British. Their bodies were hauled by the POWs one mile uphill near the train depot where they were to be cremated. The ashes were collected later, put in a small wooden box, and labeled with a soiled piece of cloth inscribed with the prisoner's number. The process was overlooked for a while, and the cremains stopped coming back. This was an oversight Tokyo command noticed, too. Specific orders came for Nakajima to send POW ashes to headquarters with their identifications. Compliance followed quickly. British POW officers at Mitsushima were ordered to construct twenty small boxes. The human remains, however, had not been retrieved, so the guards filled the boxes with the kitchen's fire debris, attached names, and sent them along to Tokyo.[36] The British- and American-trained Japanese doctors would stop into camp every now and again but not often enough to keep up with the prisoners' maladies, and medicine was not brought in on

17. The Worst Winter

a regular basis. Many of the deaths could likely have been prevented if the prisoners had been given better medical treatment and food.

Louis, Errett's father, spaded the garden in their new Santa Fe home as Errett enjoyed the first night that the temperature at Mitsushima rose

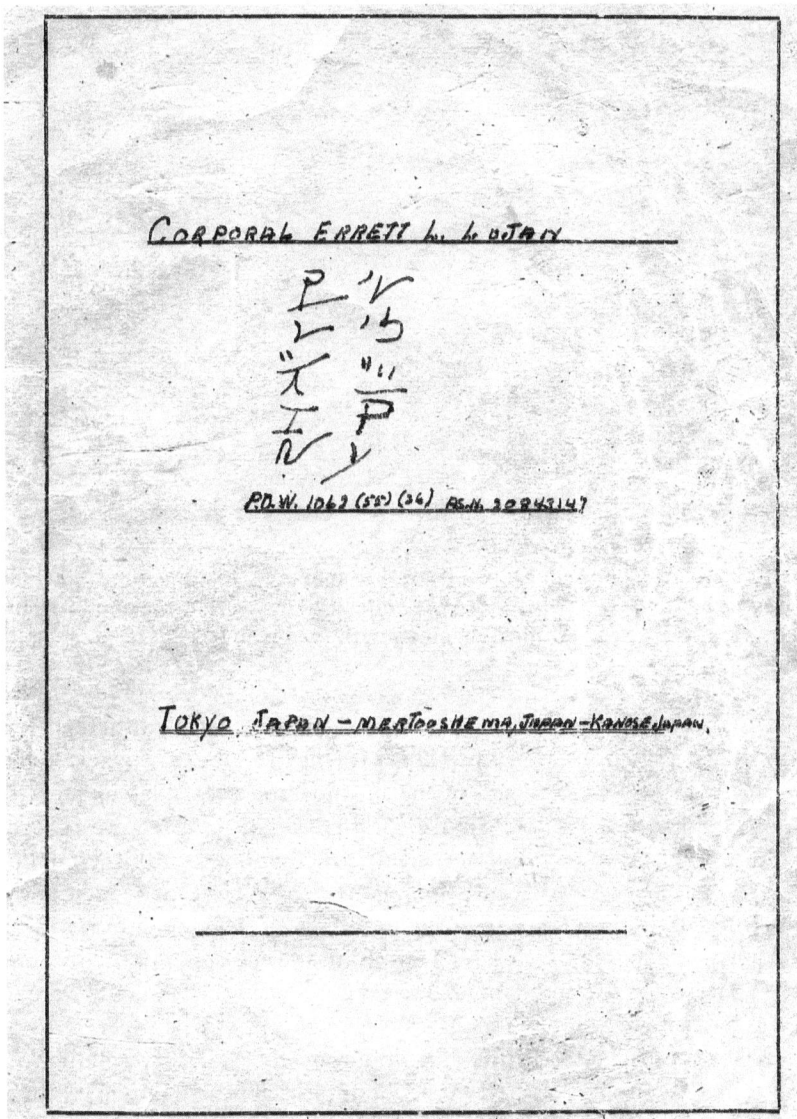

Errett's authorized diary he was ordered to keep by his Japanese captors. It was periodically read by them to ensure the POWs did not write anything critical about their treatment.

Errett's small diary he kept hidden from the Japanese. The stub of the pencil he used to write in the diary is now in the collection of the New Mexico Military Museum in Santa Fe, New Mexico, along with the blade he kept to sharpen its point.

above freezing. Jess was still mailing letters to her son telling him the news of the days. In the one dated April 26, 1943, she described their new home on a corner lot at the crossroads of Navajo and Taos Streets. It was actually two lots comprised of a main house with five rooms on the ground level and two in the basement. There was a detached garage as well. A smaller three-room house was adjacent. The Lujans rented it out for $35 a month. Some information was forbidden such as the War Department's notification approving her application for a family allowance under the provisions of the Servicemen's Dependents Allowance Act of 1942. Payments were to be paid retroactive to June 1, 1942.[37]

A few months after Bruns Hospital opened, a top-secret endeavor, the Manhattan Project, started in the mountains about forty-five minutes away by car from Santa Fe in a town established for the project and named Los Alamos. Their goal was to create a nuclear bomb for use in the war. The project was overseen by army general Leslie Groves and the scientists were led by Robert Oppenheimer. Secretary of War Stimson ordered the takeover of the property by eminent domain in a letter dated November 26, 1942.[38] Congress approved a $31 million budget for the project for the 1943 fiscal year.[39] The facility took over Los Alamos Ranch School on the Pajarito Plateau that Oppenheimer had visited and he championed this particular location among several being considered. It was an ideal site for security purposes and had beautiful vistas. The official papers enacting the taking were signed by New Mexico attorney Howard Houk,[40] a man whom Errett did not know but would soon be his brother-in-law. A sense of urgency dogged the Manhattan Project. It was believed Germany was well down the path of nuclear research and might develop a bomb before the United States could. Los Alamos and the Manhattan Project were strictly guarded secrets, and steps were taken to ensure no information leaked to the public.

In mid–April, a package of recreational items sent from a neutral country arrived at Mitsushima. It contained a ukulele, two mouth organs, two chess sets, five books on learning the Japanese language along with one Japanese dictionary, and twelve decks of cards. Once Mush Mouth helped himself to his share of books and half the cards for the guards, he turned to the ranking officers to lay out the rules for using these things: only in the afternoons on rest days and only in the officers' billet.[41] Mush Mouth's support of having recreation gave the POW officers an idea. They each contributed some money and handed it over to him. Mush Mouth did as asked and used the fifty-two yen to buy them a guitar from the next village. V.R. Fernandez, one of the POWs from Kuala Lumpur, Malaya, was a talented guitarist.[42]

Bruns Army Hospital in the southwest corner of Santa Fe was one of one hundred such installations authorized by the War Department to be built across the country to handle war casualties. Bruns was one of the fifty-one general hospitals built. Like the structures in Los Alamos erected for the Manhattan Project, Bruns was never meant to be a permanent facility. They were constructed using wood and plasterboard and almost every building identical, the average size being 25 feet by 160 feet. The army's policy was to place the new facilities about four hundred miles inland from any coast to reduce their vulnerability, yet be close enough to transport patients from a port within a day. Climate, terrain, utilities, transport systems, communication systems, available labor, housing, and accessibility to large training camps were also factors considered. Santa Fe was deemed perfect, and the hospital's doors opened to its first patient on April 19, 1943. Five hundred officers and enlisted men were transferred in to staff Bruns, and at its peak, it employed one thousand civilians.[43] The facility was about a mile from Louis's new house.

Within days of opening, Louis landed a job at Bruns's canteen stocking shelves and keeping track of the inventory. He truly enjoyed the work, the staff, and the patients, and it gave him a sense of helping with the war effort. Within a month, two of his brothers, Carlos and Ernie, joined the Bruns employment ranks; however, Ernie left four and a half months later for his tour of military service in the U.S. Army. The hospital was named for the late Earl Harvey Bruns of the army medical corps, who was an internationally known authority on pulmonary disease and thoracic surgery. Brigadier General Larry B. McAfee was its longest tenured commander. In its first year, staff at Bruns treated 1,352 patients and performed upward of one thousand surgeries.[44] The number of patients soon grew to 1,500.

Local women dropped in regularly to instruct patients interested in learning Spanish, knitting, drawing, or other things. Sometimes they simply read to them or just talked. A post orchestra formed and played for local dances. The post exchange was a combination general store, restaurant, fountain, and drugstore where one could get a haircut, clothes laundered, checks cashed, and clothes tailored. The patients reveled in its social atmosphere.

As expected, the mood and expertise at Bruns worked wonders on the tortured bodies and souls of its patients. A radio system, the Bruns Broadcasting System, was piped into every ward. Patients attentively listened to accounts of D-Day in Europe, and those well enough to walk spent most of their day at the post exchange or out and about town on a furlough pass.

18

Remaining Months at Mitsushima

Errett's feelings teeter-tottered between desperation and optimism in his diaries. "Don't worry, this will all be over soon and I will be back home." "Don't worry, Bill. I'll see that your mother gets your ring." But what if it was not over soon? What if he died here? "Lord, how much longer is this mess going to go on?" It was on one of those blue days when he had his second fight, somewhat rougher than his first, but he fared better. If Yoshizawa had seen him fighting, he would have thrown him in the guard house for ten days, but Errett knew Mush Mouth was away. Another POW caught stealing food from the kitchen got off relatively easy. Errett saw him the next day, a little beaten up, walking through the barracks with a sign hanging from his neck saying, "I am a sergeant, but I am a thief who steals the mezor from the Cook House. Would you mind laughing at me for my conduct?"[1]

A few of the American POWs did everything they could almost every day to pick a fight and usually succeeded. Private Verble Jones, POW #38, from Selma, Alabama, was one of those guys. None of the POWs had anything good to say about him. He was a thorn in everyone's side. If Verble was not harassing one of the POWs, he made trouble other ways like screwing up the count at *tenko* or stealing whole bags of rice from the cook house or heating a thermometer so he could claim a sick day. His pranks at roll call cost the whole barracks an hour standing at attention at night, often in a cold drizzle.

Nostalgia engulfed Errett in early May. He was to turn twenty-one two days before Mother's Day as a POW. He thought constantly of home and his heart was tormented by a ravenous yearning to be home. Then a small miracle was thrown into the mix of anguish, heartbreak, hatred, pain, and cruelty he was living. An old Japanese man outside the fence motioned him closer one night as Errett headed for the latrine. He paused once at the corner of the building. No one was looking his way. He slipped behind it instead of going inside. Cautiously, he approached the old man and discovered he was not alone. With him was a boy who looked to be about twelve or thirteen. The old man's arm moved almost imperceptibly as a small pack flew from his hand and over the fence. Errett squatted down still looking at them, felt for the package, and picked it up as he slowly stood up. It felt familiar. He looked. Yes, just as he thought. It was a package of local tobacco, what the POWs called horsehair. He looked up to see the two slipping away but motioning what Errett interpreted as a promise to return another time. And he was right.

The old man, his wife, or the boy came back several times over the next several months tossing Errett various items over the fence, always under the cover of night—cigarettes with ten to a pack, horsehair to smoke in his pipe, rice balls deliciously flavored with fish heads, chili, a small bottle of wine, black pepper, and other items for which Errett was unboundingly grateful. On the heels of this miracle came another. Much to Errett's amazement, Pasty Face, one of the civilian guards at the dam site, took it upon himself to share his rice cakes with him. "Just shows," he wrote about the benevolence of his new Japanese friends, "that some of these people are human." Other edible treats came his way when Corporal George Piel from New Orleans occasionally shunted a baked potato or two from the cook house his way on the sly.

Usually, he enjoyed extra food just as soon as he got it. Being caught squirreling food was risky and would probably result in solitary confinement. He had no wish to be laid into that coffin-looking wooden box as the lid locked shut for various lengths of time based on the temperament of the captors. Some men were confined for days, others for hours. Some did not survive the experience, and he was not interested in testing his resilience. The wine from the old man was a different story, though. It came nine days before his twenty-first birthday and he intended to save it for that celebration. He loosened a wall plank next to his bunk space and slipped the bottle in for safekeeping, where it stayed undetected until the night of May 14, when he drank it all.

The night before his birthday, Errett lay in his bunk thinking back to before all this mess started. He had seen the *Wizard of Oz* four years ago. It was just a fanciful story full of things that would not ever happen. Nonetheless, he repeated the mantra, "There's no place like home, there's no place like home, there's no place like home," just in case there was such a thing as magic. When he awoke the next morning, no magic had turned the tide. He was still living a nightmare, but whether it was the wine or reality, Errett felt his twenty-first birthday was better than his twentieth and hoped like hell he would be home for his twenty-second. He entered a mildly disillusioned sentiment in his diary: "a heck of a place to spend your 21st birthday."

18. Remaining Months at Mitsushima

He might have made it home if New Mexico U.S. representative Clinton P. Anderson's hopes of a prisoner exchange, which the congressman conveyed in a letter to Jess, had materialized, but it did not.[2] Instead, Errett did what he could to make himself feel better, and the one thing that did help was collecting a small bouquet of wildflowers in honor of Jess on Mother's Day. He pestered Mike Chavez to do the same for his mom when he went to collect his broken pipe that Mike was repairing. Errett tried twice to fix it before giving up. It was a lot of work to put into a contraption that was so small it used up in two drags all the horsehair that could be stuffed into the bowl. But the Korean tobacco horsehair was less expensive and easier to come by than cigarettes.

From Errett's birthday through the remainder of May, he worked mixing cement one day of hard labor after another. The cement chute blocked up once and work was called off early. The guards were in a rage about it and planned to blast it open. Errett hoped they would blow the whole damn works up, but that did not happen. The next day, it was functioning again.

The Japanese pipe with case and container for "horsehair" tobacco. Errett etched into the metal bands around the container: "No. 36 E.L. Lujan" "1942 POW 1945" "Kanose, Japan."

Around this time back in the United States, a new offensive strategy was being tested involving incendiary bombs. It was the brainchild of Dr. Lytle S. Adams of Pennsylvania and inspired by a trip to Carlsbad Caverns where the 200th had visited nearly two years prior during their convoy maneuvers. The dental surgeon developed an idea to use bats to carry incendiary bombs that would target the paper-and-wood structures in Japan. He sent his idea to the White House. President Roosevelt referred Adams's communiqué to the army's Chemical Warfare Service, who referred it to the army air force, who referred it to Dr. L.F. Fisser of the National Defense Research Committee. Dr. Fisser drew up blueprints for a half-ounce bomb that would burn for four minutes. The small bombs were strapped to bats and dropped from airplanes in the early morning. Theoretically, the nocturnal bats were to immediately seek shelter in designated targets similar to Japanese houses and gnaw through the twine holding the bombs to them. The results of this first test put an end to the project. A general's car was blown up, half of the bats did not survive the air drop, and unintended structures burned to the ground when the bats ridded themselves of their cargo.[3]

If Errett had known of this bat venture, its amusement might have lightened his day. As it was, his grueling task of mixing cement continued without levity. His hands were in really bad shape, hurting just like they did one time as a boy when they were warming up from the verge of frostbite. He knew asking for medical help was useless.

To deal with those in need of clothing, and there were many, the guards ordered an accounting of all clothing items with the intention of redistributing them so equal numbers were had among the POWs. Errett put his pants, shirts, jacket, and socks out along with everyone else. When the tally was done, his pair of blue pants was confiscated. The next day, Little Glass Eye entered Errett's barracks. Other guards had been reassigned out of Mitsushima, but Little Glass Eye remained and decided to conduct an inventory of underwear. This time, nothing was taken from Errett, nor did the sadistic guard send Errett's clothes to a heap on the floor with a swish of his arm as usual.

The six hundred copies of the *Nippon Times* and *Tokyo Times* that arrived in camp for the POWs in mid–April were making the rounds among the men. They were printed in English and spanned a little more than three recent weeks. From them, Errett gleaned that Turkey was now a staunch ally on their side, that the Americans had reclaimed the Aleutians when the Japanese military abandoned the last Japanese-held island of Kiska, that B-24s off the USS *Hornet* were bombing Japan, and that Allied forces were in complete control of North Africa. What the papers did not carry was the death of Admiral Yamamoto, commander of the Imperial

18. Remaining Months at Mitsushima

Japanese combined fleet and director of the attack on Pearl Harbor. He was successfully targeted by the Allies' Operation Vengeance planned after intercepting information revealing the admiral's travel itinerary in the Solomon Islands. The plan called for American pilots to intercept and shoot down his plane as it crossed over the southwest edge of Bougainville on April 18. The precision with which the operation was carried out was perfect.[4] What made it all the sweeter was that the admiral went down in the plane on the first anniversary of Doolittle's raid on Japan. The newspapers, seemingly reliable sources, and the recent kindness from pop, as he called the old Japanese man, helped not only Errett's constitution but also his spirit. Somehow, others were doing better, too. The sick barracks had fewer and fewer POWs, and deaths at Mitsushima slowed to a temporary halt and not another one occurred until mid–June 1943. Accidents at the dam site, however, were on the rise. By mid–May, eight POWs had been injured.

Mush Mouth returned in early May from Tokyo with new instructions for the POWs: empty your pockets, put all money aside, and those without money purses will make one.[5] Fortunately, Errett had a wallet. The others set about fashioning paper money bags that were carefully inspected the following day after which all POWs were ordered to carry their money in them and on their person at all times.

As the weather warmed, more cigarettes were issued, and volleyball games began. With the warmer weather, though, came a dramatic increase in the fly population. Mush Mouth assessed this as a health problem, assigning the medical orderlies and light-duty POWs the task of killing one hundred flies daily.[6] Each day, they turned in their pile of flies to verify their work. Most of the POWs helped out in the campaign, and while Errett doggedly swatted flies, he also collected their larvae, which he packed into his and others' wounds to keep infections at bay. Those little buggers cleaned the wounds real good, better than any medicine available to them.

This remedy worked well on wounds other than those on their feet. Errett looked down at his. They were scraped, sore, and raw from the wooden clogs issued to him in late April, which had not held up since there was little left of them. The next morning at *tenko*, he and a few other POWs were issued a new pair of shoes and, as far as he was concerned, just in time or he would be walking to work with nothing between his feet and the ground. Although the shoes were straw, they were better than what he had and they fit, unlike most POWs', who were of greater stature and therefore had longer feet. He supposed that his new shoes were made by the POWs not well enough to work the dam site since that task was assigned to them.

Volleyball games were fashioned by utilizing a basketball the British brought with them. Even though it was great fun, Mush Mouth often cut the games short. Just another reason to resent him. Errett scoffed a few indignant words: "Seems like you have to get permission to take a shit these days. Boy, I sure would like to lay one on that fish mouth of his," and Errett did not even play volleyball. At least the guards had yet to interrupt their nightly blackjack game, although Errett was not a very good player. His mind wandered too often to his fiancée, Lily. He always did think about girls more than almost anything else other than food.

The end of May had some pleasurable moments after the camp was inspected by a Japanese naval officer. Errett penned a card to his family back home, took a hot bath followed by a cold shower, ate two bowls of rice and two bowls of beans in one meal, was issued ten cigarettes, and missed a few days of work due to rain. Waving six letters above his head, the interpreter announced they would soon be distributed to the POWs. Half were for Americans and half were for the British. Errett figured the large portions of beans and rice were planned to raise the POWs' weights. Errett tipped the scales at 131 pounds. The issued cigarettes were in addition to a pack Errett scooped up when an old Japanese man at work pulled his gloves out of his pocket and the fags fell out. The POWs drooled but were denied anything from a recent Red Cross shipment from South Africa containing thirteen 100-pound sacks of sugar, two 150-pound sacks of salt, 528 one-pound tins of peas and beans, twenty 7-pound tins of cocoa, and forty boxes of dehydrated soup mix. Magnanimously, the twenty-five Tarzan and Mars science fiction books included in the stash were allowed to be read at night in the entertainment building.[7]

The pleasure pendulum swung the other way, hard and fast, on Thursday, May 27. Everything just happened at once. Errett had to work in miserably rainy conditions. He spilled his supper on the ground before ever taking a bite. The card he wrote home was returned for improvement. Although he had not broken the rule of asking for clothes, food, or medicine or printing in block capital letters, he had put more than thirty letters on some of the eight lines on the card. All totaled, he was four letters over the 240 allowed. He was told he could rewrite it or just forget it. He was not about to forget it, but he wondered when his would actually be mailed since it would be turned in so much later than many others. As a group, they were allowed to turn in only thirty cards a day. Worst of all, Errett's hands hurt so badly that he could barely feel them. They were raw and sore. His skin was shedding as if he were peeling off rubber gloves, which, if he had some, might have kept his hands in relatively good condition. At lunch, he went to the river to soak them in the cold water, but as soon as he stuck them in, Bill's ring fell in and swiftly disappeared.[8]

18. Remaining Months at Mitsushima

"Oh, Lord! Oh shit!" He moaned, he cried, he pounded his hurting fists. "How did I let that happen?" He would rather have had one of those sadistic bastard guards kick the shit out of him than lose Bill's ring. Anguish consumed him; torment clutched his heart. He loved his mother so much and he knew she loved him with all her heart, just like Bill and his mom. There was one horrible difference in their stories, though. Bill's sister was killed in a car accident just days before Bill shipped out.[9] Now his mom had no children left.

Errett sat with a heavy heart looking at the blank card on the table. He had to get a note sent home, but he had to make it upbeat to pass the Japanese censors. So, it was time to write and get it perfect no matter how tormented he felt. On May 30, 1943, he wrote,

> DEAR MOTHER AND DAD, HOPE THIS CARD REACHES YOU SAFELY. I'M O.K., DON'T WORRY. PLEASE WRITE. IS MERLE MARRIED YET? I BET CLAIRE IS QUITE A YOUNG LADY NOW.
> I PRAY THE WAR WILL SOON BE OVER SO I MAY RETURN.
> HELLO TO ALL MY FRIENDS. HOPE TO BE HOME SOON, SO CHINS UP. PRAY ALL ARE WELL. Errett Louis Lujan

His signature was not counted against the 240 letter maximum, so his card had only 210 letters. He addressed the card on the reverse to Mrs. L.G. Lujan, 716 Gildersleeve Avenue, Santa Fe, New Mexico. He did not know his family had moved to another house across town bought with a $1,000 down payment Louis was given by his mother, Isabel, from the sale of her ranch in Oklahoma, where she had lived for the past six years since her husband, Lorenzo, died. When Errett handed in his card to Mush Mouth, he learned that letters would be allowed at a later date, possibly on Christmas Day. Four of the six incoming letters for POWs were handed out. Two were postmarked nine months ago, and the ones Paul Grassick and James Groves received were posted a full year ago! Errett's May 30 card home made better time—according to Merle's letter to Errett of September 7, 1943, it arrived at the Lujan residence the first week of September—but he had yet to receive any mail.

Not receiving a letter struck Errett's heart like the blade of a knife in his chest. He prayed to God for mail. If he had been one of the lucky recipients, he would have known through all of Jess's and Merle's letters in May and June that Merle was dating attorney Howard Houk. He would have known about his family's new home, their victory garden, the many letters posted to him, and their growing rabbit population (fourteen with more on the way) aiding in their protein intake. Jess wrote in a June 29, 1943, letter to Errett, "They sure are good eating!" but the letters were withheld.

Errett was also not getting enough to eat. Since he was not working as hard as before, his rations were cut. He was hungry all the time. Piel in the kitchen noticed and sneaked him a can of sugar and a little extra rice. On the plus side, he was pulled off the cement mixing detail because his hands could not do the work. His new duties included hauling dirt to the gardens inside the compound, cleaning latrines, and an array of miscellaneous work at the dam site but not cement, at least not until mid–June.

Mush Mouth addressed the POWs, providing an update of sorts. Errett listened. Shoidisan (Smiling Sergeant) and Sakamoto (medical sergeant) were to leave soon. Only when he added that he, too, would be leaving did the POWs holler.[10] Errett gave a loud whoop, but it was indistinguishable among the cheering from every other POW. When the cacophony lowered, other news was imparted. An inspection by a Japanese colonel and other officers would be in a few days, so clean everything.

The POWs always groused about inspections, and this time it paid off. The upcoming inspection probably had more to do with it than their complaints. Corned beef, pears, five pieces of fried fish, and cigarettes came their way. Errett also received pay of $7.80 for two months of hard labor. After looking around the camp, the inspection entourage made its way to the dam. The Tokyo colonel was extremely pleased with what he saw at Mitsushima and conveyed to the POWs a piece of news he knew they wanted to hear. At that moment, he said, seven hundred thousand pieces of mail for Allied POWs were in Tokyo[11] being reviewed, after which they would be distributed. On average, that would mean about twenty letters for each POW in Japan. Errett deduced that surely one would come his way. Euphoria engulfed the camp except for the guards who felt no such contentment. They were given other news. All of them, they were told, would soon be leaving. They were needed to fight.

True to their word, by mid–June, most of the guards were reassigned and new, old-looking Japanese men replaced them. Heavy off-and-on rains over three days greeted the new guards. The tunnels at the dam site flooded. Everything was a sloppy mess everywhere. When Errett and the others got the worksite cleaned up, he was reassigned to cement mixing. Thankfully, that was followed by a Red Cross issue of corned beef and pears and pay for two weeks in June along with five pieces of fried fish and extra salt. The extra food helped his stamina. He did not want to end up like poor Private Elmer Engle from Lexington, Kentucky. Engle had diarrhea like almost all of the POWs, but his case was particularly bad and he was barely strong enough to make it to the latrine. On his last trip there, he passed out, hit his head on a log, and crumpled to the ground. The log apparently dislodged and rolled onto his chest, suffocating him.[12]

Another Red Cross representative showed up at Mitsushima the last day of June 1943, this time from Switzerland. Again, the canteen was

18. Remaining Months at Mitsushima

stocked with all sorts of items that had been locked up for months. And again, the canteen was cleared out ten minutes after the Red Cross representatives departed. They did leave behind musical instruments that added immensely to the entertainment nights put on by the British. Following this was a decree from the camp commandant that all POWs could swim between 5:00 p.m. and 6:00 p.m. A couple of weeks later, the POWs witnessed the Smiling Sergeant lecturing another guard for an hour during night *tenko*. The POWs in formation decided that whatever problem the Smiling Sergeant was having, it had nothing to do with them. So, the 190 POWs sat down to wait it out. Smiling Sergeant turned his rage to them and marched them into the fourteen-by-twenty-foot guard room where they stood for another four hours, except for the sixty who could not fit into the room and stood at attention outside.[13]

July was sultry. Rumors and newspapers arriving at camp spread news among the POWs. They read them as fast as the rivulets of sweat tracing over their bodies: Sicily was nearly in Allied hands; Kumi Electric Company would take over running the Mitsushima camp in August; MacArthur was in New Guinea; Churchill's bomber losses over Europe thus far was 6 percent; and intense fighting was going on in the Solomon Islands. The good news sure pleased Errett, but he was crestfallen when another batch of about fifteen letters, five to twelve months old, arrived for the POWs[14] and none were for him.

19

Changing of the Guards

Before the military personnel left Mitsushima, Nakajima ordered a photographic record of the POWs created. Propaganda shots of boys just having fun were taken. The prisoners were ordered to swim, play music, garden in the tomato patch, and fish as their pictures were taken. Individual mug shots were done after shaving their heads and beards and their clean, unsoiled identification patches sewn on their jackets. Four months later, Errett was given the photo of himself, which he carefully posted in his diary.

Errett did not pose in the group photos but later wondered if he should have, just in case his family might see him in one. They missed him as much as he missed them. Since Errett became a confirmed POW, Jess received periodic, infrequent information from the government. The latest, in mid–July 1943, was a form letter instructing on how to package and send Christmas parcels to the POWs in the Orient and what to send. The government sent her two labels around August 1. One was for the outside of the package and the other was to be put inside the box. The box could not be larger than four-by-eighteen-by-forty-two inches or weigh more than eleven pounds. Once packed, the box was to be wrapped so it could easily be opened for inspection. The contents of the box must be listed and attached to its exterior. The arrival date in New York City for Christmas parcels was September 15.[1]

Jess immediately began working on her box for Errett. It was the hottest summer in Santa Fe in the past sixty-five years, but she barely noticed. She went shopping right away and put together a collection of towels, socks, shirts, vitamins, cigarettes, sweets, and various other items. She wanted to pack some gum, but it had not been on the store shelves for some time now. However, Louis succeeded in acquiring several packages by purchasing them at Bruns Hospital where he now worked. Merle described in her letter of August 22, 1943, to Errett how Jess packed and repacked the box three times before she got the weight down to just under eleven pounds after she removed one shirt, one towel, and a pair of socks. She wrapped it with twine, attached the contents list, placed the label on top, and gave it to the clerk at the post office on August 21. Ten days later, the War Department notified her that Errett had been transferred to another camp near Tokyo,[2] which was not the case. The Japanese military had simply changed the number of Camp Mitsushima from Tokyo Camp #3 to Tokyo Camp #2 to correct an administrative error.[3] Nonetheless, having an incorrect address on the package doused the flame of hope she felt when she imagined him opening it.

New communication opportunities from the POWs were being orchestrated by the Japanese military. Captain Hewitt and Major Allen Cory of the Fifty-First Infantry Battalion were ordered out of their barracks and they were marched away. When they returned a short time

The camp commandant at Mitsushima ordered all POWs to have their heads shaved and stand for a picture just before moving several of the POWs to Kanose POW camp on 16 April 1944. This is Errett's mug shot.

later, the POWs learned they each sent a radiogram home. Mush Mouth announced that friendly American POWs and those who worked diligently at their jobs would be allowed to do the same at the rate of two POWs per month. After the propaganda messaging work was accomplished, the guards turned to collecting military equipment to take with them when reassigned to the battlefield. This included the POWs' bowls given to them for beans and rice. Officers were exempt from turning theirs in, but Errett was not.[4]

At the beginning of 1943, the POWs had to turn in any foreign money to the guards so it could be exchanged for Japanese currency at the rate of 95 sen for one British pound, 99 sen for one American dollar, 8.75 yen for five pesos, and thirty sen for 1 guilder.[5] Apparently, the Japanese military did not use the going rate of exchange since one American dollar was equivalent to 345 sen. That reduced Errett's wallet by a tidy sum. He had hardly any money when he arrived in Japan and he was not going to earn much when the average pay was 3 cents for a day of work.[6]

The impending departure of the Japanese guards and officers was celebrated with a party arranged by the Japanese. POWs were included in the festivities and treated to a half gallon of sake.[7] It did not go very far among so many men, but they were happy enough just to see the likes of Mush Mouth and other sadistic men leave. The exact date set for the departure of the Japanese military at camp was not shared, but it spurred Errett into selecting a time to exact his revenge on Little Glass Eye. He and two others hatched a foolproof plan, or so they thought. They would subdue him at night after one of his drinking binges, pull out his glass eye, plunge a needle into his brain through his empty eye socket, and replace his fake eye.[8] They chose the night of the next rest day, Sunday, August 1, to execute their plan. Errett anticipated with great pleasure ridding the earth of such a loathsome creature. It was only a few days until Sunday, and while he waited, he played the upcoming scene over and over in his mind.

At morning *tenko* on the Saturday before they were to put the plan in motion, Errett was handed a bombshell: Little Glass Eye and some others were to leave that day.[9] There would be no opportunity to carry out his assassination.[10] All he could do was trudge to work at the dam site. By August 1, all current and former military personnel were gone except Nakajima, whose time as camp commandant would last until the end of next year.

Macheta, the new interpreter, was the antithesis of Mush Mouth. He spoke very good English, not too surprising since he attended Davis Agricultural College in the United States before the war, studying psychology and philosophy; he was polite, seemed quite nervous, and bowed all the time, even to the POWs.[11] Nakajima did not tolerate Macheta's kindness for long. The gumzokos, as the Japanese administrators were known, beat Macheta for ninety minutes, then ordered him to stand naked in front of the guard room after each workday for thirty consecutive nights. As this was impossible to live through, the penance he endured was less than two nights.[12] They could not afford for him to die, as interpreters were not easy to come by.

With the new regime at Mitsushima came an influx of sorry-looking Koreans all wearing tattered clothes. They were drilled all day for a solid month before they gained a few liberties. They were treated slightly worse than the POWs, who suffered fewer punishments, had more food, and were allowed nightly entertainment under the new camp management. The Koreans outnumbered the POWs but were crammed into a smaller area with too few latrines that quickly turned vile.[13] It was clear to Errett the Japanese hated the Koreans.

Errett's living quarters had its own set of problems and topping the list were fleas. He was bitten and itching all over and fighting a losing battle. Sleep was never longer than a couple of hours, and when he got up, he had more bites. He had bites on top of bites; they all did. He was certain those nasty little bugs were on the verge of inheriting the earth. To alleviate the problem, Nakajima ordered all blankets and mats taken to the river edge to air out for a day.[14] Supposedly, fleas did not like fresh air and would leave in search of new hosts. It lured some of the fleas away but not nearly enough. So, as they suffered through their flea infestation, the POWs sat each night to hear the Japanese civilian camp doctor deliver a lecture on things like "chew your food"[15] for optimal digestion.

Toward the end of the month, Errett was issued just under eight ounces of dried pears. At the time, they tasted better than anything Errett could remember. His time outside camp revealed to him that the nearby Japanese civilians were suffering to aid their cause in war. The privations endured by the populace toughened Nakajima's position on identifying those POWs stealing food from the Red Cross supplies, and he ordered the POW officers to find the stolen food, return it, and provide the names of the men who took the food. Captain Hewitt found two tins of meat and vegetables and asked the culprits to come forward after evening *tenko* to avoid every POW being subjected to punishment. The captain was stunned when five men came forward. He must not have found all the missing food but handing in the five men's names was enough to keep the rest from reprisal. Nakajima said he would think over what punishment he would mete out. Several days passed without a punishment decreed. As it turned out, none was ever administered.[16]

Errett was bewildered at the novel techniques the Japanese invented to improve his health as a POW such as wrapping a blanket piece around the midriff while sleeping and keeping all doors and windows shut at night.[17] Later, a lieutenant POW serving in the British navy as a doctor was transferred to Mitsushima from a Tokyo hospital. Comforts at camp, due partly to him, were expanded. POWs were to be allowed more cigarettes, more toilet paper (four sheets a day), more face soap (one every two months), more toothbrushes (one every three months), more tooth powder, and more wash soap (one every month).[18] However, Nakajima still maintained control of all aspects at camp, including medical challenges. When sickness spread with the cooling of the weather, he insisted those in sick bay have a single burn inflicted on their upper arm. The resulting scar was a ruse to trick others into believing they were vaccinated against whatever ailment they suffered.[19] Errett was thankful he was well enough to escape such treatment that would leave him with a souvenir from Mitsushima for the remainder of his life.

The British doctor also arrived with news he surreptitiously acquired while working at the hospital in Tokyo. The *Lisbon Maru*, another Japanese hellship, sank and one hundred of the POWs being transported escaped through China. More important, he arrived at Mitsushima with a batch of letters from home for the POWs.[20] From here forward, mail arrived about every four months, but most was withheld from the prisoners.

At the end of September 1943, Errett received twenty-four maggot-riddled pears, tobacco, a bar of soap, a pencil, a notebook, a toothbrush, and a spoon. Macheta ordered the POWs to keep a diary, but it could not exceed one hundred pages. It was to be sent to their families if they died at Mitsushima. As the quantity of food at Mitsushima improved slightly for Errett, New Mexicans were in a deep grieving period while enveloped by record-setting high temperatures in July and August. Names of deceased troops from New Mexico, dozens of them, were printed in the newspapers throughout the summer and into the fall. One of the Lujans' neighbors sent Errett a St. Christopher medal in hopes of calling on some kind of divine protection for him. If the saint's powers worked, they did it from afar since the medal never reached him. Louis worked in the garage fixing up his newly purchased Model A station wagon. All he needed was a car to get to work, but pride in fixing it up made him feel good. "He thinks it's as fine as a Cadillac," Jess wrote in a letter penned by her and Louis on August 22, 1943. Jess used the bus for her errands.

Looking at the big picture of what the defenders of the Philippines accomplished shows that the price paid allowed them to gain ground in the Pacific theater and forestall Japan's advance to Australia. Allied troops in the South Pacific were finally on the offensive even though Europe was still a priority for the United States. That would change but only after victory in Europe was achieved nineteen months later. For now, the Allies relished one big success—control of Sicily, invasion of Italy, and a signed armistice for that region by September 29, 1943.

During the first week of September, POWs at Mitsushima were given paper and envelopes so they could write home. They were to follow the same instructions as before, but copies were no longer required. Ten letters a day could be turned in for review and mailing. Errett handed over his second missive home on September 5, 1943, the same date his family received the first letter he wrote to them on March 10, 1943, using their old address. Santa Fe was a small enough town then, about twenty thousand people. Someone at the U.S. Post Office recognized the old address on the envelope, knew the Lujan family, and called them so they could get the letter sooner rather than later. Merle raced to the post office and even faster home with the small treasure, telling Errett all about that great day in her letter to him on September 7, 1943. For Jess, it was a God-sent missive as relief pushed Jess's anxiety over Errett to the periphery. At last, she had a shred of hope of seeing her son again.

Merle read Errett's letter aloud with the whole family surrounding her including Jess's aunt Abbie Nisbeth, whose mother immigrated from Ireland. Her husband, John, was a veteran of the Spanish-American War and died on the same day Errett surrendered in the Philippines. Tears traced pathways down their cheeks each time she read aloud the fifty-eight words Errett had painstakingly printed. She read it over and over, and the crying quietly continued. Merle left the house to see other families with men in the 200th CA. She had to let them know they had received correspondence from Errett. It signaled hope to the entire town. It was the first letter from the Orient to reach Santa Fe from a prisoner in Japan, although a few families had received cards. Since its mailing, Jess and the other Lujans had sent one Red Cross cablegram and written eight letters to Errett. He had yet to see any.

Errett took advantage of a new contract program, *komodi*, in which a group of POWs agreed to perform a certain amount of work before the normal end of the workday. On his first *komodi* workday, he awoke at 4:30 a.m., dressed, made his bed, ate a small amount of watery rice soup for breakfast, cleaned his mess gear, and fell into formation for *tenko* at 6:00 a.m. These days, the POWs stood in formation according to their work party. After roll call and being checked out, he moved with his group to the dam site. They all worked diligently, hoping for an early return to camp. They rested one hour midday during their lunch break, returned to their concrete, and completed their contracted work at three in the afternoon, one hour and twenty minutes ahead of the usual stopping time. Errett was glad to return to camp early. The next day, he was back to camp even earlier, at two fifteen in the afternoon.

He looked forward to a third day of quitting early, which he got but for another reason. The commander of all Tokyo POW camps was to inspect Mitsushima in two days and their camp must be spotless. This, Errett was told, would require much *tokusan*, or cleaning. To make the camp look recreational, Japanese staff issued a volleyball, net, and medicine ball to the POWs.[21] The Tokyo commander arrived at seven thirty, minutes after morning *tenko* on October 9. The POWs stood in rank formation and were ordered to take off their shirts and shoes. The commander looked Errett over down to his fingernails. The POWs redressed while the inspection continued in their barracks followed by a look at the worksites at the dam.[22]

The inspection went well, and the POWs were rewarded a couple of days later with the option to buy three apples each at the cost of thirty sen. Errett gladly paid the guard. These were the first apples he had tasted since leaving the United States. Two POWs who decided they would steal food from the kitchen instead of buying apples were caught. Kimura, The Punk, in charge of the kitchen determined their punishment. He selected certain POWs to form two parallel lines. The thieves, Corporal James and another POW, walked slowly through the lines naked while they were smacked on the backsides with wooden laths.[23] The beltline weapons were unlike the guards' weapon of choice, which was a curved oak limb shaped into a sword.

Mid–October was rough. Errett was weak, unable to do much work, and wore little clothing since the interpreter had confiscated his blouse and winter shirts. Notwithstanding those depredations, Errett received a bar of soap and a pen with two nibs to use with ink from one of the three bottles in his barracks. Five POWs, however, managed to work at the diligence level and earned tokens that could be used as money to purchase horsehair, medicine, cigarettes, towels, and other coveted items. In the diligence system, POWs were given one red chevron for every hundred diligence citations earned and a blue chevron for not missing a day of work between paydays.[24]

The POWs had yet another inspection from the brass in Tokyo on the last Friday in October.[25] To put the POWs in good spirits, they were given Red Cross Christmas boxes from the previous year containing sugar, mabela, and a tin of corned beef. In a matter of a couple of days after eating the sugar in the Red Cross boxes, those afflicted with beriberi had little to no symptoms. This uplifted Errett's spirits, but the real reason he felt so lighthearted was the latest rumor—the war had ended. Could it be true? He thankfully prayed to God and asked for a little more protection, just enough to get him home. Two days later, a new rumor supplanted the first—the war would probably end in seven months.[26]

Despite the latest gifting of Red Cross food, the immediate improvement in their health did not last. Chicken pox infected two of the POWs, and other illnesses cropped up with a vengeance. Robertson, sent to a Tokyo hospital with tuberculosis, died while nineteen others from Mitsushima remained hospitalized.[27] Prisoners were still very hungry, and stealing from the kitchen increased even though punishment, if one was caught, would be severe.

While Errett stood at *tenko* in the days approaching Thanksgiving, he was not surprised to see the high mountaintops wearing a mantle of snow. It had been getting noticeably colder each day, cold enough for one-eighth of an inch of ice to form in their water buckets. He shivered slightly while listening to Macheta tell them that no POW could sport a mustache—that luxury was reserved for the camp commandant only. He also wanted to identify any POW with experience in repairing airplanes. He ended his address with embellished war news—the United States recently lost forty-five ships in New Guinea.[28] He failed to acknowledge that the United States had taken control of the Makin atoll. Several of the men handed their names in in response to fixing planes. Errett wondered if they would be sent somewhere with better conditions.

Errett penned another card home to his family and handed it in on Thanksgiving Day to be sent via the Red Cross. The Lujans were busy writing, too, adhering to the recently received instructions of the Japanese as conveyed through the U.S. Department of Army. They printed each word in block letters or typed them. They kept each letter to twenty-five words or fewer, but of course, their letters were much longer, so they simply started a new letter every time they had about twenty-five on the page and then mailed them separately.[29]

Much to the surprise of the POWs, they were allowed to conduct a commemorative service for those who had died at Mitsushima over the past year on their next rest day, the day after Thanksgiving. POW officers crafted British and American flags for the service. The service was solemn. Boxes containing ashes, one to represent the British who had died and the other Americans, were covered with the respective flags of the two countries. Paper flowers were placed on each box and a few words were said. All but twelve prisoners who were in the hospital attended.[30] Errett sat among the other POWs, trying not to think about the past year and a half, about the beatings, about the deaths, about Bill, about losing Bill's ring, about tomorrow. After the ceremony, each prisoner was given one tin each of mabela, meat, and vegetables along with three mandarin oranges.

Errett's outlook improved slightly as did his family's in Santa Fe when they were pleasantly surprised with a letter from Thomas Foy, the father of Tom Foy who sailed with Errett on the *Nagato Maru* to Japan. It contained information they heard on a broadcast from Tokyo, Japan, by Tom on November 18. In part, they were told that their son "mentioned your son, Errett R. Lujan, and also the fact that he was in good health."[31]

Heavy rain fell often in November and December, producing several unscheduled rest days. Frost greeted them every morning, but Errett was spared the three feet of snow on the ground he endured last year at this time.[32] It was still colder than blue blazes, though. Less than five hours of sunlight hitting the camp each day did little to warm the camp. Gloves were issued to those who worked outside of camp,[33] but they were not the kind Errett could use in his work. Although the weather was somewhat milder than last winter, sickness among the POWs rose. Currently, five were down with pneumonia.[34]

Nakajima wrote out a message defending his treatment of POWs at Mitsushima. It was, he ciphered, because Japanese nationals in the United States had been jailed, raped, and were soon to be sent to prison camps. Baths were to be every five days and only on the 5th, 10th, 15th, 20th, and 25th of the month but only if those were not workdays. Before December 16, all POWs were to have their hair cut. Big Glass Eye was to take chest, waist, and feet measurements of each POW and record the metrics.[35] Then Errett listened to another directive from the camp commandant via Macheta. As he listened, one of his constant wishes had come about. His family received one of his cards mailed from Mitsushima.

New rumors spread through the camp from various sources. POW William J. Findley of Devonport, England, returned from the Tokyo hospital with news that the Allies were sinking two Japanese ships for every American one.[36] The POWs' clandestine radio announced that Formosa had been bombed by twenty American planes. Errett welcomed this little bit of news along with an issue of oranges, mabela, corned beef, a tin of meat with vegetables, soap, toilet paper, cigarettes, and tobacco the first week of December. He paid 2.97 yen for his six and a half oranges and 30 sen for the tobacco and cigarettes. Just before Christmas, some good news leaked out. One hundred letters for the American POWs had arrived. Errett was elated and hopeful that at least one would be for him even if it took the full sixty days anticipated to pass through the camp censors.[37]

Errett woke Christmas morning hoping some good to come of the day. He attended the morning church service and then received his share of a cigarette and tobacco issue. The highlight, though, came at suppertime. Like always, he had food on his mind, and some relief in that plight came. Errett savored two bowls of beef stew, oranges, some pie, and coffee. He practically licked his mess kit clean, not wanting the meal to end. With what could pass as a full stomach these days, he listened to the POWs sing Christmas songs in a satiated bliss.

The pleasantness from Christmas settled on Errett like a big, fluffy down comforter for a week until tragedy struck. A big snow on New Year's Eve collapsed a barracks. Eight POWs were killed outright and another sixteen to eighteen were badly hurt. The loss deflated his bubble of relative well-being. The POWs had few details these days on how the war was going outside the camp, but their situation was definitely not going well for them. If they could see the big picture, they would know they were part of the 117,142 casualties and missing from the American army in both theaters of war at the end of 1943. On the other hand, they would be pleased to learn that the war had catapulted the United States into being an eminent economic and military power in the world and a force to be reckoned with as evident throughout the United States, even in small places like Santa Fe.

19. Changing of the Guards

By 1944, Bruns Hospital had grown to 196 buildings. Outdoor facilities included a handball court, volleyball court, badminton court, shuffleboard, clock golf, tennis court, horseshoe toss, football field, and softball field and had notables such as Olivia de Havilland and Helen Keller visit the patients. It was redesignated as a specialized center for chest diseases and ex–POW treatment facility for those soldiers returning. About 750 beds were allotted for tuberculosis patients, and seventy-five German POWs were brought in from Roswell, New Mexico, as maintenance workers for the hospital.[38]

In the middle of February 1944, a convalescent reconditioning annex to Bruns opened nearly ten miles away from the main hospital. It had recently been operating as the Santa Fe Inn and was set on seventeen acres. Their success rate was impressive. All of the men who received treatment at the annex returned to duty. The big lounge at the inn was used in the winter for indoor athletics and calisthenics, but the principal components of the rehabilitation facility was its physical therapy clinic, occupational therapy shop, and physical and educational programs. Therapy treatments were those familiar today: shortwave diathermy, infrared and ultraviolet lamps, electrical stimulation, whirlpool baths, massage, and passive and active exercise by professional physical therapists. After hours, the lounge at the annex served as somewhat of a nightclub with beer, other cold drinks, crackers, pool tables, phone booths, and a jukebox.

As snow piled higher at Mitsushima in January and February, temperatures dropped. Snow remained on the hillsides and shadowed places through the winter, creating ripe conditions for the POWs to have an occasional snowball fight.[39] Despite the cold, the POWs were warmed by messages from home. In early January, two men received parcels, making them happier than they had been since the surrender. Two weeks later, on January 19, Errett received five of the eleven letters from home sent thus far to Japan—two from Jess, two from Merle, and one from Claire.

He felt he had hit the jackpot. It was the first he learned of their new home on Taos and Navajo Streets they purchased a year earlier. He read them over and over while he ate his portion of food from two Red Cross boxes he shared with two other prisoners. Secondhand information of a tantalizing nature originally suggested by the interpreter seemed astonishing—POWs over thirty-two years of age were to be sent home.[40] If true, and they highly doubted it was, only a handful would be leaving. Macheta was looked down on by other Japanese in the camp,[41] so Errett believed he simply made things up he thought the POWs might like to hear to gain their favor. Errett spent his first rest day in February 1944 cleaning the camp for an inspection by a Japanese commander, a colonel, from Tokyo. The commander arrived late in the day on the 7th, a day earlier than expected.

A studio photograph taken in the latter part of 1940 of Errett and his sisters before Errett's regiment was activated. Claire is in the middle and Merle to the far right.

Errett fell in for evening *tenko*, removed his shoes as ordered, and stood on the cold snow-covered ground until the colonel had inspected everyone's feet. The next day, he returned with a purported civilian Japanese prince accompanying him. The prince attended Oxford in England and said he was fond of the British culture; however, the war forced him to return to Japan. The colonel came a third day but only spoke to the American doctor to inform him he was to be detailed elsewhere for three weeks.[42]

On March 12, 1944, Errett replied to the letters from his family given him in mid–January. He was anxious to answer them, but that was the earliest he was allowed to do so. "I'm in fine shape. I spend a lot of time planning things we will do. I received five letters but no packages yet. How's the new home?" Nakajima grudgingly handed over Red Cross boxes to the POWs in mid–March.[43] Errett opened his as carefully as if it contained delicate china. On top was a pair of gloves set on a neatly folded handkerchief. On the bottom were a sweater and pajamas. What would have been empty spaces were filled with socks.

The POWs happened to get fairly reliable information almost daily one way or another. At roughly the same time, March 20, while Grandma Lujan was visiting her son and his family in Santa Fe, the Lujans received their third letter from Errett. It was the one he wrote on September 5, 1943. Errett spent the last few months of winter in Mitsushima working at the dam, cleaning the camp for another inspection, enjoying two extra rest days, and handing in another letter to be mailed home. On one of the rest days, he managed to enjoy a hot bath, giving him the one and only time he was comfortably warm during the winter. A different surge of warmth came on St. Patrick's Day when he received another letter from home. In late March, he was issued another skimpy blanket, but it did little to keep the cold out of his bones, and even though the winter of 1943–1944 in Japan was the coldest in forty-two years, Errett felt he was in better circumstances than the previous winter.

The local papers in New Mexico from January through March were packed with news of advances being made in the war. Achievements such as the American planes turning the tide of the war in Europe by causing significant damage to the German air force to the stepped-up bombings of Tokyo, Nagoya, and Osaka in Japan reassured the Lujans. Six-pound napalm-filled bombs were dropped for hours on end on these Japanese cities. The fire glow of Tokyo could be seen one hundred and fifty miles away, too distant for Errett to see from Mitsushima. However, if he could have climbed the mountains surrounding Mitsushima, he might have seen Nagoya aglow in the night. American pilots in Operation Iceberg achieved another success a month later when the Japanese ship *Yamato* attempted a run to Okinawa. It was blown to pieces, and nearly four thousand Japanese sailors died at the cost of twelve Americans and their ten aircraft. Overall at Okinawa, nineteen hundred Japanese *kamikaze* planes attacked American navy vessels during the battle.[44]

The same papers had other articles quite disturbing to the families of the 200th. Word was getting out about atrocities committed by the Japanese. The ordeals of Bataan began to surface but were left uncorroborated by the U.S. government. In fact, pictures of graves and beheaded American and Australian POWs reached Washington, D.C., by mid–May 1944, but the information was not released until a year later shortly after VE Day.[45]

20

The First Leg at Kanose

Rain fell often the first week of April. Errett slipped on one of the handmade grass raincoats and plodded off to work even though it did not keep him from getting soaked. One of the guys in line ahead saw no practical reason to put it on. Buick took offense to his outright insubordination and slapped the poor man on one side of his head for an eternity. He went deaf in that ear. Amazingly, Buick caught hell from his sergeant.[1]

Two POWs returned to Mitsushima from the Tokyo hospital in early April 1944. Errett pondered the wealth of news they brought as he dried out once back from the dam site: Truk, Guam, Rubul, and Wake were taken back by the Allies; attack on the Philippines was imminent; Russians were sixty miles into Poland; seven Japanese planes had been shot down over China for every Allied one lost to their guns; half of the Japanese ships leaving the Philippines had been sunk; seven thousand Japanese surrendered in New Guinea; the English coast evacuated to five miles inland; and most astonishingly, thirteen nations, including Germany, had sent messages to Japan protesting treatment of POWs in their care.[2] But it was news of his family Errett mostly wanted. He would have relished knowing that twenty-nine-year-old Merle had married Howard Houk on April 8, 1944.

Two more Japanese at Mitsushima were reassigned elsewhere in the war. Medical secretary San and Limpy (Kitasawa San) left camp. Limpy's emotions ran high as he slobbered on POWs saying goodbye. Information regarding POWs seemed to those at Mitsushima to be getting out. Errett could only surmise that his family was being kept somewhat informed, and he knew that for now, they knew he was alive. When offered the opportunity, he felt it prudent to sign up for the $10,000 life insurance policy the American Red Cross was offering.

Then the biggest news of all came a few days later. Macheta lined everyone up and, one by one, rolled black ink over their fingertips and pressed them onto cards—twice. One set would be sent to Tokyo headquarters and the other kept with the POW's camp medical record. Four

20. The First Leg at Kanose

days later on the following Saturday, forty-nine British and forty-nine American troops (Errett included) and two Chinese of the Singapore Technical Corps were ordered to Barracks #1 with all of their belongings at midday. All other POWs were sent to Barracks #2.³

Errett fetched his things, unsure of what was going on. Once all one hundred were in the barracks, Nakajima addressed them. Japan's POW Management Bureau had sent orders to send them to another camp. They had been selected because of their better discipline and health than the others, although some were noticeably ill,⁴ to be sent to a camp located in a cooler part of Japan on the northeast side of Honshu. Errett could not imagine how cold he would be there given his experience in the slightly more southerly Mitsushima.

First, they turned in their work clothes and then were issued some Red Cross food. Errett was given milk, a rarity. Then they were ordered to take six blankets each and add them to their belongings. Each man was to carry his full kit of dishes, soap, clothes, and so forth and the six blankets. Errett tried this way and that to manage his load but failed, as did most of the other POWs. The unwieldly baggage was obviously too much to carry, prompting a new directive. Errett followed the instructions along with the others, rolling nine blankets into one bundle, keeping only one with their belongings. When the twenty-six bundles were finished and their personal items inspected for contraband, Nakajima festooned them with more food and their last pay for work on the dam.⁵

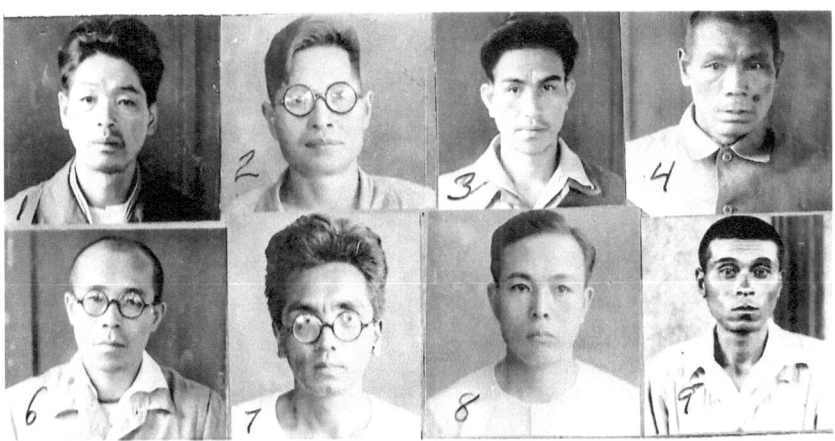

Eight of the 20 mug shots taken in April 1944 of Singapore Technical Corps (STC) POWs who numbered at least 90 at Mitsushima POW camp. Most members of the STC POWs were of Chinese origin who moved to Malaysia before the war, but some were native Malayans (Photographs were part of Errett's collection.)

The men in Barracks #1 embarked on a celebration of sorts. Errett joined the others chowing down on a meal of bully beef, spaghetti, and cocoa. They were ordered into their bunks by eleven to get a good night's rest before being awakened well before sunrise for an early departure. They marched out and headed for the train depot at five in the morning on April 16, 1944, through the gate they first entered seventeen months ago, leaving the rest of their fellow prisoners at Mitsushima.[6]

Errett, the other ninety-nine POWs, the twenty-six bundles of blankets, and all of their other gear were piled into one train car a little after six that morning. Half of the men had to stand in the cramped conditions. One Arm and Big Glass Eye were also transferred to the new camp and accompanied the prisoners. Errett guessed his new home was not on the beaten track as the train transfers mounted up, six in all. About halfway, three feet of snow on the ground could easily be seen through the windows. They disembarked at Kanose in the Niigata Prefecture at nine that night and immediately began their half-mile walk to their new prison camp, Tokyo POW Branch Camp #16-D.

As the crow flies, Kanose is just under two hundred miles from Mitsushima, but because of the mountainous terrain, Errett traveled about three hundred miles to reach his new camp. Kanose is on the north side of the hundred-and-thirty-mile-long Agano River and nearly thirty miles southeast of the coastal city of Niigata, the largest in the prefecture on the Sea of Japan side of the main island of Honshu. Spanning the Agano River, which was much wider than the Tenryū, Errett spotted a hydroelectric dam. This one was complete and running. He was sure glad there was no work to do there.

Judging from what he could see in the cold and bleak night, Kanose appeared to be a smaller village than Mitsushima, perhaps around four thousand people, and where the schoolchildren, Errett discovered, were taught as if they were in military training.[7] The camp itself was closer to the dam than the village of Kanose, which lay above and out of sight of the POW camp. It merged with three neighboring villages in 2005 and is now known as Aga. The cold crawled through Errett's body and into his bones as he trekked through this last leg of his day. He warmed up a little inside the barracks where there was a wood fire. Shortly, they were served rice and stew. The facility had better lavatories and washstands than Mitsushima. Nonetheless, the place was cold and bleak and a crust of snow covered the ground. His new barracks were unlike the last. This one was a large warehouse mostly made of tin. Partitions cordoned the space inside into six rooms with a connecting corridor. Three of the rooms served as billets, each to accommodate thirty-three POWs according to their newly assigned POW number. Errett looked at his number, 36, saw his name misspelled, and weighed the importance of asking it to be corrected. At #36, *sano-jū-roku*, on the sequential roster he was in the middle partitioned billet. On the floors of each billet were rice mats for beds. Errett sat and sewed his new POW number on the front and back of his green jacket, then he wrapped everything he could around him, lay on his mat, and closed his eyes hoping for sleep to come quickly. It did.

The routine at Kanose, Errett discovered, was very much like that at Mitsushima starting with assembling in the morning but without roll call, followed by breakfast, and then work. Half of the POWs went to work their first day in camp, but Errett was not one of them. Showa Denko, a company manufacturing carbon rods, was his new "employer" and listed the POWs who worked for them as "volunteers."[8] The company provided shelter and food for work done in their factory from 8:00 a.m. to 4:30 p.m. with an hour for lunch. The work was simple—loading ore, stoking furnaces, stirring the pots of molten ore, or unplugging the vat to release the liquid. It took a tremendous amount of electricity to attain a temperature high enough to smelt the ore. That power came from the nearby dam across the Agano River. The process required attaching a round globule of carbon on one end of a long rod. After heating it up, it was dipped into the ore to melt it. In making the carbide (a compound of carbon and metal) into a heavy liquid, a tap directed the hot mixture into kettles when a worker unplugged it with a long rod.

While Errett stood at attention after morning formation on the third day in camp, the camp commandant, a colonel, inspected their living quarters and then addressed the POWs. All were to report for work today. Compared to the others in charge of the various POW camps Errett had been in, the commandant seemed a gentleman. His interpreter, Keitaro Fukijima, began addressing the men. It was not the tirade of Japanese superiority or ridicule as Nakajima regaled them with on their arrival at Mitsushima. Instead, the tone was somewhat more respectful. The oration began with the standard "do as you are told" and "stay healthy" instructions and the fact the camp had no doctor or medicine. Then the tone softened. They will be treated according to law, they will be allowed recreational activities, have daily baths after their work shift, and since they fought a good fight as was their duty, they will be treated as heroes. They were also informed that one hundred thousand letters and parcels for POWs arrived in Tokyo on April 1.[9]

There was no mention of punishments if they disobeyed. That is not to say they had none. The men knew better than that and they certainly found out they were right, but some of the punishments were less severe than at Mitsushima. Nonetheless, Errett met a new guard who earned a reputation of being particularly violent toward the POWs—Kiromitzu Saito, nicknamed "The Bulldog."[10] In contrast, Private Matt Braun was caught hiding beans on a shelf behind his bunk. These beans had not yet been distributed and Matt had been cooking them on a small railcar of hardening liquid carbide rolled into the barracks after work. The cooling carbide doubled in providing smokeless heat in the room that lasted twenty-one hours. Two others were found to also have Red Cross food not yet issued. They were called into the commandant's office where he delivered to Matt a somewhat gentle slap on his cheek and told him, "Next time you steal, don't get caught."[11] The other two had their next Red Cross parcels given them two days later than everyone else. After the commandant concluded his remarks, hot baths were had and Errett retired for the evening with a few more blankets allotted him from the 256 sent from Mitsushima.

A new work schedule was imposed on the POWs. They were divided into four groups. The first three groups rotated eight-hour shifts, one after another, in stoking the furnaces. The first shift was 8:00 a.m. to 4 p.m., the next 4:00 p.m. to midnight, and the last midnight to 8:00 a.m. The fourth group loaded ore from 8:00 a.m. to 5:30 p.m. Initially, several workers suffered injuries due to a lack of eye protection and proper footwear. The camp commandant responded to complaints relatively quickly. Soon the company issued work suits, mitts, face masks, and towels. However, shortages occurred time and again, and more were injured. Military protocol such as saluting, roll call, and so forth was followed at the mill, and on-site managers seemed reasonable. However, seeing very young Japanese children forced to work at the mill was unsettling. The new schedule lasted less than a week. It required the factory overseers to work twelve-hour shifts, something they did not like, so the 8:00 a.m. to 4:30 p.m. schedule resumed for all. In early May, Errett was asked whether he preferred to work twelve-hour shifts followed by twenty-four hours off or eight-hour shifts with no rest days. It was a survey being conducted at the commandant's request. He along with the other men elected to work the eight-hour schedule.[12]

It did not take Errett long to know the civilian guards Tokio Minagawa and Kiyoji Ishibe who worked under the direction of Shotaro Kanagawa, the company honcho who was nearing fifty, and he came to know the thirty-year-old Estu Origasa who also worked there. The guards often cruised by him while he stoked furnaces, five minutes on the clock, then ten minutes of rest. The downtime gave Errett the opportunity to look around. To his astonishment, he noticed a variety of American-made General Electric and Westinghouse products everywhere. The generator was U.S.-made. The breakers were U.S.-made. Even upstream at the dam, he saw U.S.-made switches that distributed power.[13] His work was not terribly labor intensive, but the heat was blistering and the air smelled toxic and stagnant since the half-mile-long mill was built in a mine shaft. In fact, manufacturing carbide at Kanose filled the workplace with residual chemical dust and dense fumes of ammonium nitrate, hydrochloric acid, and sulfuric acid.[14]

One week after arrival, a new and much younger camp commandant, former army soldier Hiroshi Azuma, arrived. His demeanor was strict, and his first address to the POWs contained more do-nots than the commandant he was replacing. Proudly wearing his second lieutenant insignia, he sternly looked over the men while Fukijima repeated his words in English, "We will treat you well.... You must respect the rules.... Lights and fires must be out at 9:00 p.m.... You must obey orders or be punished,"[15] while guards, such as Kanemasu Uchida looked on. The POWs soon realized Azuma could speak enough English to carry on a conversation. Each POW was then made to sign a document stating they would not try to escape. Errett had no intention of trying to escape. Where on earth could he go here that would be safe?

The company had built a new kitchen in camp for the POWs and let them know they were in the process of purchasing tobacco for them, too. Azuma ordered each prisoner to be issued a toothbrush, pencil, and half a pack of tooth powder[16] but sold one pack of tobacco at sixty sen to be shared by five POWs. To aid the Kanose POWs and all other Allied prisoners of war, the United States created a monetary relief account sending U.S. dollars to Switzerland to be spent on humanitarian aid. In the end, it was not used for that purpose, but after the war, some POWs from Allied countries were allotted compensation from it. The United States was the only Allied country to ban its ex–POWs from requesting compensation for the slave labor they performed.[17]

Errett received a fair number of gratis items in May after forty Red Cross parcels for American POWs arrived along with over three hundred letters from home. The parcels' contents varied from box to box and included razors and razor blades, tooth powder, shaving soap, sewing kits, toothbrushes, pencils, combs, shoe polish and laces, soap, razor blade sharpeners, scissors, pipes, cigarettes, and tobacco, and every POW received ten bean-paste biscuits, pens, and toilet paper. Various medicines also arrived.[18] Unbeknownst to Errett, the odds were fairly good that letters for him might be in the batch. His family had mailed forty letters his way since August 1943. Errett and four other American POWs shared the contents of two allotted boxes. Errett picked out and gathered his items— tobacco, cigarettes, shaving cream, soap, and a comb.

As letters piled up at Kanose, the Lujans penned even more. Merle wrote two on Mother's Day, May 14, 1944, as it was also Errett's birthday. It was too much for Jess to do, though. Mother's Day was doubly difficult for her. All she could think about was the Mother's Day he was born twenty-two years ago.

Antityphoid inoculations and pills were administered as an increasing number of POWs suffered from that disease[19] as well as diarrhea, boils, ulcers, and inflamed, bruised, and bleeding feet for lack of shoes. The carbide company augmented these gifts with some of their own, mostly consisting of cigarettes and tobacco, given to workers they identified as industrious.

The newly arrived Azuma involved himself with the POWs by leading their physical training himself and procuring things requested by the men such as tea, cocoa, soy, pepper, seaweed, mustard, curry, fish powder, vitamins, and bread.[20] Errett was really surprised when a Ping-Pong table showed up on the same day one of the British officers requested it[21] in spite of Fukijima telling them that Azuma was not an army man and Kanose was not an army camp, making it difficult to get supplies such as recreational items.

Why treatment was better here, he did not know, but it was, and so far, the commandant seemed to Errett to be a decent fellow, given the circumstances. For instance, the punishment for the recent theft of onions from the garden was insignificant. No one confessed to the theft, so Errett and the others were told to stand in formation and close their eyes. The punishment for not fessing up was usually harsh like the belt line or holding buckets of water with outstretched arms for an eternity or being locked up in the coffin, and so forth. Instead, each received a mere tap on their cheeks.

Then Fukijima read a message from the camp commandant at Mitsushima. Errett stood in disbelief at the audacity of the missive. The POWs were succinctly thanked for their work in building the dam.[22] This from a man who felt the POWs were barely human. Then the topic of the recent theft of food from the cook house came up. They were not asked who stole the food, nor was a confession asked for, nor were they lectured. They were only told to keep their eyes closed. Errett noticed Matt Braun was held back after others were dismissed. Fukijima asked Matt why his eyes were not closed. Matt claimed he did not understand the interpreter and that was enough at this camp under this commandant this time to shift blame to the interpreter and away from the POWs.[23]

Two goats and five small pigs were brought into camp in May. Those animals and all food harvested from the camp garden were promised to the POWs.[24] This made the task of filling the honey bucket with human waste, hooking the bucket to an ox, and dipping the fertilizer along the garden rows somewhat less offensive. They had seen this method of fertilizing crops everywhere they had been in Japan.

Perhaps the explanation for better treatment was as simple as

20. The First Leg at Kanose

different personnel running things at Kanose, or could it be the changing tide in the war slowly going against Japan, or were there new developments in a POW exchange? In mid–May, rumors had it that Tōjō had agreed to a prisoner exchange with Churchill and Roosevelt,[25] and for such a purpose he would, no doubt, want prisoners who had been in the care of Japan to be in better shape.

Pressure on Roosevelt from his advisers for the exchange increased as news of the Japanese beheadings of American POWs finally reached Washington. Concurrent rumors of an exchange, fifty Allied POWs for one hundred Japanese POWs, were surprisingly circulating through Kanose camp by May 26, along with a postscript that Burma was now in Allied hands.[26] This new rumor of a prisoner exchange evaporated like the others, but in the meantime, about four hundred letters for the POWs were distributed. Errett looked on as some of the men received as many as thirty. He sure was happy for them. Finally, one was handed to him.

Errett's optimism again elevated during the first week of June as apples were portioned out at 11 cents each, limited to one per POW, and American Red Cross boxes filled with shoe repair materials were made available.[27] Errett welcomed the apples as they were a nice change from the whale meat and blubber meals of late.[28] During an inspection immediately after by a colonel from Tokyo and Major Hamada, only one question was put to the prisoners. Do you like this or the last camp better? The unanimous reply was Kanose. It pleased Azuma so much that he issued three more apples to each POW. What excited Errett the most, what excited everyone at the time, were the newspapers published the second week in June circulating in camp describing Allied troops and paratroopers landing in France during Operation Overlord, widely known today as D-Day, and Allied forces gaining control of Rome.

Elation among the Kanose prisoners was palpable even though they attempted to conceal it as rumors circulated that a Japanese envoy was being sent to talk about peace. The POWs were warned against talking about the war, so as Errett moved among the workers in the furnace, he simply offered a knowing smile to his fellow POWs. They conveyed their feelings without a word said. Suddenly, the butt end of one of the long metal rods being used to stir the molten ore clocked Errett in the face, knocking out the jubilation he felt just a moment before and part of a tooth. The company guard took note of the accident and reported it to Azuma at the end of the work shift. Soon afterward, Errett was summarily escorted to the dentist in town who had a poor reputation among the POWs. He returned with a silver-colored cap covering his broken front tooth. It fit well enough, but he felt branded. He hated it and vowed it would be the first thing to go once he returned home no matter how much it cost.

The defensive positions of the Axis nations' military apparently changed Azuma's and previously friendly guards' moods. They began distancing themselves and employing a more tyrannical approach toward the POWs. The smallest violations of the rules, perceived or real, was met with a rampage of slapping and clubbing. The men were slapped for wearing hats inside, not washing their hands after using the latrines, being slow to *tenko*, talking to the guards about the progress of the war, not bowing properly, and other infractions. Fire drills came often. Blackout conditions for the camp and the factory were ordered at night starting at nine.[29] All the POWs were pressed into digging up all available land within the camp for gardens, the explanation being that one hundred additional POWs would soon arrive. The current POWs, they were told, were to educate the new ones on camp life and rules.[30]

Kanose enjoyed a record of no POW deaths up until late June when Private Frank Brancaticano succumbed to pneumonia. He was to be cremated like the ones before at Mitsushima. A group of American POWs were assigned to carry his body and wood to the next village eight miles away. The somber men trekked away toward their destination following the river. Over the months at Kanose, they had felt hopeful that no more POWs would die. After all, it was the first in nearly a year and the first one at Kanose,[31] and only a few each day, about six to eight, were out of work and another four to six on light duty with health problems such as pleurisy, boils, rheumatism, and diarrhea.

Other aspects were improving, although only slightly, in Errett's opinion. His pay, as a noncommissioned officer, was raised to 25 cents an hour. The accolades for the POWs' work were joined by a lecture from Azuma to heed the rules by admitting wrongdoing, not making excuses, not citing international law for a defense, and not making fun of the Japanese.[32] Errett was happy just to be allowed to send another card home, which he did at the end of June.

The B-29 Superfortress bomber made headlines in the *Santa Fe New Mexican* in mid–June with "SUPER-FORTRESS BLASTS JAP HOMELAND." Jess and Louis could almost hear the words shouting off the page. In this, its first combat mission, the bomber rained down destruction on the Yawata Steelworks located on the southern-most Japanese island of Kyushu. Forty-seven of the seventy-five planes made it to the target completely intact. The B-29 was a formidable weapon with four engines, a payload capacity of up to ten tons of bombs, machine guns in four remote-control turrets, a tail turret with two more machine guns, and one 120-mm cannon. It could also fly more than twice the range of a B-17 Flying Fortress.

Headway was also being made in the Mariana Islands, the Carolines,

20. The First Leg at Kanose

and Peleliu. Minister of War Tōjō's miscalculation of his enemy's strategy and indifference to the huge losses of Japanese lives caught up with him. He was certain the next target the United States planned was Palau and the Philippines. Much to his surprise, it was Saipan on June 17, immediately followed by Tinian, both in the Mariana Islands. The battle for Saipan was simultaneously on land and in the Philippine Sea. Toward the end of June, the Allies won a pivotal battle, nicknamed the Mariana Turkey Shoot, in the Philippine Sea, destroying the Japanese navy and costing Tōjō his position as premier and Admiral Ozawa, the lead officer in the battle, his life along with approximately four hundred planes, their pilots, and three aircraft carriers. Tōjō was replaced by army general Kuniake Koiso, the Governor General of Korea, on July 18, 1944.

In mid–June 1944, an Englishman, Dr. Lane, and two medical orderlies, Wilkinson and Kingen, arrived at Kanose. A German raider captured Lane in May 1942 in the Indian Ocean while Lane was serving aboard SS *Nankin*. Wilkinson was captured in Hong Kong and Kingen in the Philippines. They worked at the Shinagawa Hospital Camp before their arrival at Kanose and brought with them varying accounts of the war. Lane reported the Allies had captured Normandy and Burgundy in France, Russia had all of Romania, and there had not been any fighting in the Pacific for a couple of months.[33]

A little over a week later, another 103 British POWs removed from two camps along the Burma-Thailand railway were ushered into Kanose losing not a man along their one-month-long voyage. They were allowed hot baths, their first in two and a half years. An estimated six thousand of the sixteen thousand Australian and British POWs died as they laid train tracks from Bangkok to Moulmein. About twenty-four arrived with severe cases of beriberi. One, Captain Janis Morris, spoke fluent Japanese, which enabled him to hear some terrific news he passed on to the Kanose prisoners.[34] Americans were producing more aircraft than the rest of the world combined, he relayed. Also, the Americans were clearly gaining the upper hand in the Pacific. More and more American bombers filled the sky, one flown by the internationally known Charles Lindbergh. Errett felt a burst of pride and a sense of renewed hope hearing the news.

News of the horrors yet to come in the next few months failed to reach the POWs at Kanose, including the Battle of the Bulge, The Great Marianas Turkey Shoot, the discovery of about 500,000 people (mostly Jews) killed at Majdanek concentration camp in Ukraine, and suicides in Saipan. Fortunately for the allies, the U.S. prevailed through some of these horrors. It was felt that with these gains, some information could be released by the U.S. government about cruelty meted out to American soldiers during the Bataan Death March two years ago. The sparse news of the death march nonetheless was enough to motivate the country into providing U.S. troops with assistance for those who would return. So with solid support from the public, Congress passed the GI Bill. It was signed into law on June 22, 1944.

The Showa Denko company created new work groups and shift schedules in an attempt to curb the increasing hostilities between the American and new British POWs. In shift 1, Errett and a few other Americans went to work at midnight accompanied by the new British arrivals. Shift 2 was comprised of the remaining British and shift 3 the remaining Americans. Men in shifts 2 and 3 often suffered heat exhaustion. Errett's group worked the carbide crushers and pulverizers and periodically found themselves having to duck for cover from the explosions in the factory that typically occurred at night. The decrepit machinery often could not contain the carbide, and when it leaked into the water, it went off with a terrific blast.[35]

Fortunately, Jess and the others at home were unaware of Errett's dangerous work conditions as they collected strawberries by the buckets in their backyard. Instead, Jess wrote on August 27 to Errett as she reflected, "The Japanese should remember how we helped them in that terrible quake. Hope they will treat you boys like we treat theirs." It was a nice thought but not the case for her son. It had been a year since their last card from him.

Almost frantically, the Japanese government looked for ways to bolster the resolve of their country, especially as word circulated about the fate of Japanese civilians in Saipan. They sent artists and writers to war zones to document how well their forces were doing. Scenes of Japanese soldiers mowing down the enemy by the dozens from spider holes (i.e., foxholes) would go far to uplift the people. Talk among the Japanese at Kanose headquarters was in agreement that the war would soon end, but they were clearly uncertain about their impending victory.

A two-day Ping-Pong tournament was organized for POWs at Kanose as part of the promise from Azuma to allow more recreation. The winner won four packs of cigarettes. Errett did not play in the tournament. He could get lots of tobacco from the canteen, and although it was not a cigarette, there was plenty, so he was happy with that. He still had a few of his ten cigarettes given to every POW four days earlier. What he really would like to happen was to be as lucky as the bloke who was rewarded with a full loaf of bread when he answered the question "What is the last thing you think of when going to bed?" His reply: "Tomorrow morning's breakfast."[36]

Errett probably would not have done very well in the tournament anyway. He was exhausted, still working nights, arguing with the newly arrived acrimonious Brits, losing weight, and being gnawed on by fleas

20. The First Leg at Kanose

while trying to sleep, but he was determined not to be added to the forty or so POWs on the sick list. He heard Azuma say that there were too many sick and that he wanted to send them back to Misushima from where he believed all would be transferred somewhere else in October. The other impediment to sleep was construction noise from building five new air raid shelters. Errett considered this a prudent endeavor since air raid sirens blared often, causing even the carbide plant to shut down for hours at a time. The new shelters were ready in late fall and used regularly until they collapsed in mid–December, rendering them unusable.

Errett became despondent about his perception of unequal work assignments. He thought the new arrivals were working only four hours. He did not know that once they finished their four hours at the furnaces, they spent another four hours hauling ore.[37] What he did know was that the Americans and the new English arrivals were not hitting it off. The British seemed cocky and had little respect for the Americans. Soon, rumors ran rampant about how the Americans would be served a bashing if they did not watch their step around the new POWs. Even most of the British first to arrive at Kanose were not getting along with the new guys. Errett was glad when he was reassigned to work with the Americans around August 1. But fighting for one reason or another was a frequent event among all. Errett watched as Private First Class Burlin Cupp from Ohio gave Private First Class David Dement from Louisiana a black eye because he called him a thief, and of course, Verble Jones was always picking a fight with someone.

Errett got a bit of rest when water mechanics at the plant silted up from two weeks of rain. The problem shut down work for a few days. The water flow problem was soon fixed, but before going back to work, Errett stopped at the canteen and bought one cucumber, left the place with three stuck in his clothes, and made his way to his barracks. He ate one and hid the others, but it did nothing to alleviate his lethargy. In fact, he nearly passed out on the job in the middle of his shift. The next morning at *tenko*, he reported in sick. The medical staff recommended a half-day rest after examining him, so he stayed in camp that morning and went to work in the afternoon. When walking into camp at the end of his half shift, he felt just as worn out and tired as he did in the morning.

Fortunately, a series of brief respites came his way when his work time was cut short several days in a row. This pause in work was interrupted by the Japanese sergeant who annoyed him and every other POW in camp with a battery of questions: When were you last home? Where is your home? Where do they live now? What kind of food do you like? What Japanese man do you respect the most? What are your favorite drinks? Is your family living or dead? What is your profession? Errett answered most of the questions and some even honestly. Then he went back to what he was doing beforehand—watching a new fence being built around the camp and ceiling being installed in his barracks. They ran out of fencing material halfway around the complex, so its completion was delayed until early September. Errett did not think it mattered at all if it was there or not. He was sure that escape would sentence him to starvation, but he was grateful for the ceiling because winter temperatures were just around the corner if the war did not end by then.

Japan continued on the defensive in August 1944 as their homeland was systematically being destroyed. Just over one hundred miles in six major cities totaling 105 square miles were obliterated, killing 240,000 Japanese. The pace of the Allied incursion frightened and angered Japan's military, and a message went forth to all POW camps from the Japanese high command: "It is the aim not to allow the escape of a single one [POW], annihilate them all and do not leave any traces."[38] The guards at Kanose, however, pointedly reassured the POWs that when the war ended, they would be sent home.

Corporal Frank Smith of Liverpool, England, usually served as concert director of the many shows at Kanose, and most of the entertainment cast was British. He set the plays and skits to the music of a three-piece band. The men dubbed the first concert "Kanose Follies" in which the actors and singers dressed as fairies using mossy nets as their clothes. They constructed wands from the silver paper in tea packets and even managed to put something over the lights to cast different colors. The second night previewed the "Gold Rush Review," which was equally good and starred "head tucked underneath her arm." Less than a week later, another, "Whoopee,"[39] was put on after which Verble Jones picked another fight, this time with Private First Class Charles Gavord from Errett's regiment, the 515th CA.

Mid–September 1944 brought a delightful surprise. A bunch of eighty letters or more arrived for the POWs, adding to the pile already on hand.[40] Now, unlike before, many were distributed quickly, and of the 150 handed out, the most recent was only six months in transit, although Errett's ten, six from Jess and four from Merle, were written over a year ago. Merle's letter of September 7, 1943, told Errett that his letter to them was the first from a POW to be received in Santa Fe and she included a couple of snapshots. It was a rest day, so he had lots of time to read and reread them as much as he liked. Their delay in reaching him did not detract from the profound connection to home that welled in his chest. One in particular tugged at his heart. It was from his mother and dated October 31, 1943, her birthday last year.

Some POWs unobtrusively scrounged materials from around Showa

20. The First Leg at Kanose

A postproduction photograph taken sometime between May 1944 and August 1945 of 31 of the (primarily) British POWs who wrote, directed, and staged plays while at Kanose POW camp. Note that they have a guitarist and violinist. The guitarist might possibly be V.R. Fernandez (Photograph sent to Errett after the war by Captain Janis Morris who was also held at Kanose).

Denko grounds and assembled a one-tube shortwave radio receiver and rigged an antenna in the rafters of their barracks. They picked up station KFI broadcasting out of Los Angeles the first time they listened to it. It was all they could do not to whoop and holler when they heard Paris had been retaken[41] by Allied forces after Supreme Commander Dwight D. Eisenhower and General Omar N. Bradley entered Paris on August 27. Hitler responded with an order to invade Poland on September 1. When it was not being used, they took the radio apart and hid the various components in the barracks. Only a few of the POWs were privy to where the components were stashed and Errett was one of them. He put some of the parts behind the new ceiling slats above his bunk. He knew, as they all did, that if they were found out, they would be executed.

In the eastern theater, General MacArthur planned and executed the next major campaign of the Pacific—the invasion of Leyte island, which he believed was both a moral and a military necessity. Admiral William Halsey commanded the naval fleet working toward the same goal. The timetable set for invasion had been moved up a couple of months after Halsey gained information from a Japanese pilot shot down and captured by one of his crews off the island that, at the time, there were far fewer Japanese troops than they expected.

The Japanese knew MacArthur had his eye fixated on the Philippines. What they did not know was where the enemy would attempt a landing. They guessed it would be the island of Luzon. MacArthur held off invading Luzon, or Operation Mike I, until January 9, 1945, when he sent the Sixth Army in against the 275,000 Japanese there. Instead, he directed troops to Leyte first.

The Battle of Leyte Gulf began on October 20, 1944, when 202,500 of MacArthur's troops landed on Leyte three weeks after Japan began its mass removal of POWs via transport ships. MacArthur waded ashore on Leyte as the iconic "I shall return" picture was snapped. Japan had stationed two hundred and fifty thousand troops on Luzon in the Philippines, but only twenty thousand of them were at Leyte at the time the Americans invaded. Japan drew up plans for its defense of the archipelago, called Operation Victory, which was to avert MacArthur from establishing a foothold there. If he got in, the Allies would have another essential doorway to Japan. Nonetheless, after three days of fighting, losses on water were twenty-eight Japanese ships and six U.S. ships. It seemed that the coveted doorway would soon be as wide as a four-car garage. Leyte was officially declared liberated on July 5, 1945, clearing the way for the newly promoted five-star general MacArthur to move into the main island of Luzon.

Statistics at Palawan on December 14 were not as favorable for the Allies. In keeping with the orders received in August from high command, guards there herded the POWs into a trench, covered it with branches, doused it with gasoline, and set it afire. Those POWs who ran out of the trench were shot. In that one act, 139 POWs were burned alive or shot; only 11 escaped.[42] The person responsible for the massacre, Captain Kojima, was the Japanese delegate who signed the Geneva Convention on behalf of Japan.

Keeping the twelve furnaces at Kanose functioning was a challenge. Huge transformers changed the value of incoming electricity to that required by the carbide factory. The strain on the transformers was enormous, and they kept burning out and parts were difficult to come by. On September 6, 1944, all but one furnace was shut down, and Errett's work was retasked to digging them out to clear built-up debris and then thoroughly cleaning them so repairs could be made. His work hours also changed. He now worked midnight to eight in the morning. It was hard work but far less dangerous than working the crushers. Food at this time was in critical supply for everyone in Japan. The POWs' diet consisted of soybeans and nothing more. Errett and about half of the others bloated up like balloons filled with bad gas. He spent most of the time in the latrine nowadays.

In the midst of the furnace cleanup, mealtime slightly improved when two pigs killed at the local slaughterhouse were brought to the prison camp cook house to butcher. The POWs were given the heads and skins. The rest went to the four thousand villagers to share. With a dearth of protein, the Japanese in the area were soon killing cats for food.[43] Errett shared with the other POWs a few horse bones with a little meat on them from the next village over. The added sustenance, however meager, improved Errett's condition. He felt a little stronger and more rested.

On September 28, 1944, only four days after receiving his ten letters, he was handed another two from home and four days after that, one more. In one were two pictures. One was of his younger sister Claire and one was of their last year's Christmas tree centered in front of the living room window. Presents were randomly placed underneath, but what stood out was a framed picture among the gifts. Claire had rushed in while Merle focused her camera and propped the picture on the floor below the tinseled branches.[44] It was an eight-by-ten black-and-white head shot of Errett. He appreciated the sentiment, but he would rather have been sent a picture of the whole family. He lingered over the picture of Claire standing next to the fence at their house he remembered so well on Gildersleeve. One of his bunkmates, Eugene Dunn from Tennessee, walked up to admire the petite young lady in the photograph. Errett introduced him to Claire.

"I'm sure glad to have a picture of my little sis," he confessed in a nostalgic voice. Eugene replied by producing a four-by-five-inch piece of paper and a pencil. He sat next to Errett and sketched Claire's face. This guy had a talent for art, Errett thought. It was perfect. He had captured her exactly even though her face in the photograph was rather small. Errett then produced a photograph loosely stuck between the pages of his notebook. It was of his fiancée, Lucille Bodillo, whom he fondly called Lily, and he asked him to sketch her, too. Errett pasted them across from each other in the center section of his journal. He was grateful for the talent expressed in the drawings and knew he would cherish them always. They were both swell renderings.

Errett's appetite started to wane. He did not have any other symptoms of an illness, but he needed no one to tell him what was wrong. It regularly occurred among the POWs. Finally, the worm in his intestines passed through his bowels. There was a betting pool each week to see whose worm was the longest. At twelve inches, Errett had a good chance of winning this week! After he had it logged into the record book, he went to the medical orderly for the mysterious worm cure. He had no idea what was in the concoction and was glad not to know, but one gulp was all it took and he was rid of them, for the time being anyway. He did not get enough to eat for himself and surely had no inclination to share his rations with a worm.

The day before the POWs were weighed once again on October 9, they were each issued four dried pears. Errett was unsure why they were weighed so often. Did they think the prisoners were gaining weight? That certainly was not the case. Were they hoping they were shedding pounds given the food shortage the Japanese were experiencing themselves? Despite their condition, Errett had no doubt about what Azuma said—they would fight to the last man, woman, and child or commit suicide. Errett hoped the second part of the commandant's statement would come true— they would stop fighting if the emperor ordered it.[45] The camp commandant reiterated the point of fighting to the last person. It was a statement that the POWs were encouraged to use when sending a radiogram home. Japan's staunch mindset on fighting to the end was added to other "facts" in their 150–200 words allowed in a radiogram such as being well treated, Japan is following the terms of the Geneva Convention, and the United States should ask for a peace settlement.

A sketch done around October 1944 by a fellow POW of Lily Bodillo, Errett's fiancée to whom he became engaged while training at Ft. Bliss, Texas.

Six POWs were the first ones selected at Kanose to record such messages. Three Americans (Captain Hewitt and Eugene Dunn, both from Tennessee, along with Staff Sergeant Frank Wilson from La Loma Ranch, about fifteen miles north of Santa Fe) and three British.[46] Frank, sixteen years older than Errett, had a quirky outlook on life in general and government specifically, leaving Errett wondering what he might say. If it was not the mantra adhering to the rules, it would never be released. The opportunity would not be wasted if he had been picked instead, he thought.

While these men were away working on their recordings, the Japanese sergeant in camp began fervently boasting about a big sea battle near Mindanao in the Philippines during which, he said, the Allies lost eleven carriers and twenty-two battleships and cruisers. He went on and on about Japan's victory, then inexplicably asked a British soldier if the POWs would go after him after the war.[47] If they were doing as well as he said they were at Mindanao, why would the prisoners even have a chance to go after them? The truth of the matter was why. The United States and its allies had the upper hand in the Pacific theater. The most sensational loss the Japanese suffered was the sinking of the seventy-thousand-ton *Shinano*, the largest aircraft carrier in the world, by the U.S. submarine *Archer-Fish* seventeen hours into its maiden voyage. It went under off to the east of the southern tip of the peninsula Kii that juts southward from Osaka, Japan, into the North Pacific Ocean. These events had much to do with Germany reneging on its agreement with Japan to send U-boats to the Indian Ocean. One Arm summed up his forecast after enjoying another skit, "Cinderella," put on by the prisoners—the POWs would be "home soon now."[48]

Azuma ordered his staff to put a lid on talk of how the war was going. That lasted one day. The sergeant was back to the subject with more spurious details as he assisted in issuing each POW a towel, soap, toilet paper, and a jock strap. The Allies lost 150 warships and 700 airplanes in the big battle and one battleship and some 120 planes in another, he said. Other sources provided a less robust and more accurate rendering of the battle. Only twenty-eight Allied ships were lost, including three aircraft carriers, ten battleships, and fifteen cruisers.[49]

It seemed clear to the POWs at Kanose that Japan was on the ropes and their psyche in turmoil. Japanese women were trying to do their part, much like Rosie the Riveter in the United States. The military needed metal for their weapons, equipment, and ammunition. Japanese women began removing iron and steel from railings, bridges, and other structures, replacing what metal they scavenged with wood and cement. They were overseen by Japanese men constantly administering "swats with a switch"[50] to keep them working.

Errett had his best treatment since becoming a guest of the Japanese in November and December 1944. There were still punishments administered for minor infractions such as not dressing properly, not owning up to a wrongdoing, fighting, and stealing food, but they were less severe now and Azuma usually made a nice gesture after the punishment like sending a hot meal to the culprit.[51] Errett was selected to record a radiogram and did so on November 17, 1944, the night of the first hard frost at camp. He was given plenty of time to write out what he was going to say and stayed within the 150-word limit. As it happened, it was not aired until five months later, but it was picked up by Mrs. H. Mark Earl in Idaho Falls, Idaho, who made it her business to monitor and record all radiograms from POWs in the Orient. It was the 454th such message she recorded. She completed the form letter with the time (12:35 p.m.), date she heard the message (April 13, 1945), and Errett's words, which were,

> Dearest Mother and Father, I am lucky to be able to send you this.
>
> Was happy to receive your letters and parcel. Little sis must be quite a girl now. I hope you have been receiving my allotment. I am sure Merle has been looking after my insurance. Send love to my dear old grandmother.

Mrs. Earl also included her personal message: "I would love to hear from you about your son."[52]

Within days of Mrs. Earl's correspondence, the Lujans received a Western Union telegram concerning the same broadcast heard by a military post, but their wording varied slightly from hers. It read,

> Dearest Mother and family. I am happy to have the privilege of sending this. May it reach you with care and safety. I was happy and proud to receive your letters and photo. I was surprised at my little sis working. I imagine her as a quite grown lady. Was surprised to hear of Merle not married. I hope you have been receiving my allotment. I am sure Merle has looked after my insurance. Happy to hear of the new home and new job. I send my love to my dear old grandmother and the rest. Chin up.[53]

Recording a radiogram gave Errett a sense of relief. He knew if his family heard it, they would be assured he was okay. As it turned out, one of his dear old grandmothers, Bessie Dyson, Jess's mother, had been living with the Lujans since August 1944 and was thrilled to get his message. He assumed it aired soon after its recording and was better off not knowing it was not broadcast until five months later. His mood was low enough just before Thanksgiving as he wrote in his diary, "This will make Christmas #4 away from home."

His mood soon changed when more letters from home were handed to him. They were among the 156 recently received in camp.[54] He basked in the pleasantness of reading them. It was a welcomed Thanksgiving gift. If he had been back at Mitsushima, he probably would not have received most, if any, of the letters from home, but he would have enjoyed the post–Thanksgiving sight of eighty-eight U.S. bombers flying in formation over his previous camp[55] on their way to destroy the Nakajima aircraft engine factory ten miles from the Japanese Imperial Palace where forty-eight bombs were dead on target. The factory supplied 30 percent of Japan's aircraft engines.[56]

Goodwill continued his way on the Sunday after Thanksgiving when he was given a full Red Cross box, his first he did not have to share. He marveled at its contents—seven packs of cigarettes, eight ounces of cheese, six ounces of pâté, twelve ounces of beef, nearly a pound of butter, half pound of sugar, twenty-four ounces of luncheon meat, six ounces of jam, two packages of chewing gum, one box of vitamin C, nearly eight ounces of salmon, one pound of prunes and raisins, eight ounces of chocolate, coffee, two bars of soap, and one can opener. The only item that seemed to be missing was a pound of canned milk, which the commandant withheld to give to those in sick bay since that population was slowly increasing.[57] With the contents of the Red Cross box and working inside, he barely noticed the first snow, a heavy and wet affair, on December 3, followed by snow and rain every day for two weeks, which left two feet of snow on the ground and compromised the newly built air raid shelters. They all fell in, leaving Errett with nothing better to do than ignore the three air raid sirens they were having nearly every day in mid–December.

Errett listened to Azuma's news and what he deemed disingenuous recitation of stricter consequences to be implemented due to poor behavior on the POWs' parts. Carbon fires in the billets were no longer allowed. Rest days were a thing of the past including Christmas. The sick and officers were to get half rations because they did not work at the mill.[58] His skepticism was on target. He heard everything clearly, but something was off. Perhaps the tenor of the commandant's delivery did not match his body language. Maybe he recognized there was less than the usual passion in his cadence. Whatever it was, Errett felt Azuma lacked earnestness, and in a couple of days, some things improved. Officers and POWs in sick bay had full rations. Parcels from home were issued to POWs on Christmas Eve. Each barracks had a small Christmas tree decorated with ornaments the POWs made along with a meager number brought in from Niigata by Azuma himself.[59]

On Christmas, Errett received a second Red Cross box of goodies containing much the same as the first and this one had a pound of milk. His spirits were buoyed as he ate his share of rice, fried beans simmered in pig fat, and a generous helping of thick, savory bone soup for breakfast. He still had to work, but better food than normal was prepared for lunch—potatoes and carrots in an oil mix served with bread.[60]

Errett and the others cleaned themselves up and were told to pose around their dinner table to be photographed. He looked pretty good except for the dark circles under his eyes. He was shorter and in better health than most of the other POWs in his billet, so he was positioned standing in front. The weakest of the bunch sat in chairs at the table. Just before the shutter snapped, Errett thought the picture might be seen by his family, so he mustered a bit of a smile. In the other barracks, Azuma joined his top staff and three POW officers for a photograph. Then all were served a veritable feast of pork, biscuits, onions, and potatoes covered with thick onion gravy followed up with two oranges, a pear, and one turnover. The entertainment committee put on two pantomimes for the camp, "Babes in Wood" and "Aladdin." The audience, including twenty-five men from the village and factory, concurred—the performance was very good.[61] Afterward, Christmas carols were sung and coffee and cake put out for everyone.

As Errett's treatment generally improved, Japan's losses increased despite their four million armed forces against about one and a half million Allied troops in the Pacific theater. By December 1944, the Japanese had lost at Guadalcanal, Kwajalein, Eniwetok, Truk, and their surrounding seas and the losses may have been the impetus for a change in work at the carbide plant in Kanose. All but two of the carbide-producing furnaces were shut down, and an eighth furnace for the manufacturing of aluminum was being constructed.[62]

In the United States, some changes for the better occurred for enemy aliens and evacuees rounded up in accordance with Executive Order 9066 when the government loosened restraints they were previously subjected to. At this time, all were indexed into three groups. In the first group were 109,000 given clearance to go anywhere in the United States after January 20, 1945. The next group of 4,963 were males who had renounced their American citizenship and demonstrated their malcontent. Their applications renouncing American citizenship were speedily approved and most were being held at Tule Lake in California. Within this group, 1,098 who renounced their citizenship and 318 who were non–U.S. citizens were

A propaganda picture taken by the Japanese on Christmas 1944 at Kanose POW camp. The weakest POWs are sitting around the table. Errett is standing, first on the left (Photograph sent to Errett after the war by Captain Janis Morris who was also held at Kanose).

transferred in increments ranging from 70 to 650 people at a time to the Department of Justice internment camp in Santa Fe. The third group was comprised of the last 4,810 men who were displaced from their homes on the West Coast but remained peaceful in their confinement. Most wanted to remain in the United States as expatriates of Japan.[63]

21

The Last Leg at Kanose

Errett sat on his bunk intent on writing a card home the first week of January 1945. It was just as cold inside as it was outside where about six feet of snow covered the ground, but he did not feel as cold as he did at Mitsushima. The frequent air raids led Azuma to ban all fires in the POWs' barracks. Errett was unaware this would be his last opportunity afforded him to contact home from the camp. In fact, the card he carefully wrote out according to the strict guidelines was piled with others handed in for mailing but never sent on. They simply vanished at the end of the war turmoil. Thirteen of his fellow American prisoners, however, were chosen to dictate a cablegram destined for their homes.[1] The activity became somewhat routine in February, but they doubted any made their way overseas.

Not only was outgoing POW mail piling up in camp, but so was the incoming correspondence. About 130 came in between January 10 and the last day of February. The new bunch of correspondence was added to the pile in camp headquarters for distribution later. Errett was one of the lucky ones to get several letters two days in a row in late February, and no wonder; Jess, Merle, and Claire wrote to him constantly over the months. Added to their letters were three that Sister Gloria, a cousin working at St. Clara Orphanage in Denver, Colorado, penned.

Despite their overwhelming numbers in the Pacific theater, Japan was losing one stronghold after another, garnering only an occasional victory. Most U.S. troops were in Europe, far fewer in the South Pacific, and no army divisions remained in the United States for deployment. MacArthur, with more than two hundred thousand troops at his disposal for the fight of the Philippines, ordered the Sixth Army into Luzon through the Lingayen Gulf to do battle with two hundred and seventy-five thousand Japanese. As MacArthur's troops moved inward on Luzon through strategic military might, one hundred and fifty rangers from the First Cavalry stealthily moved into Cabanatuan prison camp and liberated close to five hundred American and British POWs on January 30, and Luzon was controlled by American forces by March 3.

21. The Last Leg at Kanose

The *Santa Fe New Mexican* was quick to announce in the January 30, 1945, edition the names of those from the 200th CA (AA) who were rescued from Cabanatuan and on their way home: Private First Class Don Adams (Artesia), Staff Sergeant Ben T. Chavez (Seboyeta), Private Joe D. Chavez (Belen), First Sergeant Orville Drummon (Clovis), Private Burnise L. Fay (Albuquerque), Corporal Albert Hayes (Lordsburg), Second Lieutenant Daniel C. Limpert (Albuquerque), Corporal Albert T. Parker (Deming), Private Alfredo G. Sanchez (Clayton), and Private First Class Earnest S. Serrano (Coyote). The news lifted the hearts of the Lujan family even though Errett presumably remained a prisoner. They imagined how they would have felt if Errett was among them. Louis celebrated by taking his younger daughter Claire to the Old Western Dance in Clayton, New Mexico, where Claire won best costume. She literally sent kisses to her brother in her next couple of letters, all of which are dated February 16. She painted on her bright red lipstick and kissed the paper hoping it would put a smile on Errett's face when he saw it.

Captain Donald Robinson, a U.S. Marine doctor who arrived in late January at Kanose and replaced Dr. Lane, also brought war news to the POWs. Military targets in Tokyo were being bombed regularly and at Yokohama, Formosa, Hong Kong, and Osaka even more so. Allied advances on the island of Luzon were going well. He also said an order went out from the Nip headquarters for POWs to be treated better. The sad news was the statistical report on POWs transferred out of the Philippines—at least half were dead.[2]

Robinson advocated for cleaner billets as a way to improve the health of the POWs. The Japanese medical orderly was eventually convinced of the rationale, and an order to clean the quarters came down. They were indeed filthy and needed a good cleaning.[3] The twenty-eight deaths at Kanose their first winter there might have been higher had it not been for Captain Robinson.

Indeed, American advances in the Philippines were by leaps and bounds in February. U.S. forces seized Subic Bay, Los Baños, and Corregidor and liberated the POWs from Santo Tomas University and Bilibid Prison in Manila as Manila itself began to fall into American hands. Two thousand men, women, and children in the Philippines were swiftly liberated by the Eleventh Airborne Division and Filipino guerrilla fighters. Corporal Rubel Gonzales was the first Santa Fean to survive the Bataan Death March and return home. He was liberated from Santo Tomas on February 3 and arrived in Santa Fe on March 8. While MacArthur was busy with regaining the Philippines at the cost of one hundred Japanese for every American soldier, U.S. Marines from the Fifth Fleet landed at Iwo Jima under the leadership of Admiral Raymond A. Spruance. America's first B-29 bombers landed on the eight-square-mile island a mere nine days later. On February 23, Joe Rosenthal of the Associated Press snapped another iconic photograph from World War II as marines raised the U.S. flag on Mt. Suribachi, the extinct volcano and highest point on the island. Three weeks later, Iwo Jima fell from Japanese control in exchange for just under the cost of seven thousand American lives.

Errett unknowingly celebrated the day enjoying his Red Cross parcel given to all but fifteen POWs and reenvisioning the sky four nights ago as a B-29 flew over Kanose. The withheld packages were punishment for stealing or possessing contraband items in the last couple of months. Verble Jones, as always Errett acknowledged, was one of those men, and Don Martindale of Salt Lake City, Utah, ran a close second to Verble when it came to getting in trouble. Such behavior antagonized the ruthless guard, Sergeant Hisao Kaneyama. He drank himself drunk at night and wreaked havoc with the POWs.[4] He beat, kicked, stomped, tortured, and clubbed many POWs, rendering some almost unconscious. After clubbings, especially in the cold months of winter, he sometimes marched them outside at night where he ordered them to stand at attention holding a block of ice until it melted.[5] He invented ways to mete out punishments for small infractions such as playing cards in the barracks.

Kaneyama led a couple of surprise barracks inspections looking for contraband and he found some, lots of rice and items from the factory but not the radio parts that he was looking for, having found a headset earlier. He went on a tirade yelling in their faces while pacing back and forth. Fortunately, all men promised not to steal in the future, and that ended their punishment. A third search a month later uncovered very little[6] and his mood was foul, but the POWs could tell he was pissed off about something else.

Kaneyama probably felt even more angst when Tokyo suffered its most damaging air attack in the war on the night of March 9 and 10. One-quarter of the city was destroyed with seventeen hundred tons of six-pound napalm-filled incendiary bombs let loose over the course of three hours. It created a fire storm visible one hundred and fifty miles away and burned to ashes sixteen square miles of the city's primary industrial area, killing about eighty-three thousand people. It became known as the fire raid. The United States lost fourteen of its 334 B-29s in the assault. The following night, the United States put into action a massive bombing of Nagoya, Osaka, Kobe, and Yokohama. That raid was equally devastating in human casualties. Collectively, about one hundred thousand died, one hundred and twenty-five thousand were wounded, and one million rendered homeless in the four cities.[7] However, damage to Japan's military industry itself was far less effective.

21. The Last Leg at Kanose

The more radical Japanese internees made up the majority of the twenty-one thousand in the Santa Fe Department of Justice camp, in addition to those at the Tule Lake compound in California. They sported shaved heads, rose each morning to face the rising sun, and prayed for the emperor and success of Japan's military in the war. One *nisei* who would not renounce his U.S. citizenship was beaten by the radicals interned there. The only raucous incident at the facility in its history occurred in March 1945, when the Tule Lake group wore contraband sweatshirts bearing emblems of Japan's march to victory in the war. Thirty border patrol officers arrived from El Paso, Texas, to find and forcibly remove the shirts. Two days later, guards attempting to transfer three of the leading troublemakers out were met with interference by two hundred and fifty to three hundred internees. Guards quickly tossed tear gas grenades into the rioting crowd. The internees responded by hurling rocks at their assailants and at the administration building. At that point, all guards were called in to regain order. They carried submachine guns, riot guns, and other weapons and surrounded the complex to secure the perimeter while sixteen officers with night sticks and gas billies entered the compound. Eventually, they dispersed the group, breaking up the riot. Several rioters were injured, but all recovered in short order. A month later in April, one attempted an escape but was unsuccessful.[8]

In mid-June while Tokyo was afire, the Kanose POW camp experienced a bit of an upheaval. Errett was at work in the mill when he heard blood-curdling cries somewhere behind him. He did not rush in the direction of the melee. That was not allowed. He found out soon enough, though, as word traveled fast among the POWs. One of the side taps broke away, dousing three British soldiers with hot liquid carbide. John Foster of Angus, Scotland, John Buchan of Middlesex, England, and Jack Crowdell of Leicester, England, were immediately transported to the hospital. Corporal Harold Rogers, also of England, was slightly burned. Foster and Buchan clung to life a mere two days before dying. Amazingly, the worst burned, Crowdell, hung on for slightly more than two weeks after their deaths. The Japanese laughed for days about the accident, but in a perplexing juxtaposition, they put on quite the show for their memorial service.[9]

Just after the official start of spring, Azuma called all of his staff and civilian Japanese plant workers to the carbide factory for a 3:00 a.m. meeting. He had become anxious listening to the radio all day. Rumors quickly spread among the POWs about peace talks initiated by Germany and Japan.[10] There was no lack of news to hear, but none was good for Japan. Bombing of Tokyo continued, and Iwo Jima was secured by Allied troops. Whatever the circumstances of the war, Errett thought, he would surely know for certain what was happening either through the newspapers coming in, from their radio they periodically used, or from the guards. In the meantime, each POW was issued one sheet of paper to write home, but these were never collected.

Sergeant Kaneyama became fed up with the war and felt taking his own life,[11] or seppuku, according to the conventions of Bushido, was his only alternative. Apparently, he did not envision things turning out well for Japan. He told Les Chater, an officer in the British POW ranks, that if the cook house honcho and factory representative slapped any of the POWs when in their billets, they were to be slapped back, tied up, and taken to him so he could tie them to the tree outside their barracks.[12] He was clearly fed up with everything. The only internal news directed to the POWs from Azuma was about work at the carbide factory. Another furnace would be starting in a few days and that would require twelve more men for each shift.[13] Four groups were to work twelve hours and have twelve hours off. Verble Jones and Don Martindale, locked up for a previous theft from the cook house, were caught at it again as soon as they were released and sent back to the guard room.[14]

War activities in April 1945 brought triumphs and tragedies, courage and cowardice. For Errett, who was putting in his time on the twelve-hour shifts off and on, it brought welcomed letters from home as the last bunch in camp was distributed on April 3. The influx had a more positive effect than the cut in rations' negative effect. By that time, the Lujans had received three letters and two cards from him. Merle sat at her desk at work, layered several sheets of paper with carbon paper, copied word for word each of the three letters, and mailed them out to relatives and friends.

A week later, another hundred and fifty letters for the prisoners arrived and Azuma took them home to censor.[15] Knowing there might be more news from home, however old, made Errett's arm seem a little less sore from a smallpox vaccination the day before.[16] Kaneyama did not resort to seppuku at Kanose. He and the medical secretary were reassigned to the battle front. Errett wondered if the sergeant would make it through the war, be killed, or die by his own hand. He never knew while he was prisoner. The sergeant's replacement, a quiet man, arrived four days later.[17]

U.S. forces invaded Okinawa at four in the afternoon on Easter Sunday, April 1. The assault stabbed like a dagger through the heart of the Japanese. Japanese civilians discovered the consequences of the impending invasion when they were ordered to commit suicide just before enemy ships came ashore. The battle was a hard-fought bloodbath that continued into June before American troops wrested the island from Japan. Unreported to those at Kanose was the death toll at Okinawa that reached 107,000 Japanese and 12,500 Americans including correspondent Ernie

21. The Last Leg at Kanose

Pyle when he took a bullet in his head. The Imperial Japanese Navy lost fifty-eight submarines in June alone, which was more than in 1942 and 1943 combined. The United States declared Okinawa secure on June 21.

Several high-profile deaths occurred in April. The day after President Roosevelt was informed that the Allied forces had taken back Vienna, Austria, he complained of a "terrific pain in the back of my head"[18] on April 12, 1945, while having his portrait painted in Warm Springs, Georgia, and died of a cerebral hemorrhage. He had been in poor health for several months, but it was nonetheless shocking. The next day, American planes bombed Tokyo, destroying the Riken laboratory and Building No. 49, ending Japan's atomic bomb program.[19] News of Roosevelt's death was sent to troops in the Pacific and European theaters of war the same day. The guards at Kanose announced it the next day, and Japanese newspapers a couple of days later confirmed it for the POWs.[20] Their concert that night was good but lacked its usual lighthearted pizzazz. In Europe, things were quickly unraveling for the Axis powers. Benito Mussolini was captured and killed by Italian citizens on April 28. Hitler and his new wife, Eva Braun, committed suicide on April 30 in Hitler's underground bunker in Berlin nine days after Soviet forces forced their way onto the streets of Berlin.

Air raid sirens blared through Kanose at ten thirty in the morning the day after Roosevelt died. Three minutes later, a single B-29 bomber flew directly overhead at about thirty thousand feet. Errett did not hear or see any Japanese planes or antiaircraft respond. All he saw were four contrails tracking behind the eastward-heading plane. The Japanese guards immediately put them to work digging new zigzag shelter trenches for themselves.[21]

Michael Gilewitch, another POW laboring at the nearby coal yard in Niigata thirty miles from Errett's camp, happened to witness a disturbing scene involving a large group of Japanese women who worked in support of their military. He was at a train station in Japan when the women, escorted by their male supervisor, walked under the coupling of a train near him to cross the tracks. The train was stopped, but the coupling on the cars came loose, knocking down a woman who, at that moment, was ducking under the connection. The uncoupling caused the train to move. Gilewitch watched as it rolled over the woman severing both of her legs through her thighs. The other women in her group still on his side of the train stopped, pointed at her, and laughed hysterically as she lay screaming and spurting blood. No one approached her, gave her comfort, or tried to help her. Her death stunned Gilewitch but not as much as the callousness from every Japanese person around her.[22]

Azuma called the POWs together to talk to them in mid-afternoon on one of the last days in April. The POWs watched panic zip through their captors when air raid sirens sounded a week before. They fully expected the commandant to rationalize subjecting them to some type of worse treatment since Japan's homeland had been relentlessly bombed. Instead, he asked what they would do if the camp was bombed and warned them not to taunt or laugh at Japanese people if Japan were defeated. The POW officers in camp also talked with the other POWs urging them to comply with all Japanese directives because of the implied looming threat of being attacked by villagers and civilian factory workers.[23]

If the POWs were better behaved, it had little effect to assuage anxiety among the Japanese at Kanose. In between Germany surrendering Italy (May 2) and Denmark (May 5), administrators at the camp searched every POW and all of their barracks unannounced. They collected all razors, knives, tools, and anything else that could be used as a weapon. POWs were still expected to shave, so razors were handed out and collected again every day. The guards' anxiety affected their attitude toward the POWs in an odd way. They were more cheerful, even friendly, most of the time. All but three of the 103 Red Cross parcels that came in in early May were issued to the POWs four days after arrival, giving Errett his fair share of half a box. A Japanese general arrived immediately following the search and conducted a cursory inspection of Kanose. Before leaving, the general shook hands with Technical Sergeant John C. Roy of Nashville, Tennessee.[24] This demonstrated to Errett that even the highest ranking officers were acting strangely and probably for good reason.

The war in Europe was declared officially over on May 8 after surrender papers were signed in Rheims, France, the preceding day. The next morning, all the Japanese at Kanose camp were up earlier than usual and no one was allowed in the administration building.[25] No doubt it was known that most POWs liberated in the Philippines were back in the States. All the news was unsettling for the Japanese, and no POWs were allowed to venture into the administration building for over a week. Errett and the others knew Japan might not be able to hold out much longer. Oddly enough, the Japanese pretended they had no worries, at least when they were around the prisoners. Kaneyama's demeanor remained unchanged as he continued meting out cruelty to the POWs. In mid–May, he clubbed Captain Hewitt on the side of his head, causing him to lose his hearing on that side.[26] It would be difficult for Kaneyama to ignore the sense of defeat on the horizon. Tokyo factories were regularly being bombed, and by the end of May 1944, half the city, fifty-six square miles of it, was totally destroyed.

In May, Azuma put thirty-seven POWs per shift to work in the carbide factory, reducing the number of guards to one per furnace[27] since the call to arms in Japan had reduced the number of Japanese guards at Kanose. The new sergeant kept the POWs busy when they were at camp, but his disciplinary actions confounded Errett. For instance, one POW was put in the guard house for giving gum to a woman at the factory, but no punishment was given to another caught stealing from the cook house.[28] A new civilian interpreter was in camp, but he shed no light on the sergeant's rationale. Azuma ordered the POWs to perform another concert on June 3, but it did not take shape then.

Ninety additional POWs were transferred to Kanose on June 5, 1945. Most were Javanese, others were Dutch, and all were relocated from the Kawasaki camp. They brought with them war news like others joining them from places with better access to information. They related the scorched earth condition of a swath of land measuring about twenty-five miles long between Tokyo and Yokohama as well as large areas of both of those cities along with Osaka, Kobe, Niigata, and Moji. In one of the more recent raids, five hundred B-29s attacked Yokohama and only one was shot down. They also reported that 95 percent of Japanese civilians were now worse off than the POWs at Kanose with regard to available food and shelter.[29]

Explosions in Niigata were now common and caused mostly by mines dropped in the bay that took out ship after ship. Over forty cylinders chock-full of magnetic mines were disgorged from U.S. planes into the bay in one flyover, and more were soon added.[30] Japanese ships in Niigata Bay that encountered a mine blew to bits and sent a five-hundred-foot geyser shooting straight upward. In no time at all, thirty Japanese vessels were sunk. The hundreds of mines off Niigata were a problem for the Japanese from June through August.[31] Immediately after Okinawa fell, all Japanese civilians ages fifteen to sixty (males) and seventeen to forty (females) became compulsory enrollees in the civilian volunteer corps and trained in the use of hand grenades, swords, halberds, firefighter hooks, and bamboo spears to combat American troops expected to invade their homeland.[32]

The number of internees in Santa Fe fluctuated but steadily grew. At its peak in 1945, twenty-one hundred internees were in the Santa Fe camp, most of whom were Tule Lake transfers but also removed from places across the United States and other parts of the world including Hawai'i, Alaska, Peru, Bolivia, Dominican Republic, Haiti, and Panama.[33] Slightly over half of them were awaiting repatriation to Japan as they had requested. Ultimately, four thousand of the six thousand who had renounced their allegiance to the United States and requested to be repatriated to Japan sued the U.S. government, asking for their renunciations to be canceled.[34]

In preparation for the few thousand internees held there in 1945, improvements had taken place. There was a new recreation hall, a new electric sterilizer in the hospital, improved clothing supply house, a new judo gymnasium, a new outdoor wrestling ring, new Ping-Pong tables, a new beer hall, a new soccer field, new equipment for the shop, a new shoe stitcher, four new latrines and six washbasins, improvements to the golf course, an addition of 778 books to the library along with shelving, new screen doors, and more than a dozen other upgrades.[35]

The *Santa Fe New Mexican* ran an article on June 9 recruiting one hundred more civilian employees to work at Bruns Hospital. The army mandated the expansion of all its hospitals between May and June 1945 to handle the wounded soldiers slowly arriving back in the States from the war zones. One hundred and fifty Italian POWs the United States held were being treated for tuberculosis at Bruns. They were repatriated in July to make space available for returning U.S. soldiers in need of treatment. Newspapers assured people that the United States was maintaining the upper hand in the war in the Pacific. The U.S. infantry landed on Saipan on June 17, and on the 30th, the Philippines was declared liberated with the campaign officially ending on July 4. Japan had lost four hundred and fifty thousand troops.

Nothing like the improvements at the Japanese internment camp in Santa Fe were seen at Kanose, but screens were finally put in the cook house windows,[36] and the latrines received an overdue cleaning. Sirens continued once or twice over seven different days throughout June. The alarms meant real possible danger as each was usually followed by one or two U.S. bombers at high altitude. A couple of times, no planes were seen, but they were undoubtedly not too far away. Errett was reading the several cards and letters he received the day before, June 28, while snacking on a few salted cherries that came with his meal. Coincidentally, the Lujans were picking and simultaneously enjoying fresh-picked cherries from their trees in the backyard. Errett heard planes above but no siren. There was something odd about the sound and he soon discovered why. Overhead flew fifty decrepit Japanese biplanes.[37] They sputtered and jostled along. More followed the next two days. It made Errett smile. What a joke they were compared to the American bombers.

Around July 1, guards discovered potatoes stolen from the camp garden. POW officers and billet leaders bore the brunt of the punishment in lieu of someone coming forward admitting guilt. They were to stand at attention until the guilty party came forward—days if need be. Seven thirty that night, a heavy rain began, and the Japanese sergeant dismissed them on the condition they ferret out the miscreant by noon the next day. By judgment time, no one turned himself in. The POW officers resorted to writing a letter to Azuma condemning the theft and agreeing that the guilty party was mean as he was willing to let others suffer for his action. Stunningly, the punishment was revised. All POW rice rations were reduced for nearly a week.[38]

21. The Last Leg at Kanose

During the week, two POWs were caught with bamboo, another infraction and very much frowned upon. They were made to stand at attention for two hours.[39] Errett was relieved his bamboo stick was not found. It was how he and the others surreptitiously siphoned rice from bags stacked in the cook house. The hollow bamboo cane was slipped down the inside pant leg of the two pairs he wore. The legs of the inside pants were lashed closed just below his calf. He stuck the open end of the sharply carved stalk through the pocket. He stood next to the bag of rice and poked the bamboo into it to create a funnel for the rice to flow. When his pant leg was full, he plugged the hole in the bag. For him, having the extra food was worth the risk.

A few days later, all POWs were ordered to stand at attention for an hour and all Americans for half an hour the next morning. Errett endured the punishment but did not know what infraction had been committed this time or by whom. It was thankfully a short time, but his arm still hurt from the typhoid and dysentery inoculations administered a couple of days before. The next day, the medical technician drew blood for testing. Just as the soreness wore off, they gave him another shot. He was starting to feel like a pin cushion. Despite this, his mood was elevated. Eighty-four more letters for the POWs came in. The most recent was postmarked February 1945.[40] Of course they were to be reviewed before handed out, so it might be a while before he found out if any were for him.

One of the better guards, nicknamed Chinless, was sent to the front lines on July 1,[41] and with him the relative quiet of June receded. Nearly four times the number of alarms sounded in July than the month before, but listening to the gramophone occurred nearly nightly in the officers' quarters.[42] The sirens blared mostly at night and several warnings came close on the heels of others. Alarms sounded for three reasons. A long blast was a caution alarm. A wailing siren meant raiding planes were in the vicinity. The all-clear signal was a long blast but only sounded after a wailing blast.[43] POWs began experiencing sleep deprivation given the frequent disruptions. Errett and the others had to get up and wrap their clothes and beds each time a wailing siren went off at night.[44] They came out of the shelters when the all-clear was given and lined up for roll call before returning to their barracks.[45]

Shotaro Kanagawa, the carbide plant honcho, kept calm among the increasing chaos. One day, Kanagawa's fourteen-year-old son entered the workplace to bring his father his lunch box. When the son found Kanagawa, the latter was completely encircled by a crowd of POWs. The boy stopped in his tracks and stiffened. He feared his father was in danger of being torn apart at any moment in the clutches of the POWs. He searched for some weapon, any weapon, to save his father but saw nothing, so he approached the group as quietly as possible. His father squatted in the center, and the POWs were leaning in, their gaze fixed on Kanagawa. The boy watched as his father carefully divided one cigarette into four pieces and then held them out in one hand. Instantly, the pieces disappeared, and were lit, and shared. The workers were obviously pleased. The circle of men disintegrated into an amorphous group. The boy scooted the lunch box to his father and turned to go home. As he exited the plant, he felt a sense of pride in his father.[46]

Air raids intensified in frequency and proximity. Azuma lost whatever composure he had left in mid–July after enemy planes in the area hit Niigata several days in a row. Errett heard the sounds of war clearly. Menacing but ineffective antiaircraft guns belched shells into the sky, allowing devastating bombs to hit the ground. Flashes of light filled the sky northwest of Kanose. The commandant seemed to panic. He jumped up and down waving his sword at an unseen foe. After settling down, he addressed the prisoners with a few warnings: "Dangerous time from now till fall … danger of stealing from gardens … still under control of [Japanese] army … useless to try to escape … probably killed if caught." He also deduced that the planes bombing Niigata were coming from carriers just offshore. This led him to think that an invasion of Honshu was imminent at Niigata, and if that happens, he said, you will all be taken to Tokyo and shot. Some POW officers in camp seemed to think that that threat was said to prevent the more ruthless guards from killing the POWs right there and then at Kanose.[47]

During all of this, the new Japanese sergeant was rarely seen. He stayed hidden in the administration building. On the few occasions he was seen, he appeared to be no more than a shy, self-conscious kid.[48] Errett had a sense Azuma was becoming desperate and it probably had to do with how the war was going.

Azuma ordered doors be put on the air raid shelters and had all medicine put into one particular shelter. The doors were to prevent water from entering the air raid shelters but did nothing to alleviate the problem. They were all constructed in low-lying areas and water naturally flowed in. He also ordered no more *tenko* after the raids. There were far too many and too much work to be done in salvaging food and clothing, running the bucket brigade to remove water, demolishing dilapidated buildings, and so forth. All of this was in addition to performing a written inventory of the animals in camp after every raid. He also changed the work schedule at the factory.[49]

As bad as it appeared to be in Niigata, other cities such as Tokyo, Yokohama, Nagoya, Osaka, and Kobe continued to be hit hard. Food was scarce, and what might have been available was blocked from transport because of the bombings, and available trains packed with Japanese troops

21. The Last Leg at Kanose

instead. The soldier-laden trains passed through Kanose regularly[50] as all able-bodied men were called up. Japan's response was not to capitulate. Instead, they called on all citizens, every man, woman, and child, to bear arms with whatever they could find to use as weapons in preparation of an invasion.[51] They would be the last defense of the country.

The arrival of three hundred more letters on July 24 in the midst of their chaos astonished the POWs.[52] Everyone focused on the mail. What are the postmarks? From where were they mailed? Are they mostly for British or American soldiers? The camp buzzed with such talk, and with their attention drawn there, they almost overlooked the five POWs who ate some wild berries and became violently ill.

POW Staff Sergeant Arthur J. Mitchell of Klamath Falls, Oregon, accompanied the mail back to camp from the Tokyo hospital. He brought a few news nuggets. He verified that Tokyo was frequently raided with one raid having eight hundred American planes. Rebuilding bombed factories commenced immediately after the flames died down, rendering about one-third back into operation in short order. He watched civilians whose homes had burned scavenge tin from other buildings to erect makeshift dwellings. Kawasaki steel works from where the Dutch and Javanese POWs at Kanose came earlier in the month was bombed, killing over thirty Dutch, American, and British POWs.[53] Apparently, Mitchell was not in a position in Tokyo to hear the BBC radio message picked up by the POWs' clandestine radios reiterating the August 1944 annihilation order of POWs in Japanese hands[54] or Churchill's recent defeat to Clement Attlee as Britain's prime minister.

Errett was assigned to work on fixing the air raid shelters on July 26. He started at eight in the morning and spent the day there, then joined the night shift at the carbide factory. One long siren filled the air that night, but before he could do anything or go anywhere, three terrific bomb blasts reverberated through the walls. They were the first bombs to explode near him since he became a prisoner and the concussion left his ears ringing. Work at the factory did not resume, so Errett lined up for *tenko* in front of the barracks and then made his way inside as his feet shuffled through bomb fragments. His quarters were a mess. The bombs shattered all the glass windows. Even the frames were broken. Items from shelves were strewn across bunks and the floor. A large chunk of rock had been propelled through the roof. Some of the men not working at the time said they saw a big four-engine plane fly over, then bank back and let loose its payload. Smaller two-engine planes with tapered wings flying lower also crossed over.

Miraculously, no POWs at Kanose were seriously hurt, but the bombs that blew through the camp unnerved Errett. Surprisingly, the Japanese at the camp seemed not to take it seriously. Azuma asked some of the POWs into his office and asked what response they should have to air raid sirens. The suggestion put forward was to head for the shelters only in the day and not at night. Azuma considered this and proclaimed something of a compromise. The prisoners could ignore an initial siren but must bundle up their things, get into their assigned groups, and go to the shelters on subsequent alarms. The very next night when the sirens alerted them to incoming planes, the POWs reacted just opposite of instructions. They hurried over to the shelters for the first alarm and stayed in their beds for the two on the heels of the first and for every night alarm thereafter. Bombs seemed to have been dropped about thirty miles away. The close call left everyone else jumpy, and it showed a couple of nights later when alarms, shouting, gonging, and whistleblowing filled the morning hours. It was a welcomed relief when no planes were sighted.[55]

Errett had to wait only a week for the newly arrived letters and telegrams to be distributed, with the most recent being the past March. He was over the moon when seventeen from the pile came his way. In one was a photograph of Merle. The changes he saw in her appearance underscored just how long he had been away from home. To compound his melancholia, he figured the POWs he heard had been liberated in the Philippines were probably home by now with their families. If he had only stayed there, he would be home, too, instead of the possibility of being obliterated by his own team's bombs like at the steelworks factory. The sadness of it all firmly planted itself in the depths of his soul.

22

Liberation

The winds of war continued to blow steadfastly into the face of Japan in August 1945. Their backs were pushed against a wall of failure built block by block by the many defeats since the Battle of Midway. For most Japanese, these losses bolstered their resolve to fight harder. Likewise, the United States was determined to end the war on their terms by way of two major offensives. First was the U.S. invasion of Japan dubbed Operation Downfall. The Joint Chiefs of Staff approved the plan, which was to start with MacArthur leading Operation Olympic, on May 25, 1945. The plan's final touches were approved just the day before. Japan called its defense operation for the anticipated U.S. invasion *Ketsu-go*, Decisive Battle for the Homeland.[1] Part of their strategy depended on about one hundred midget submarines they had placed in reserve for their defense. Another part called for an invasion of cities on coastal California where they were to release plague-infected fleas on September 22, 1945.[2]

The United States chose Okinawa, less than four hundred miles from the Japanese mainland, as base of operations for Operation Downfall. The war was not put on hold while the two sides prepared for the invasion. On August 1, the POWs at Kanose witnessed fires burning thirty-five miles away as Nagaoka went up in flames after an intense raid just after day turned to night. The prisoners were uneasy. They felt the carbide factory would be the next target either right away or at least within four days. They hunkered down in the shelters. The guards and other Japanese staff, Errett noticed, partied until after midnight.[3] The following night, U.S. bombers loaded with napalm-filled incendiary bombs laid waste to six Japanese cities. On August 3, the U.S. Navy established a blockade surrounding the ever-weakening Japanese homeland.

As early as June 1945, MacArthur expressed his optimism for Operation Downfall.[4] The administration in Washington, D.C., felt the same. What pressed on everyone's mind was the human cost. Toward the end of July, Chief of Staff George Marshall projected deaths from Operation Downfall to be somewhere between one-quarter and one million people on each side of the fight.⁵ Even without highly accurate numbers, though, the cost of human life to invade Japan was expected to be high. In anticipation months before, the military began increasing the number of draftees in January to pay the price. The United States, of course, continued to monitor Japanese defenses and within a month suspected the death toll might be on the higher end of the spectrum.

The second U.S. major offensive pursued to end the war in the Pacific was the development of the atomic bomb. President Harry Truman decided rather early on to use it. He mulled over the information for several days and listened to the opinion of the interim committee considering the same issue. On June 1, 1945, a full two weeks before it was tested, Truman decided to use the new weapon⁶ to halt the fighting and lower the number of deaths in war, but it would be some time before he gave the order to employ it. The Manhattan Project began as a race with Germany to see who would be the first to have a usable atomic weapon, and it had been an expensive project.

The first atomic explosion happened on July 16 within an eighteen-by-twenty-four-mile expanse in the Jornada del Muerto, or Journey of Death, of white sand in the northwest sector of the Alamogordo bombing range, a federal installation in southern New Mexico. When the plutonium bomb exploded, people saw the early morning sky light up brighter than anything they had seen before. A half ball of fire morphed into a giant mushroom cloud clearly visible a hundred and eighty miles away. Robert Oppenheimer, the scientist in charge of developing the bomb in Los Alamos, applied the code name Trinity to the test. Neither he nor his colleagues were certain it would work as they predicted, but it did. Four hours after the fireball dimmed over the Trinity site, the *Indianapolis*, a U.S. cruiser, sailed with its cargo under the Golden Gate Bridge and headed for Tinian. Its cargo was Little Boy, the first uranium atomic bomb that would be used in war against an enemy.

The success of the atomic bomb test gave President Truman a rather large arrow in his quiver of weapons and reassurance of ultimate victory relatively soon. He ordered a radio broadcast of the Potsdam Declaration concerning the Japanese a little over a week after the Trinity test. It was an ultimatum to surrender unconditionally, end the war, and avoid the final onslaught the United States was prepared to deliver. It was aired directly to the Japanese people. In it was also a warning of consequences. If no surrender came, the Japanese people should be prepared to evacuate cities before bombing resumed. Hearing aircraft on July 27, they looked to the sky. They knew it would not be their country's airplanes even before they could see them. The planes came in very low, but the whistling sounds of bombs were absent. Instead, papers filled the air. The leaflets released

22. Liberation

to them listed cities that were in the crosshairs of U.S. pilots, and people "should evacuate."[7] About a week later, more leaflets floated onto Japanese soil. Some six million leaflets papered forty-seven different cities with the same warning.[8]

Some refugees from the newly burned-out cities relocated to Hiroshima in preparation for more attacks. They were ordered to wear air raid hats of cloth hoods when outdoors and to carry small amounts of medicine with them at all times. They tore down closely spaced wooden buildings to reduce the fire potential. They widened streets and practiced drills to scramble to air raid shelters. Very few actually evacuated the target cities.

As the clock ticked closer to Operation Downfall, President Truman came closer and closer to giving the order to use the atomic bomb. Four potential targets were selected for destruction using the new mega bomb: Nagasaki, Hiroshima, Niigata, and Kokura. Tokyo was an unlikely target since its prewar population of eight million had already been reduced to two hundred thousand by August 8. The last week in July, President Truman wrote in his diary, "The weapon [atomic bomb] is to be used against Japan between now [July 25] and August 10th."[9] This in no way stalled preparations to invade Japan. MacArthur was assembling an invasion force during the first week of August to go into Kyushu on November 1 as part of Operation Downfall. He sent Army Chief of Staff George C. Marshall a message that the total troops to be involved in the invasion would be 681,000.

On Monday, August 6, 1945, three Superfortresses left Tinian in the Marianas in response to Field Orders No. 13 dated four days earlier. They were to proceed with delivering the atom bomb to Hiroshima (the primary target) or Kokura (the secondary target) in accordance with Truman's directive as planned by the Joint Chiefs, and an alternative was Nagasaki. The *Straight Flush* headed for Hiroshima, *Jabbit III* flew to Kokura, and *Full House* struck out for Nagasaki to check the weather.[10] As they flew away, a crane on the Tinian airstrip lifted the ninety-seven-hundred-pound bomb, called Little Boy, into the forward bomb bay of another Superfortress, the *Enola Gay*, as pilot Colonel Paul Tibbets ran the checklist before taking off. He lumbered off the ground with the heavy payload, and once steadily airborne, a cordite explosive charge was inserted behind the bomb's uranium slug. When activated, it would initiate an uncontrolled nuclear reaction changing matter (uranium) into energy equal to ten thousand tons of TNT. Two other B-29 Superfortresses accompanied Tibbets, No. 91, the photo plane, and the *Great Artiste* carrying sensors to measure the force of the blast once the bomb detonated.

The first of the weather planes to call in an "all clear" was *Straight Flush*. With that, Tibbets and his two escorts set their course for

Hiroshima, the seventh largest city in Japan with a population of about three hundred and eighty thousand but with no aircraft industries, which was the first priority for the United States in selecting targets. It had not yet been bombed, which is why refugees sought it out during the nine months of the U.S. strategic bombing campaign.

Tibbets entered the sky above Hiroshima at an altitude of 31,600 feet on a bright and calm morning as the crews of the three airplanes slipped dark welder goggles on seconds before Little Boy dropped from the bomb bay of the *Enola Gay* at a quarter after eight. Instruments were simultaneously let loose from the *Great Artiste* and they floated slowly downward tethered to parachutes. Little Boy exploded forty-three seconds later at nineteen hundred feet above the city creating a fireball thousands of times hotter than the surface of the sun, killing one hundred and forty thousand people by the end of 1945 and destroying all means of communication. Another two hundred thousand people perished within five years from the effects of the bomb.[11]

It was not until late in the afternoon that Japan's military was aware of the bombing. Once the reports were in, it was clear to them that it was a nuclear explosion. Their scientists, headed by Dr. Yoshio Nishina, had begun work in 1943 on developing a nuclear weapon for Japan. Two things put an end to their atomic program: first, the uranium ore they contracted to receive from Czechoslovakia via submarine never arrived, and second, the B-29 air raids in March and April 1945 inadvertently destroyed their research facilities.[12]

New Mexicans read about the bomb in their Tuesday morning edition of the *Santa Fe New Mexican* (August 7, 1945): "U.S. ANNOUNCES ATOM BOMB," "HOPE FOR EARLIER END TO WAR." Five articles on the front page described the atomic bomb, and indeed, Truman felt sure that the demonstration of such destructive power would leave the Japanese with no other option than to unconditionally surrender. Truman put forth a statement directly to Japanese citizens pushing for surrender since the Japanese Imperial Army quashed the audio message with radio-jamming equipment. Beginning one day after Hiroshima was bombed and for the eight days following, sixteen million copies of the message, written in Japanese, were delivered by air drop to forty-seven Japanese cities having a population of at least one hundred thousand, or about 40 percent of the total population. In part, it read,

> TO THE JAPANESE PEOPLE: We are in possession of the most destructive explosive ever devised by man. We have just begun to use this weapon against your homeland. If you still have any doubt, make inquiry as to what happened to Hiroshima. If our terms are not accepted you may expect a rain of ruin from the air, the like of which has never been seen on this earth. Before using this

bomb to destroy every resource of the military, we ask that you now petition the Emperor to end the war.[13]

A half-million Japanese-language newspapers detailing the results of the atomic bomb on Hiroshima, including grim graphics, were also dropped over the country.[14] With such news delivered directly to the Japanese people, President Truman was sure their surrender had been secured. He waited anxiously to hear a response from Japan, but none came. The Supreme Council for the Direction of the War continued debating their options at the Japanese Imperial Palace. News of Hiroshima did not come to Kanose before the United States dropped the second atomic bomb, but air raid sirens frequently sounded at the camp. Errett and the others paid no attention to them, and none of the guards seemed to care.

The crew at Tinian loaded a second atomic weapon into the forward bomb bay of *Bock's Car* on August 9. This bomb, Fat Man, was a plutonium implosion bomb like the one tested at Alamogordo. Major Charles Sweeney, the pilot, lifted off just before two in the morning, despite the meager two hours of sleep he managed to get, and headed for Japan. The target potentials: Kokura or Nagasaki. The *Great Artiste* followed with its blast-measuring instruments. The mission had been moved up two days due to a typhoon forming in the Pacific between Tinian and Japan.

This mission did not run as flawlessly as the first. *Bock's Car* ran dangerously low on fuel due to a malfunctioning fuel pump, the rendezvous with one of the camera planes was missed, factory smoke at Kokura (the first target assessed) obscured visibility despite clear weather, and flak pocked their airspace. Sweeney turned toward Nagasaki only to find visibility marginal due to clouds. Being dangerously low on fuel left him with only one option—release Fat Man based on radar bearings. Their preferred target was the Mitsubishi shipyard where suicide weapons were being built. Instead, all they could lay eyes on was a stadium that ended up being about two miles from their prime target.

The bombardier released Fat Man from 31,000 feet. It detonated at 1,540 feet a couple of minutes past eleven that morning. The blast killed more than forty-five thousand people, injured about sixty thousand but lacked the firestorm seen with Little Boy, thus saving the lives of tens of thousands of people despite Fat Man's predicted power to be twice that of Little Boy.[15] Nonetheless, seventy thousand died by the end of the year and a total of a hundred and forty thousand within five years.[16] Again, Truman anxiously waited to hear from the Japanese government, and again, no response.

At 7:33 a.m. on August 10 Japan time (Tokyo is thirteen hours ahead of Washington, D.C.), an American military radioman intercepted the unofficial text of Japan's foreign minister stating that the emperor desired an end to the war but under one condition. The looming question holding up the surrender regarded the fate of Emperor Hirohito and Japan's request that he remain emperor without charges brought against him.[17] By August 12, Japan was told the emperor could remain in power but subject to the supreme Allied commander,[18] who everyone knew would be MacArthur. The process, however, remained stalled until 10:30 a.m. on August 14, when Hirohito informed his cabinet as they met in the Gobunko, the palace library serving as an air raid shelter, that he would accept the terms of unconditional surrender later in the day. He also directed them to draft an imperial rescript he would read to his citizenry over a radio broadcast.[19]

The news of an impending surrender urgently broadcast by the Domei News Agency was picked up at the U.S. Navy radio station in Guam.[20] The development, although not confirmed through official channels, optimistically scrubbed recent orders to carry out a massive assault on Japan from the air. Instead, U.S. planes took to the skies dropping five million leaflets to the Japanese people exposing their government's agreement to surrender.[21] Truman capitulated to Hirohito remaining emperor mostly on the advice and persuasion of MacArthur and forwarded the draft surrender document to Allied heads of state.[22] The only change made from their feedback was at the suggestion of Prime Minister Clement Attlee of Great Britain who thought Emperor Hirohito should not be required to appear in person to sign the surrender document.

Despite the ongoing negotiations, Japanese military operatives were still attacking U.S. personnel where they could, and Japan's cabinet remained deadlocked in accepting/rejecting the surrender as written. Truman felt he had been patient long enough and ordered air strikes on Japan to continue "with everything we've got!"[23] Niigata was hit once again. An alarm rousted the POWs out of their barracks at seven in the morning. The guards announced U.S. fighters bombing and strafing near Niigata, and four planes were shot down.[24] Other talk referred to a "kilo bomb" and "oki bomb,"[25] both meaning big, big bombs. Something big was definitely going on. Work at the Kanose factory was limited to one furnace and the crusher, and the Japanese civilians were getting only half the food the POWs received.[26]

It was not until August 14, Washington time, late in the afternoon that President Truman received word via the Swiss that Japan would surrender and Hirohito would address his people over the radio. The emperor had announced to his ministers just the day before that the Allies' reply was "evidence of the Peaceful and friendly intentions of the enemy."[27] A small rebel faction of the Imperial Japanese Army vehemently opposed

22. Liberation

surrender and plotted a coup to take control of the palace, ransack it to find the emperor's recorded rescript, and destroy it. They failed.

An early morning radio message on August 15, 1945, Tokyo time, went out on station NHK saying, "His Imperial Majesty the Emperor has issued a rescript. It will be broadcast at noon today. Let us all listen respectfully to the voice of the Emperor."[28] Utility workers were authorized to unblock electrical current to those places shut off from it during the day so that the emperor's message could be heard by all.

At ten in the morning, Azuma rushed out of his office at Kanose wearing his sheathed sword in hand and holstered gun. He was agitated and confused as to what to do. He ordered the POWs to return from the factory. After they arrived, he ordered them back to work but immediately reversed that order. Instead, he assigned them work around the camp.[29]

Every radio in Japan had swarms of people around them when noon rolled around. Everyone was eerily quiet and stood stiff upright when the announcer began, "All listeners please rise." Some of the Kanose POWs outside the camp saw villagers paying rapt attention as they huddled around their radios as Hirohito began with addressing his "good and loyal subjects."[30] Hirohito's words of defeat stunned his countrymen, but his command to refrain from any rash acts that could lead to strife and confusion was clear. As conciliatory as this appeared, he did not order a laying down of arms until September 2, but his words thwarted hundreds of young *kamikaze* pilots ready to strike Americans in Okinawa.

The air raid post on the hill above the Kanose camp was shuttered before the day ended and flags taken down.[31] Errett was among the seventy thousand Allied POWs held in Japan and another thirty thousand in Japanese territories when the surrender occurred.[32] The Kanose POWs themselves were stunned for the remainder of that day but went into town at night singing. This blatant act of disregard further unsettled the camp commandant. The next day, the POW officers at Kanose were called in to meet with Azuma. None of the parties explicitly said the war was over; it was simply assumed by all. Now confirmation of the bombs and war's end was given after the meeting with Azuma. The weapons-clad Azuma told the officers that POWs found outside the camp would be shot. Basically, he was at a loss as to what to do because no instructions had come from Tokyo headquarters save one: POWs "were not to work" but could have a concert tomorrow. The POWs treated themselves to a show in camp the next night. It included a Dutch hula dancer and a skit, *The Picture*.[33]

Errett and a few other POWs heard as early as August 10 about both atomic bombs via their radio. A sense of imminent freedom set the POWs on a new track. They began culling their belongings, throwing out old stuff like winter clothes, cleaning kits, and anything else they would expect not to need over the next week or two. Azuma became incensed at this. He still had no official word about how to manage the camp, and items being discarded could be used by the Japanese who were in desperate need. Three days after the emperor's radio message, Azuma packed up in a hurry and left for a meeting in Tokyo of all camp heads.[34] Looking around, Errett could see a change in the Oriental faces surrounding him. They looked less strained and somewhat friendlier but tenuously so.

When Azuma returned two days later, he seemed more stressed than when he left. He went into a fit yelling at the POWs lazing around and not coming to attention when he appeared. He ordered wood gathering and garden details. Errett was alarmed at his countenance. With him came a new interpreter who spoke perfect English and provided the interpretation as Azuma hollered. The war is not over. No peace accord has been signed. The POWs are still under the direction of the Imperial Japanese Army who has the authority to tell them what to do and when. More guards were to arrive that night to maintain control, and indeed, they did—one officer with thirty men. The last bit of news hit hard: it will probably take three or four months before they could return home.[35]

On August 22, the Japanese sergeant carried a roster of POWs at Kanose to Tokyo while the prisoners stayed in camp. Evidently, work details had ended. They spent their time sorting through all the Red Cross clothes and whatever had been confiscated by the Japanese during the war that had accumulated in their storage area. They could have anything from there they wanted except boots. Azuma was having those sent to Tokyo, and the POWs, he said, could pick a pair up there. Instead, all POWs received British tennis shoes and whatever jackets, trousers, underpants, socks, and shirts they wanted from the stockpile brought back from the next two villages he had sent them to.[36]

Errett was in dire need of clothes the past winter but not now. He was, however, interested in a particular item—a British army tunic presumably picked up in Singapore. He tried a few on and settled for one that was a little beat up but fit him well. Two Japanese soldiers walked in from the train depot the next day and directed the POWs to paint "PW" on one roof. It was something to do while the water and lights were off all day.[37]

When the Japanese sergeant returned from Tokyo on August 26, he brought with him instructions Azuma had hoped for. The pact for armistice was not yet, but soon would be, signed. The POW officers were now in charge of all the POWs in camp, but there were rules to follow. First, if any trouble were to start with Japanese civilians, the POWs were to retreat to the air raid shelters. They were to begin taking their own roll calls twice daily, once at 7:30 a.m. and again at 5:00 p.m. Otherwise, they were free to go anywhere but must have a Japanese escort if they left camp. There was no

22. Liberation

mandatory times for lights to be turned off. Everyone in camp, Japanese and POWs, were to be issued the same food in the same quantities. Most anticipated was the current estimated date they could return home, and that, they were told, was in about a month. If the POWs wanted anything, they were to ask, but of course, the Japanese had little they could offer.[38]

Several POWs took advantage of these day trips. One was to the dam upstream,[39] but Errett passed on that excursion. He had spent enough days at the dam at Mitsushima to last a lifetime. Instead, he took his new tunic into town and found a tailor who fixed the jacket just like Errett wanted. Missing buttons were replaced, the ragged bottom was evened out and hemmed, the sleeves removed, and the armholes neatly finished. He put the vest on and wore it every day.

Eight U.S. planes flew over Kanose between August 27 and 28. The POWs jumped up and down and waved their arms but in vain. The pilots gave no indication of seeing their small "PW" sign or them. To add to their frustration, they learned that four B-29s flew over the nearby Niigata camps and, in one day, dropped eight canisters the size of forty-four-gallon drums filled with clean new uniforms, food, medical supplies, cigarettes, and other items. The Kanose POWs were determined to catch the eye of the next plane overhead. They gathered all the sheets they could find, ripped them into strips, and made two large "PW" signs.[40]

The Japanese sergeant's news that POWs at Amori and Shinagawa camps had already been evacuated to warships anchored offshore did not bother Errett in the least. He and the others were having too much fun celebrating the end of the war. He made his way around camp getting as many camp mates as possible to sign his vest. In the end, all of the American POWs and five British POWs signed it. The vest also sported a beautifully illustrated U.S. flag with an eagle just below the right front pocket. Of course, it was drawn by Eugene Dunn. Errett would never forget these men and his time in Japan and all of those others whose names were not inscribed on his vest to remind him of them.

Azuma met with POW officers inside his headquarters building. He still did not know when the official surrender would take place but wanted the names of the POWs who might want to stay in Japan after the war, astonishingly saying that it would be so nice because conditions for them would be different than they were during the war. He also took responsibility for any maltreatment the POWs thought they suffered while at Kanose. He alone, he said, was responsible and asked that no one mention any names to that end but his. To conclude the meeting, two bottles of sake were shared, and they all got drunk.[41]

The last POW show at Kanose was put together by the Dutch in honor of Queen Wilhemina's birthday, August 31. Azuma attended but none of the POWs paid any attention to him. The angst Errett and the others were experiencing had tapered off when, three days earlier, they had been informed that the instrument of surrender would be signed on September 2.[42] All thoroughly enjoyed the show, even the guards.

Emperor Hirohito put forth an order for all Japanese to lay down their arms. Those orders were carried out at Kanose as all the guns in camp were turned over to the POWs on September 2.[43] The same day, the surrender ceremony ending the war took place aboard the USS *Missouri* in Tokyo Bay on Sunday morning. Errett was stunned as he heard the news. He felt the best he had in three and a half years.

Captain Hewitt felt certain that none of the U.S. planes had recognized the Kanose camp of POWs or they would have had supplies by now. He went to the train depot on September 3 with one purpose in mind—to retrieve firsthand information on the status of their liberation. He returned the next day with nineteen bags of rice and a good deal more food, chocolates, and cigarettes from that drop to POWs at the Niigata camps. One Japanese woman at Niigata was killed by a drum of supplies as it struck her from above. He also had news on their departure from Kanose. They were to leave soon by train as they became available. Relief filled every POW at Kanose. They ate a good meal and then set out for town and a night out. They had no idea what to expect from the locals but found many who invited them into their homes and gave them souvenirs. No one showed any animosity toward them.[44]

Errett and the others were told that trains would finally be available to get them on September 6 to begin their journey home. Considering everything, Errett had not had an easy time as a prisoner, but there were a few Japanese people at Kanose whom he thought well of given the circumstances. He decided to say a proper farewell to them. A few other POWs felt the same, and together, they made their way to the Showa Denko plant after he stuffed his pockets with chocolate and American cigarettes until they were full. Once at the factory, he found the people he was looking for. First, he met Kanagawa. In exchange for the gifts Errett handed him, Kanagawa gave him a picture of himself with his name written in Japanese on the backside and a Showa Denko business card. The photo, however, was a boy in his early teens taken around thirty-five years ago. Next, he located Estu Origasa, who also worked at Showa Denko. They said goodbye to each other in their native languages. Origasa took the business card Errett still held and wrote her name on the reverse in pencil even though she knew Errett could not read Japanese. Origasa had always been pleasant to Errett even without the benefit of a common language. He returned to camp, ate a nice dinner, and then ventured into town with several other former POWs for a boisterous night of singing, drinking, and dancing.

22. Liberation

The next day, that glorious day, September 6, 1945, Errett snapped to attention in formation at a little before seven in the morning wearing his vest over a shirt. Everyone had been up by at least five, eaten, dressed, and packed what they wanted to carry home. Errett took very little with him—a machete, a leather Japanese whip, a wooden club shaped like a sword used by one of the guards to extract obedience from the POWs, and a few small items. These, British uniform buttons of every variety at Kanose, a pencil, his small pencil sharpening knife, a whetstone to sharpen his knife, and his diaries he carried in his pants pockets. Held secure in one diary was the picture of Kanagawa and the Showa Denko business card with Origasa's name on the back.

The British and Dutch POWs, however, carried everything they had with them in bulky, heavy bundles slung over their backs. The entire group left at 7:30 a.m., marched to the factory, then through town with the unresponsive villagers looking on, and arrived at the depot. Once on board, the train departed at 8:15 a.m., chugging toward Yokohama,[45] nine days after the first group of eighty POWs recently liberated from camps in Japan arrived in San Francisco. Errett's entire route to the airport on the southwest side of Tokyo Bay was unimpeded as all the bridges and train tracks were intact. As his train pulled into Yokohama, cheers louder than the train whistle erupted from the incoming American POWs when they spotted a glut of American women and other recently freed soldiers on the platform.[46] Errett thought there was no better sight in the world than this. With smiles bright as

Shotaro Kanagawa, the company director at the Showa Denko carbide plant at Kanose POW camp where Errett was assigned to work. Kanagawa gave this picture to Errett on his departure in September 1945 when the war ended. Kanagawa is obviously a boy and the picture was probably taken a couple of decades prior.

sunshine, the women passed out cigarettes, chocolates, and other treats before the men were loaded onto buses and taken to the docks where their physical condition was assessed, mostly by Red Cross nurses.

Errett went through the checkup stations in his turn without any major complications to cause alarm or hold him back. The treatment that garnered the most reaction was delousing. Errett walked up to the nurse feeling like he was floating in a dream. He had barely noticed those before him who had been treated. The nurse flipped a bottle upside down and stuck it down his neck, first in the front and then the back, squeezing the solution onto his torso. Fleas fluttered out like butterflies from every opening. The nurse laughed at the fleeing fleas.[47] In about an hour, he noticed a feeling of comfort he had not experienced since being in Japan. At last, he was not home to dozens of sand fleas.

The next morning at seven, September 7, Errett, having been given the okay-to-return label, rode the bus to the airport to await a flight to Okinawa. He was lucky to be on one of the early flights via a C-54 transport plane. Once back on the ground after the five-hour flight, he was assigned to a walled tent with wooden sides and floor for one night. Early the next day, he joined fifteen hundred other liberated men who climbed into B-29 bombers and settled in for their flight to Manila. The six hours in the air turned unlucky for one aboard Errett's plane when some spasmodic episode opened the bomb bay door letting one of the recently liberated passengers fall to his death.[48] It was a sad memory that stayed with Errett the rest of his life.

As soon as they hit the tarmac in the Philippines, they were segregated into British, American, and Dutch groups, and the officers from those groups formed three other groups. Before leaving Manila, the men were interviewed, mostly at night, about their treatment as POWs.[49] The ex–POWs could opt to telegram home from Manila, so Errett quickly dashed off to do so. "Home soon. Love to all. Am in Philippine Islands." The Lujans received it the night of September 25, and it was timely as Jess and family had not heard anything about Errett from the government since their last telegram dated September 19 stating, "No information has yet been received as to the return to military control of your son Corporal Errett L. Lujan."

Moving tens of thousands of ex–POWs from Manila to the States was a huge undertaking. Errett was not put on a navy transport ship until around September 25, the same date in New Mexico his family received his telegram from Manila. In the meantime, Errett relished the free beer, candy, and cigarettes issued three times daily and enjoyed the shows playing every night. Word passed through the ranks that most prisoners had now been liberated, and a combined sigh of relief swept through the men.

22. Liberation

However, Errett shouldered a deep sadness at the thought of Bill Brown not being one of those returning, nor the ring Bill had entrusted to him.

Once on board the navy ship, he had time to fatten up, which is exactly what the brass wanted to happen to avoid their skeletal frames shocking their families. Errett did his part. He did not miss a meal, not at 7:30 a.m. for breakfast or 12:30 p.m. for dinner or at 6:30 p.m. for supper, and he usually partook in all the ice cream he wanted after that. He thoroughly enjoyed the eight o'clock show in the evening, but it kind of made him wonder how the ones in prison camp could have been so good given their circumstances. One of the best things on board was the dental office. It was one of the first places he went as he crossed the open sea.[50] He could not wait to have the silver stainless steel cap on his front tooth removed and replaced with an American white one. At last, that glaring reminder of being a prisoner was gone, and he was headed home, gaining about two pounds a day over the course of the fifteen-day voyage. He took time to write one last letter postmarked September 27, 9:30 p.m. It began with "Dear Mother and Dad, In a few more days we will all be together again. I am now at sea and will be home sometime after the 15th of October." He wrote a little more about flying out of Japan and the devastating state of the Philippines.

His ship docked in San Francisco on October 8, 1945, to the sounds of a military band playing for them from the deck of a moored ship in the harbor. Others from the 200th and 515th arrived the same day. Errett made a beeline to the Western Union Office and sent a cable home to his mother at five forty that night. It read, "Arrived safely. Expect to see you soon. Don't attempt to contact or write me here. Love, Errett." He actually did not know where he would be in San Francisco or when he would be leaving for Santa Fe. The next day, he sent another cable in the evening: "Arrived safely Letterman General Hospital, Crissey Annex. Feeling fine. Being transferred home soon. Love, Errett." Mother Nature dealt a blow to Japan that same day when super typhoon Louise blew over Okinawa, then made a northeast heading, and violently spun toward a stretch of Japan from Nagasaki to Tokyo like a mercy storm trying to clear the debris of war.

Claire could not help but write Errett at Letterman Hospital on October 10. She let him know that everyone had picked a date he would be arriving in Santa Fe. Jess, of course, picked October 11 because it would be the soonest he could be in Santa Fe. The next word the family received was that Errett was on his way by train and the day he would arrive. He asked that everyone stay home and he would see them there. Louis's boss at Bruns, a colonel, made different plans. He ordered his aide to drive Louis in his official car to the four-year-old Kirtland Army Air Base in Albuquerque seventy miles away to meet Errett so he could see him and get him home as soon as possible.[51]

The aide eased the car next to the train tracks at Kirtland on the afternoon of October 15. When Louis saw the incoming train pulling in, he stepped out of the car. Errett did not expect to see anyone from Santa Fe at this point in his journey home, much less from his family. He was overcome when he spotted his father. He was speechless. After several embraces and as tears freely streaked both of their faces, they got in the back seat of the colonel's car. The ride home was mostly quiet. There was so much to say, but it was difficult for either to start. They were beyond words. Louis was able to get Errett home before the train with the other eighty or so ex–POWs reached Santa Fe. None in the family knew that Errett was arriving early. As the car rounded the corner at his house on Taos Street, Errett flung the car door open, leaped out, and ran to the house. When the family looked out to see what car had stopped in front, they were beside themselves to see Errett in his newly issued uniform heading straight for the door and Louis behind him carrying his son's army duffel. The screen door slammed shut as more tears, hugs, and laughter filled the whole house. Even neighbors were drawn to the corner. They emerged from their homes, ran over, and joined in.

Five hundred of the roughly nine hundred soldiers of the 200th who survived were admitted and treated at Bruns Hospital, including Errett. Over half suffered from tropical diseases from parasites, the most

A close-up of Errett while posing with other Santa Fe County veterans of Bataan and Corregidor on 12 November 1945, 17 days after returning home, and provided to him courtesy of the *Santa Fe New Mexican* newspaper. This is the person his wife fell in love with.

common being the roundworm *Ascaris lumbricoides* and hookworm.[52] A few stories surfaced among them while at Bruns. Tony Montoya had been given the nickname "Angel of the Hospital" in the Philippines because he continually nursed the sick.[53] Evans Garcia, it was learned, faced a firing squad rather than squeal on another POW who had stolen food he gave to sick POWs. Thankfully, he was not shot.[54]

Santa Fe had an estimated 10 percent of its male population serve in World War II. While New Mexico mourned the loss of about half of its National Guard regiment, statistics on the national level soon emerged. The entire National Guard unit from Red Oak, Iowa, was wiped out in French North Africa by Erwin Rommel, in February 1943. It was the largest proportional loss for an American city.[55] They were part of the 179,874 U.S. Army forces killed in World War II. Overall, about fifty million people died in World War II. In 1956, the Japanese Ministry of Health and Welfare concluded that Japanese fatalities due to World War II numbered about 2.3 million, not including those missing and unaccounted for.[56] On the Russian front, 45 percent of the Germans captured by the Russians died and about 60 percent of Russians captured by the Germans died. The Allied POW death rate in German camps was about 4 percent, roughly eight times better than POWs of the Japanese fared. The men of the 200th CA (AA) who did not return home were part of the total of 2,263 New Mexicans lost.

Atomic research was the most dramatic scientific development of the war, but the conflict also led to the large-scale production of penicillin, plasma, synthetic drugs, improved radar, and the jet engine. Errett's perspective was clear—the atomic bomb put an end to the war and saved countless lives, including his. The war also brought Bruns to Santa Fe, and Errett was thankful that his father and uncles had good jobs there. But the hospital's days were numbered. With the war ended and men on the mend, it was slated for closure. In September 1946, it had 644 patients. It closed January 1947, putting some four hundred civilian employees out of work. In March 1947, the War Department awarded an interim permit to the College of Christian Brothers for the twenty-two acres and fifty-one barracks that comprised Bruns. Under the direction of the brothers, it became a college.[57]

The doors of the Santa Fe Japanese internment camp closed in April 1946 after having detained 4,555 Japanese men throughout the war. The Japanese detention program officially ended on June 30, 1946, leaving a scar on this country's record of human rights. About the same time the Japanese were given back control of their lives, Errett's regiment, the 200th Coast Artillery (Antiaircraft), reverted to National Guard status.

With all the survivors of the New Mexico National Guard regiment back home, Governor Miles proclaimed November 13, 1945, Bataan Day. Since then, recognition of the regiment has been held on April 9, the day they were surrendered to the Japanese. Errett remembered writing home when the USS *President Pierce* arrived in Manila on September 16, 1941, that when he "gets home I will have a lot to tell everyone," but like so many who made it back, he rarely spoke about his experience.

Errett married Betty McDaniel Hester on December 29, 1945, after agreeing to get hitched one night while socializing at El Nido. Betty remembers the time as if it were yesterday. The marriage license cost $2.50, and when it came time to pay the county courthouse clerk, Errett realized he had only a twenty dollar bill. The clerk had already locked her cashbox for the day, so Betty paid the tab. After the Methodist minister Reverend Shropshire officiated their marriage, the couple drove to Taos, spent two nights, and then returned to Santa Fe. Errett's pass from Bruns Hospital was due to expire and Betty had to be back at work on Monday.[58]

The following year, Errett was ordered to Ft. Sam Houston to receive his discharge. The newly married couple drove there in tandem with Francis VanBuskirk and his new wife, Jeri. Both wives were around three months pregnant at the time. The Lujan couple drove to Texas in a car Errett purchased, hoping his promised check from the U.S. government would soon come in to cover the cost. He was the first ex–POW in Santa Fe

Francis VanBuskirk and Errett Lujan on horseback taking time to enjoy themselves when driving to Texas to be discharged from the army (left photo); Errett atop his newly purchased car; Errett with his wife, Betty (left), and Jeri VanBuskirk (Photographs taken in May 1946).

22. Liberation

to receive his money but not until 1950. The sum, $1,241, was purportedly calculated at $1 for every day he was a POW.

Errett was honorably discharged from the U.S. Army at Ft. Sam Houston in San Antonio, Texas, on May 15, 1946. It is doubtful he ever knew the guilt Governor Miles felt for having agreed to release the 200th Coast Artillery to active duty in the U.S. Army. The governor carried with him throughout his life a heavy burden of responsibility for the suffering and deaths among these men. With a heavy heart, he reiterated this to his son several times and added, "But for the grace of God go I."[59]

Epilogue

Errett met his future wife, Betty, by way of introduction through his sister with whom Betty worked. They spent many an evening in nearby Tesuque (where Bill Brown lived before the war) eating, dancing, and generally partying at El Nido, a favorite meeting place for throngs of young people immediately after the war. They were married around three months after he returned to Santa Fe, making Errett stepfather to her two young boys. Their whirlwind romance was fun, exciting, and somewhat typical of the time. Needless to say, his former fiancée and her family did not take this well.

One evening, just a few days after their wedding, Errett and Betty walked around the plaza in Santa Fe after dinner and passed the glass-fronted eatery of the Plaza Diner. Immediately, something caught Errett's eye on the window. It was a 10 × 18 inch "Picturegram" dated January 9, 1946, of a Japanese guard being led out of the courtroom after his sentencing for war crimes attributed to him. Errett could not believe it.[1] In the center of the photograph was Errett's nemesis—Little Glass Eye. All the feelings of hatred for the diabolical man flooded back as he stood transfixed. The owner hurriedly came out to speak with him, bringing the picture with him. The restaurateur offered his apologies as he knew Errett had been a prisoner of the Japanese, then he offered the picture to him. Errett accepted it, then read the bold print: "Little Glass Eye Gets Life at Hard Labor."

A few Japanese found complicit in atrocities related to the Bataan Death March were sentenced to be hanged, but Errett never knew their names. He did, however, know those in his camps in Japan who would pay for their treacherous deeds. Among those found guilty and sentenced to death by hanging were Matsuzaki (Scar Face), Sukeo Nakajima, Sadahara Hiramatsu, Kunio Yoshizawa, and Tamotsu Kimura. Those of Errett's captors in addition to Little Glass Eye who were sentenced to hard labor in prison were Takeo Kirishita (for life), Hisao Kaneyama (fourteen years), Hiroshi Azuma (seven years), Keitaro Fukijima (seven years), Kiromitzu

Saito (five years), Ishibe Kiyoji (two years), and Tokio Minagawa (1½ years). Richard Gordon (known as Albert Gordon during the war) speculates depravities inflicted on POWs at Mitsushima by Little Glass Eye were mistakenly attributed to Big Glass Eye, which led to the death sentence for him.[2] Others seem to agree with this assessment.

In the fall of 1947, Errett received two letters from the Legal Section of the Supreme Commander for the Allied Powers confirming the trials and sentences for other guards at the two camps where he was held. None of the names appear in his diaries, but he may have recorded them by their nicknames or, perhaps, not at all. They are Shichinobu Shichino (at Mitsushima; twenty-five years), Masanobu Michishita (Mitsushima; death by hanging), Mineo Nojima (Mitsushima; life), and Kanemasu Uchida (Kanose; brought to trial while serving five years for other crimes). Errett wrote on the September 5, 1947, letter he received explaining the upcoming trial for Uchida that Corporal James Aiken at Kanose was not tied to a tree in the snow for three hours, as stated, but "all night." In the end, the last Japanese serving a prison sentence for war crimes was released in December 1958, and others were paroled earlier.[3]

Errett had a love of horses and grew up riding them from an early age on the family ranch. He acquired a palomino mare and bred her, which led to his new and beloved colt he named Golden Boy. He kept his horses at his uncle Jake's ranch in northeast New Mexico in the winters and in the backyard of his house in Santa Fe in the summers.

After his discharge, Errett worked as a butcher and at a Pontiac car dealership. After his and Betty's second child together was born, Errett changed jobs to work for Gross Kelly distribution, a job that required a fair amount of travel throughout northern New Mexico. Soon afterward, he and three Murphy brothers opened a bowling alley in Santa Fe, featuring the first automatic pinsetters in town, a mere half block from Errett's home at the edge of town at the time. He worked tirelessly running the business and managing people over the course of nearly twenty years. The facility grew to include more lanes, billiard tables, snooker tables, a pinball machine room, a restaurant, a bar, a snack bar, and an ice-skating rink.

He and the Murphy brothers sold the business as they neared retirement age. It was at this time that Errett finally applied for a 100 percent veteran's disability due to the broken back he incurred on the *Nagato Maru* in addition to maladies he suffered from other ill treatment while a POW. Initially, he limited his disability claim to 25 percent when he was discharged, not wanting to take a handout while he could provide a living for his family. His pride prevented him from asking for it any earlier. By the time he reached retirement age, he decided he had probably earned full disability compensation for the years he had left to live. His disability status was elevated to 100 percent after review of his medical papers, and several eyewitness accounts of his ordeals while in captivity were provided.

Errett met with Bill Brown's mother not long after he returned stateside. Mrs. Brown knew about her son's death in the Philippines, but it was still difficult for Errett to answer her questions although she did not push for details. He passed on his regrets for not keeping his promise to Bill about the ring.[4] It was a brief but poignant conversation, but the heartache lasted his lifetime.

Appendix

POW Signatures on Errett Lujan's Vest

James Aikin [West Point, Kentucky]
James Archey [High Wycombe, England]
Bill [P. Beverly F.] Atnip [Boswell, Oklahoma]
Jack Atwell, Ft. Dodge [Ft. Dodge, Iowa]
Kid [William E.] Bandish [Chicago, Illinois]
Jim [James] Barry [Dorset, England]
Cullen W. Berry [Lufkin, Texas]
[P.] Bedford Bolin [Vicksburg, Mississippi]
E.D. [P. Matthew] Braun [Rome, New York]
Glenn Brokaw [Salinas, California]
Mike Chavez [Deming, New Mexico]
Major Allen Cory [Tulsa, Oklahoma]
Burlin C. Cupp [Carey, Ohio]
David A. Dement [Elm Grove, Louisiana]
Eugene C. Dunn [Newport, Tennessee]
Bill [William] Eaton [New Cross, London]
[P.] Earle Ennis [Stockton, California]
Captain Ace E. Faulkner
Bernard A. Fields [St. Johns, Kentucky]
Charles Gavord [Deming, New Mexico]
Marshall W. Goff [Globe, Arizona]
Paul A. Grassick [Mansfield, Ohio]
Captain Walter J. Hewitt [St. Paul, Minnesota]
A. Jay Holstein [Miami, Arizona]
Revis C. Hyde [Mississippi]
John B. Ivy [Huntington, Texas]
Leo L. Johnson [New Berlin, New York]
Bob Jones [England]
Eugene Jones [Dallas, Texas]

Front view of the British tunic Errett fashioned into a vest just before liberation. Signatures cover the fabric on the front, back, sides, and shoulders. The vest is currently on display at the National Guard Museum in Washington, D.C., located less than a block west of Union Station.

P. [Verble] Big Jones [Selma, Alabama]
Ray Klassen [Missouri]
P. Fred Kolilis [Tacoma, Washington]
Donald Lily [Indianapolis, Indiana]
John A. Lobe [Detroit, Michigan]
Verner Marble [Oneota, New York]
Willie Mann [Baltimore, Maryland]
Don A. (Woof) Martindale [Salt Lake City, Utah]
Arthur J. Mitchell, [Klamath Falls, Oregon]
Dorris (Bob) Pratt [Sherman, Texas]
William R. Richards [Cartersville, Oklahoma]
Joel Rogers [Bayard, New Mexico]

Samuel J. Rouse [Rocky Mount, North Carolina]
John C. Roy [Nashville, Tennessee; Miami, Florida]
Alvin Silver [Brooklyn, New York]
Osmond H. Simmonds [Wales]
Clifton Snodgrass [Junction City, Kansas]
Paul R. ("Emo") Spencer [Oklahoma City, Oklahoma]
Kenneth Stanford [Ardmore, Oklahoma]
Arvil L. Steele [Texarkana, Texas]
James Suterfield [Collinston, Louisiana]
Simone (Sam) Vallerga [Alameda, California]

Chapter Notes

FACHL = Fray Angélico Chávez History Library/New Mexico History Museum, Santa Fe, New Mexico
GJEMP = Governor John E. Miles Papers, New Mexico State Archives and Records Center, Santa Fe, New Mexico
NARA = National Archives and Records Administration
NMMM = New Mexico Military Museum, Santa Fe, New Mexico
NMSRCA = New Mexico State Records Center and Archives, Santa Fe, New Mexico

Introduction

1. Claire Guentz, Interview with author (Albuquerque, New Mexico, 5 February 2005).

Chapter 1

1. Saburō Ienaga, *The Pacific War, 1931–1945* (New York: Pantheon, 1978), 5.
2. *Ibid.*, 5–6.
3. Iris Chang, *The Rape of Nanking* (New York: Basic Books, 1997), 216–217.
4. Richard J. Daly, *Me—A Biography for My Children* (ms in possession of author, 2002), 107.
5. Ienaga, 154.
6. *Ibid.*, 153–154.

Chapter 2

1. Doris Kearns Goodwin, *No Ordinary Time* (New York: Simon & Schuster, 1994), 23.

2. Franklin D. Roosevelt, Address of the President to the Congress, Washington, DC, 6 January 1941 (NARA, copy in possession of author), 1–10.
3. Henry J. Tobias and Charles E. Woodhouse, *Santa Fe: A Modern History, 1880–1990* (Albuquerque: University of New Mexico Press, 2001), 141.
4. Claire Guentz, Interview with author (4 February 2005).
5. Francis VanBuskirk, Interview with author (Santa Fe, New Mexico, 25 October 2006).
6. New Mexico Adjutant General (NMSRCA: accession 1973–019, sub-series 18.3) pertaining to Governor Miles overcoming financial constraints to proceed with solicitations for bids and construction of a new armory.
7. John Pershing Jolly, *History, National Guard of New Mexico, 1606–1963* (Santa Fe: New Mexico National Guard, 1964), 33.
8. VanBuskirk.
9. E. Bartlett Kerr, *Surrender and Survival* (New York: William Morrow, 1985), 24.
10. *Ibid.*, 19.
11. John W. Whitman, *Bataan, Our Last Ditch* (New York: Hippocrene, 1990), 13.
12. Guentz.
13. Dorothy Cave, *Beyond Courage* (Las Cruces, NM: Yucca Press, 1992), 20.
14. Richard Daly, *Me—A Biography for My Children* (ms in possession of author, 2002), 77–78.
15. Tony Reyna, Interview with author (Taos Pueblo, New Mexico, 1 November 2005).

Chapter 3

1. War Department, *Basic Field Manual for Military Training* (Washington, DC: Government Printing Office, 16 July 1941), 1.
2. Harry E. Steen, *Experiences in WWII in the Far East* (Hamilton, ON: McMaster University, 1992; copy at NMMM; ms in possession of author), 1–2.
3. Richard Daly, *Me—A Biography for My Children* (ms in possession of author, 2002), 80.
4. Richard Daly, Interview with author (Santa Fe, New Mexico, 1 September 2005).
5. Tony Reyna, Interview with author (Taos Pueblo, New Mexico, 1 November 2005).
6. Dorothy Cave, *Beyond Courage* (Las Cruces, NM: Yucca Press, 1992), 24.
7. Betty Lujan, Interview with author (Santa Fe, New Mexico, 8 July 2002).

Chapter 4

1. Richard Daly, Interview with author (Santa Fe, New Mexico, 1 September 2005).
2. Harry E. Steen, *Experiences in WWII in the Far East* (Hamilton, ON: McMaster University, 1992; copy at NMMM; ms in possession of author), 4.
3. William Manchester, *American Caesar* (Boston: Little Brown, 1978), 174–175.
4. Elizabeth M. Norman, *We Band of Angels* (New York: Random House, 1999), 30.
5. Steen, *Experiences in WWII*, 7.
6. E. Bartlett Kerr, *Surrender and Survival* (New York: William Morrow, 1985), 22.
7. Francis VanBuskirk, Interview with author (Santa Fe, New Mexico, 25 October 2006).
8. John Pershing Jolly, *History, National Guard of New Mexico, 1606–1963* (Santa Fe: National Guard of New Mexico, 1964), 33.
9. Francis VanBuskirk, Interview with author (Santa Fe, New Mexico, 25 October 2006).
10. Tony Reyna, Interview with author (Taos Pueblo, New Mexico, 1 November 2005).
11. Norman, *We Band of Angels*, 3–4.
12. Winston Shillito, Interview with Jonathan Cohen (El Paso, Texas, 4 February 1997: Hamilton, ON: McMaster University, 1992; copy at NMMM), 4.
13. Michael Gilewitch, *Moyeh* (ms in possession of author, 1990s), 3–21.
14. *Ibid.*, 3–21/22.
15. Steen, *Experiences in WWII*, 8–9.
16. Kerr, *Surrender and Survival*, 21.

Chapter 5

1. Dominic J. Caraccilo, *Surviving Bataan and Beyond* (Mechanicsburg, PA, Stackpole: Books, 1999), chapter 5, p. 259, note 11.
2. Tony Reyna, Interview with author (Taos Pueblo, New Mexico, 1 November 2005).
3. Harry E. Steen, *Experiences in WWII in the Far East* (Hamilton, ON: McMaster University, 1992; copy at NMMM; ms in possession of author), 9.
4. John Pershing Jolly, *History, National Guard of New Mexico, 1606–1963* (Santa Fe: New Mexico National Guard, 1964), 33.
5. *Ibid.*, 38.
6. Richard J. Daly, *Me—A Biography for My Children* (ms in possession of author, 2002), 86–87.
7. Steen, *Experiences in WWII*, 10.
8. Reyna.
9. Winston Shillito, Interview with Jonathan Cohen (El Paso, Texas, 4 February 1997: Hamilton, ON: McMaster University, 1992; copy at NMMM), 8.
10. Reyna.
11. Francis VanBuskirk, Interview with author (Santa Fe, New Mexico, 25 October 2006).
12. *Ibid.*
13. *Ibid.*
14. Daly, *Me*, 87.
15. John S. Coleman, Jr., *Bataan and Beyond* (College Station: Texas A&M University Press, 1978), 10–11.
16. Richard Connaughton, *MacArthur's Defeat in the Philippines* (Woodstock, NY: Overlook Press, 2001), 144.
17. Jolly, *History, National Guard of New Mexico*, 34; Eva Jane Matson, *It Tolled for New Mexico* (Las Cruces, NM: Yucca Press, 1994), 360–363.

18. John W. Whitman, *Bataan, Our Last Ditch* (New York: Hippocrene Books, 1990), 100.
19. Michael Gilewitch, *Moyeh* (ms in possession of author, 1990s), 3-22.
20. Whitman, *Bataan*, 402.
21. *Ibid.*, 100.
22. William Overmeir, Interview with author (San Antonio, Texas, ADBC Convention, May 2009).
23. Steen, *Experiences in WWII*, 13-14.
24. Whitman, *Bataan*, 463.
25. *Ibid.*, 465.
26. Coleman, *Bataan and Beyond*, 31.

Chapter 6

1. Richard Gordon, with Benjamin S. Llamzon, *Horyo* (St. Paul: Paragon House, 1999), 41-42.
2. Richard C. Mallonée, *Battle for Bataan* (New York: Presidio Press, 1980), 35.
3. Harry E. Steen, *Experiences in WWII in the Far East* (Hamilton, ON: McMaster University, 1992; copy at NMMM; ms in possession of author), 16.
4. Mallonée, *Battle for Bataan*, 41.
5. Steen, *Experiences in WWII*, 14.
6. Richard Daly, *Me—A Biography for My Children* (ms in possession of author, 2002), 99.
7. *Ibid.*, 100.
8. Francis VanBuskirk, Interview with author (Santa Fe, New Mexico, 25 October 2006).
9. Daly, *Me*, 101.
10. Richard Daly, Interview with author (Santa Fe, New Mexico, 1 September 2005).
11. Daly, *Me*, 101.
12. VanBuskirk.
13. Daly, Interview with author.
14. Donald J. Young, *Battle of Bataan* (Jefferson, NC: McFarland, 2009), 113.
15. John W. Whitman, *Bataan, Our Last Ditch* (New York: Hippocrene Books, 1990), 411.
16. Young, *Battle of Bataan*, 20.
17. Whitman, *Bataan*, 89-91.
18. Michael Gilewitch, *Moyeh* (ms in possession of author, 1990s), 3-24.
19. *Ibid.*, 3-25.
20. Gordon, *Horyo*, 66.

Chapter 7

1. Donald J. Young, *Battle of Bataan* (Jefferson, NC: McFarland, 2009), 15.
2. Dorothy Cave, *Beyond Courage* (Las Cruces, NM: Yucca Press, 1992), 95.
3. Winston Shillito, Interview with Jonathan Cohen (El Paso, Texas, 4 February 1997: Hamilton, ON: McMaster University, 1992; copy at NMMM).
4. John W. Whitman, *Bataan, Our Last Ditch* (New York: Hippocrene, 1990), 289.
5. Shillito, 25.
6. Michael Gilewitch, *Moyeh* (ms in possession of author, 1990s), 3-34.
7. Cave, *Beyond Courage*, 100.
8. Gordon, *Horyo*, 69-70.
9. Gilewitch, *Moyeh*, 3-11.
10. *Ibid.*, 3-12.
11. *Ibid.*, 3-12.
12. *Ibid.*, 3-34.
13. *Ibid.*, 3-19.
14. Whitman, *Bataan*, 167.
15. Cave, *Beyond Courage*, 96.
16. Whitman, *Bataan*, 247-248.
17. *Ibid.*, 211.
18. Matthew Braun, Interview with author (Syracuse, New York, 11 January 2004).

Chapter 8

1. Michael Gilewitch, *Moyeh* (ms in possession of author, 1990s), 3-19/20.
2. Dorothy Cave, *Beyond Courage* (Las Cruces, NM: Yucca Press, 1992), 103, 249.
3. John W. Whitman, *Bataan, Our Last Ditch* (New York: Hippocrene, 1990), 363.
4. *Ibid.*, 360.
5. Cave, *Beyond Courage*, 109.
6. Whitman, *Bataan*, 377.
7. Gilewitch, *Moyeh*, 3-39.
8. Cave, *Beyond Courage*, 124-125.
9. Richard C. Mallonée, *Battle for Bataan* (New York: Presidio Press, 1980), 110.
10. Whitman, *Bataan*, 453.
11. Gilewitch, *Moyeh*, 3-32.
12. Cave, *Beyond Courage*, 108.
13. *Ibid.* (citation credited to Captain Jack Boyer), 111.
14. Donald J. Young, *Battle of Bataan* (Jefferson, NC: McFarland, 2009), 156.
15. Whitman, *Bataan*, 513.
16. Gilewitch, *Moyeh*, 3-32.

17. Richard Connaughton, *MacArthur's Defeat in the Philippines* (Woodstock, NY: Overlook Press, 2001), 234.
18. Whitman, *Bataan*, 462.
19. Gilewitch, *Moyeh*, 3-32/33.

Chapter 9

1. Shuji Fujii, letter to Governor John E. Miles, 8 December 1941, NMSRCA, GJEMP.
2. Miles Proclamation, 8 December 1941, NMSRCA, GJEMP.
3. Admiral Richard E. Byrd, USM (retired), to Governor John E. Miles, 23 December 1941, NMSRCA, GJEMP.
4. Governor John E. Miles to All Department Heads, 9 January, NMSRCA, GJEMP.
5. Henry Stimson to Governor Miles, 25 February 1942, NMSRCA, Santa Fe, New Mexico, Governor John E. Miles Papers.
6. George C. Marshall, General Orders Number 14, Washington, DC, 9 March 1942, copy in possession of author.
7. Bureau of Census, Department of Commerce (Tables 1 and 2, 1942) (copy in possession of author).
8. Allen R. Bosworth, *America's Concentration Camps* (New York: Norton, 1967), 56.
9. National Reclamation Association Bulletin, 20 May 1942, NMSRCA, GJEMP.
10. Eva Ammen and Mathilde Ammen to Governor Miles, 13 March 1942, NMSRCA, GJEMP.
11. C.C. McCulloh, Assistant Attorney General to John Wight, 27 May 1942, NMSRCA, GJEMP.
12. John E. Miles, Press Release, 7 April 1942, NMSRCA, GJEMP, box 5, folder 167.
13. Lloyd Jensen to Governor Miles, April 1942, NMSRCA, GJEMP.
14. Bosworth, *America's Concentration Camps*, 18.
15. Unknown to Mr. Jerre Mangione, 14 October 1943, Washington, DC, NARA, RG 85 (copy in possession of author), 1.
16. *Ibid.*
17. Mark Hummels, "Former Internee Recalls Life as an 'Enemy Alien,'" *Santa Fe New Mexican*, 22 August 1999.
18. James Matsu to Governor John Miles, 3 February 1942, NMSRCA, GJEMP.
19. Henry J. Tobias and Charles E. Woodhouse, *Santa Fe 1880-1990—A Modern History* (Albuquerque: University of New Mexico Press, 2001), 142.
20. Koichiro Okada, Japanese American Internment Camps Research Material (AC304), FACHL.

Chapter 10

1. John W. Whitman, *Bataan, Our Last Ditch* (New York: Hippocrene Books, 1990), 468.
2. Colonel Richard C. Mallonée, *Battle for Bataan* (New York: Presidio Press, 1980), 118-119.
3. Dorothy Cave, *Beyond Courage* (Las Cruces, NM: Yucca Press, 1992), 115.
4. Whitman, *Bataan*, 477-478; Cave, *Beyond Courage*, 140.
5. Cave, *Beyond Courage*, 121.
6. Mallonée, *Battle for Bataan*, 125.
7. Cave, *Beyond Courage*, 142.
8. Whitman, *Bataan*, 353.
9. *Ibid.*, 411.
10. *Ibid.*, 465.
11. *Ibid.*, 559.
12. *Ibid.*, 549.
13. Francis VanBuskirk, Interview with author (Santa Fe, New Mexico, 25 October 2006).
14. Whitman, *Bataan*, 546-547.
15. *Ibid.*, 553, 557.
16. Harry E. Steen, *Experiences in WWII in the Far East* (Hamilton, ON: McMaster University, 1992; copy at NMMM; ms in possession of author), 19.
17. Winston Shillito, Interview with Jonathan Cohen (El Paso, Texas, 4 February 1997: Hamilton, ON: McMaster University, 1992; copy at NMMM), 11.
18. William Overmeir, Interview with author (San Antonio, Texas, 2 May 2009).
19. Whitman, *Bataan*, 567.
20. Michael Gilewitch, *Moyeh* (ms in possession of author, 1990s), 3-41.
21. Cave, *Beyond Courage*, 133.
22. VanBuskirk.
23. *Ibid.*
24. Cave, *Beyond Courage*, 145.

Chapter 11

1. Dorothy Cave, *Beyond Courage* (Las Cruces, NM: Yucca Press, 1992), 170.

2. Michael Gilewitch, *Moyeh* (ms in possession of author, 1990s), 4-6.
3. *Ibid.*
4. Harry E. Steen, *Experiences in WWII in the Far East* (Hamilton, Ontario: McMaster University, 1992; copy at NMMM; ms in possession of author), 25.
5. E. Bartlett Kerr, *Surrender and Survival* (New York: William Morrow, 1985), 51-52.
6. John S. Coleman, Jr., *Bataan and Beyond* (College Station: Texas A&M University Press, 1978), 69.
7. *Ibid.*
8. Gilewitch, *Moyeh*, 4-24.
9. Steen, *Experiences in WWII*, 28.
10. Winston Shillito, Interview with Jonathan Cohen (El Paso, Texas, 4 February 1997: Hamilton, ON: McMaster University, 1992; copy at NMMM), 12.
11. *Ibid.*
12. History Channel, "The Bataan Death March," 13 February 2004.

Chapter 12

1. Dorothy Cave, *Beyond Courage* (Las Cruces, NM: Yucca Press, 1992), 125.
2. Governor John E. Miles, Proclamation, 9 April 1942, NMSRC, GJEMP.
3. Craig Nelson, *The First Heroes* (New York: Viking Penguin, 2002), 119-121.
4. Ronald H. Spector, *Eagle against the Sun* (New York: Free Press, 1985), 155.
5. War Department to Governor John E. Miles, 6 May 1942, NMSRCA, GJEMP.
6. Major General J.A. Ulio to Mrs. Jesse Lujan, 15 May 1942 (copy in possession of author).
7. Edward Brett and Donna Brett, "Santa Fe's Shameful Jap Trap," *Santa Fe Reporter*, 15 February 1984, 11.
8. Captain Antonio Martin, Report on Visit, Washington, DC (NARA, RG 59, Special War Problems Division: Santa Fe folder, box 20, 10-11 July 1944, copy in Japanese American Internment Camps Research Material (AC304), FACHL).
9. Henry J. Tobias and Charles E. Woodhouse, *Santa Fe 1880-1990—A Modern History* (Albuquerque: University of New Mexico Press, 2001), 148.
10. Governor John E. Miles, Press Release, 28 May 1942, NMSRC, GJEMP.
11. Governor John E. Miles, Press Release, 13 May 1942, NMSRCA, GJEMP, box 5, folder 167.
12. Claire Guentz, Interview with author (Albuquerque, New Mexico, 5 February 2005).

Chapter 13

1. John E. Olson, *O'Donnell—Andersonville of the Pacific* (Lake Quivira, KS: John E. Olson, 1985), 151.
2. History Channel, "The Bataan Death March," 13 February 2004.
3. Gavan Daws, *Prisoners of the Japanese* (New York: William Morrow, 1994), 86-87.
4. Harry E. Steen, *Experiences in WWII in the Far East* (Hamilton, ON: McMaster University, 1992; copy at NMMM; ms in possession of author), 30.
5. Linda Goetz Holmes, *Unprepared Regrettable Events* (Mechanicsburg, PA: Stackpole Books, 2001, chapter 3, footnote 20, 185, attributed to Sumio Adachi, National Defense Academy, Yokosuka, Japan, 1982).
6. Francis VanBuskirk, Interview with author (Santa Fe, New Mexico, 25 October 2006).
7. History Channel, "The Bataan Death March."
8. Michael Gilewitch, *Moyeh* (ms in possession of author, 1990s), 4-37.
9. *Ibid.*, 4-35.
10. History Channel, "The Bataan Death March."
11. Dorothy Cave, *Beyond Courage* (Las Cruces, NM: Yucca Press, 1992), 206.
12. E. Bartlett Kerr, *Surrender and Survival* (New York: William Morrow, 1985), 87.
13. Matthew Braun, Interview with author (Syracuse, New York, 11 January 2004).
14. Daws, *Prisoners of the Japanese*, 135.
15. Louis Morton, *The Fall of the Philippines* (Washington, DC: Center of Military History, United States Army, 1989), 561.
16. Cave, *Beyond Courage*, 191.
17. Kerr, *Surrender and Survival*, 81.
18. Linda Goetz Holmes, *Unjust Enrichment* (Mechanicsburg, PA: Stackpole Books, 2001), 23.
19. Kerr, *Surrender and Survival*, 94.
20. Gilewitch, *Moyeh*, 4-57.

21. Manny Lawton, *Some Survived* (Chapel Hill: Algonquin Books, 1984), 31.
22. Kerr, *Surrender and Survival*, 95.

Chapter 14

1. John M. Wright, Jr., *Captured on Corregidor* (Jefferson, NC: McFarland, 1988), 59–60.
2. Michael Gilewitch, *Moyeh* (ms in possession of author, 1990s), 4–42, 4–45.
3. E. Bartlett Kerr, *Surrender and Survival* (New York: William Morrow, 1985), 101.
4. John S. Coleman, Jr., *Bataan and Beyond* (College Station: Texas A&M University Press, 1978), 94.
5. *Ibid.*, 92.
6. *Ibid.*, 94.
7. *Ibid.*, 92–93.
8. Wright, *Captured on Corregidor*, 59.
9. Kerr, *Surrender and Survival*, 95–96.
10. Wright, *Captured on Corregidor*, 59.
11. Kerr, *Surrender and Survival*, 90–91.
12. *Ibid.*, 103.
13. Gilewitch, *Moyeh*, 4–43.
14. Coleman, *Bataan and Beyond*, 93.
15. Winston Shillito, Interview with Jonathan Cohen (El Paso, Texas, 4 February 1997: Hamilton, ON: McMaster University, 1992; copy at NMMM), 26.
16. Kerr, *Surrender and Survival*, 108/118.
17. Gilewitch, *Moyeh*, 4–68.
18. Francis VanBuskirk, Interview with author (Santa Fe, New Mexico, 25 October 2006).
19. Kerr, *Surrender and Survival*, 100.
20. Gilewitch, *Moyeh*, 4–53, 4–59, 4–67.
21. Wright, *Captured on Corregidor*, 53.
22. Dorothy Cave, *Beyond Courage* (Las Cruces, NM: Yucca Press, 1992), 222.
23. Wright, *Captured on Corregidor*, 53.
24. Cave, *Beyond Courage*, 220–221.
25. Gilewitch, *Moyeh*, 4–47 through 4–49.
26. *Ibid.*, 4–53, 4–57.
27. *Ibid.*, 4–54, 4–56.
28. *Ibid.*, 4–57.
29. Kerr, *Surrender and Survival*, 104.
30. Lucy L. Wilson to Merle Lujan, 7 August 1942 (copy in possession of author).
31. Gilewitch, *Moyeh*, 4–59.
32. *Ibid.*, 4–65/66.
33. Wright, *Captured on Corregidor*, 56.
34. VanBuskirk.
35. Coleman, *Bataan and Beyond*, 94, 104.
36. Kerr, *Surrender and Survival*, 100–101.
37. Linda Goetz Holmes, *Unjust Enrichment* (Mechanicsburg, PA: Stackpole Books, 2001), 22.
38. Bert Webber, *Silent Siege* (Medford, OR: Webb Research Group, 1983), 163–170.

Chapter 15

1. Linda Goetz Holmes, *Unjust Enrichment: How Japan's Companies Built Postwar Fortunes Using American POWs* (Stackpole Books, Mechanicsburg, Pennsylvania), 27.
2. Doris Kearns Goodwin, *No Ordinary Time* (New York: Simon & Schuster, 1994), 462.
3. John S. Coleman, Jr., *Bataan and Beyond* (College Station: Texas A&M University Press, 1978), 105.
4. Richard Gordon, with Benjamin S. Llamzon, *Horyo* (St. Paul: Paragon House, 1999), 133.
5. Coleman, *Bataan and Beyond*, 105.
6. E. Bartlett Kerr, *Surrender and Survival* (New York: William Morrow, 1985), 119.
7. Coleman, *Bataan and Beyond*, 105.
8. Dorothy Cave, *Beyond Courage* (Las Cruces, NM: Yucca Press, 1992), 280.
9. Coleman, *Bataan and Beyond*, 107.
10. Gordon, *Horyo*, 134–135.
11. Coleman, *Bataan and Beyond*, 107.
12. Cave, *Beyond Courage*, 280.
13. Coleman, *Bataan and Beyond*, 107–108.
14. *Ibid.*
15. *Ibid.*
16. Cave, *Beyond Courage*, 280.
17. Coleman, *Bataan and Beyond*, 108.
18. *Ibid.*
19. *Ibid.*
20. Kerr, *Surrender and Survival*, 119–120; Cave, 280.
21. Gordon, *Horyo*, 139.
22. Coleman, *Bataan and Beyond*, 108.
23. *Ibid.*, 108–109.

24. Michael Gilewitch, *Moyeh* (ms in possession of author, 1990s), 4–72.
25. Kerr, *Surrender and Survival*, 120–122.
26. Richard J. Daly, *Me—A Biography for My Children* (ms in possession of author, 2002), 131.

Chapter 16

1. Richard Gordon, with Benjamin S. Llamzon, *Horyo* (St. Paul: Paragon House, 1999), 149.
2. Les Chater, with Elizabeth Hamid, *Behind the Fence* (St. Catharines, ON: Vanwell Publishing, 2001), 82.
3. Gordon, *Horyo*, 150.
4. *Ibid.*, 164.
5. Chater, *Behind the Fence*, 82.
6. Gordon, *Horyo*, 149.
7. *Ibid.*, 149–150.
8. Captain Antonio Martin, "Report on Visit April 20 & 22, 1943," Washington, DC (NARA, RG 59, Special War Problems Division, Santa Fe folder, box 20, copy in Japanese American Internment Camps Research Material (AC304), FACHL).
9. Gordon, *Horyo*, 162.
10. *Ibid.*, 154–155.
11. *Ibid.*, 150.
12. Chater, *Behind the Fence*, 81.
13. Gordon, *Horyo*, 162.
14. E. Bartlett Kerr, *Surrender and Survival* (New York: William Morrow, 1985), 124.
15. Gordon, *Horyo*, 159.
16. *Ibid.*, 166.
17. Chater, *Behind the Fence*, 93.

Chapter 17

1. Les Chater, with Elizabeth Hamid, *Behind the Fence* (St. Catharines, ON: Vanwell Publishing, 2001), 88, 91.
2. *Ibid.*, 89.
3. *Ibid.*, 100.
4. Harry E. Steen, *Experiences in WWII in the Far East* (Hamilton, ON: McMaster University, 1992; copy at NMMM; ms in possession of author), 38–39.
5. Richard Gordon, with Benjamin S. Llamzon, *Horyo* (St. Paul: Paragon House, 1999), 164.
6. Chater, *Behind the Fence*, 91.
7. *Ibid.*, 94.
8. *Ibid.*, 95, 97.
9. *Ibid.*, 95.
10. *Ibid.*, 97.
11. E. Bartlett Kerr, *Surrender and Survival* (New York: William Morrow, 1985), 132.
12. Chater, *Behind the Fence*, 97.
13. *Ibid.*
14. Eva Jane Matson, *It Tolled for New Mexico* (Las Cruces, NM: Yucca Press, 1994), 21.
15. Holland M. Smith and Percy Finch, *Coral and Brass* (New York: Scribner's, 1949), 99.
16. Gordon, *Horyo*, 163.
17. Chater, *Behind the Fence*, 99–100.
18. *Ibid.*, 100.
19. *Ibid.*, 101.
20. *Ibid.*, 101.
21. *Ibid.*, 105.
22. *Ibid.*, 118.
23. *Ibid.*, 99.
24. *Ibid.*, 110.
25. *Ibid.*, 111.
26. *Ibid.*, 115.
27. *Ibid.*, 116.
28. *Ibid.*
29. *Ibid.*, 114.
30. *Ibid.*, 116.
31. *Ibid.*, 118.
32. *Ibid.*, 119–120.
33. *Ibid.*, 121–122.
34. *Ibid.*, 106.
35. Manny Lawton, *Some Survived* (Chapel Hill: Algonquin Books, 1984), 37.
36. Chater, *Behind the Fence*, 96, 133.
37. War Department, Washington, DC, to Jesse G. Lujan, 19 February 1943.
38. John D. Wirth and Linda Harvey Aldrich, *Los Alamos: The Ranch School Years—1917–1943* (Albuquerque: University of New Mexico Press, 2003), 157.
39. Cynthia Kelly, ed., *The Manhattan Project* (New York: Black Dog and Leventhal Publishers, 2007), 66.
40. Howard Houk, Interview with author (Albuquerque, New Mexico, 30 August 2002).
41. Chater, *Behind the Fence*, 124.
42. *Ibid.*, 124–125.
43. Gussie Fauntleroy, "Bruns Hospital Had Big Impact in Little Time," *Santa Fe New Mexican*, 29 August 1999 (Bruns General Hospital vertical files (AC704) FACHL).

44. Brother Tim Coldwell, "A History of Bruns General Hospital and Its Subsequent Acquisition by St. Michael's College: 1942–1947," research paper, 1977 (Bruns General Hospital vertical files (AC704) FACHL).

Chapter 18

1. Les Chater, with Elizabeth Hamid, *Behind the Fence* (St. Catharines, ON: Vanwell Publishing, 2001), 131.
2. Clinton P. Anderson to Jesse Lujan, 13 May 1943.
3. Thomas B. Allen and Norman Polmar, *Code Name Downfall* (New York: Simon & Schuster, 1995), 93–94.
4. Ronald H. Spector, *Eagle against the Sun* (New York: Free Press, 1985), 229–230.
5. Chater, *Behind the Fence*, 130.
6. *Ibid.*, 127.
7. *Ibid.*, 136.
8. Betty Lujan, Interview with author (Santa Fe, New Mexico, 8 July 2002).
9. *Ibid.*
10. Chater, *Behind the Fence*, 141.
11. *Ibid.*, 146.
12. *Ibid.*, 146–148, 153.
13. *Ibid.*, 154.
14. *Ibid.*

Chapter 19

1. Provost Marshal General, Washington, DC, to Jess Lujan, 10 July 1943 (copy in possession of author).
2. Provost Marshal General, Washington, DC, to Jess Lujan, 31 August 1943 (copy in possession of author).
3. Les Chater, with Elizabeth Hamid, *Behind the Fence* (St. Catharines, ON: Vanwell Publishing, 2001), 172.
4. *Ibid.*, 155.
5. *Ibid.*, 156.
6. Linda Goetz Holmes, *Unjust Enrichment* (Mechanicsburg, PA: Stackpole Books, 2001), 30.
7. Chater, *Behind the Fence*, 157.
8. Betty Lujan, Interview with author (Santa Fe, New Mexico, 8 July 2002).
9. Chater, *Behind the Fence*, 159.
10. Betty Lujan.
11. Chater, *Behind the Fence*, 159–160.
12. *Ibid.*, 173.
13. *Ibid.*, 163, 186.
14. *Ibid.*, 163.
15. *Ibid.*, 166.
16. *Ibid.*, 168.
17. *Ibid.*, 167.
18. *Ibid.*, 171.
19. *Ibid.*, 182.
20. *Ibid.*, 171.
21. *Ibid.*, 177.
22. *Ibid.*, 178.
23. *Ibid.*, 179.
24. *Ibid.*, 180.
25. *Ibid.*, 183.
26. *Ibid.*, 186.
27. *Ibid.*, 185, 187.
28. *Ibid.*, 188.
29. Prisoner of War Information Bureau, Washington, DC, to Mrs. Jesse Lujan, 15 October 1943 (copy in possession of author).
30. Chater, *Behind the Fence*, 189.
31. Thomas Foy to family of Everett R. Lujan, 26 November 1943 (copy in possession of author).
32. Harry E. Steen, *Experiences in World War II in the Far East* (Hamilton, ON: McMaster University, 1992; copy at NMMM; copy in possession of author), 44.
33. Chater, *Behind the Fence*, 191.
34. *Ibid.*, 193.
35. *Ibid.*, 190–192.
36. *Ibid.*, 193.
37. *Ibid.*, 192.
38. U.S. Army, "Bruns Annual Report, 1944"; "Bruns in Way of Becoming Finest Hospital of Type in U.S.," *Santa Fe New Mexican*, 19 April, 1945, 1, 3.
39. Chater, *Behind the Fence*, 196, 197.
40. *Ibid.*, 196.
41. *Ibid.*, 199.
42. *Ibid.*, 198.
43. *Ibid.*, 201.
44. Thomas B. Allen and Norman Polmar, *Code Name Downfall* (New York: Simon & Schuster, 1995), 85–86, 98–101, 107.
45. *Ibid.*, 154.

Chapter 20

1. Les Chater, with Elizabeth Hamid, *Behind the Fence* (St. Catharines, ON: Vanwell Publishing, 2001), 203.
2. *Ibid.*

3. *Ibid.*, 203–204.
4. *Ibid.*, 204.
5. *Ibid.*
6. *Ibid.*
7. Matthew Braun, Interview with author (Syracuse, New York, 11 January 2004).
8. Linda Goetz Holmes, *Unjust Enrichment* (Mechanicsburg, PA: Stackpole Books, 2001), 30.
9. Chater, *Behind the Fence*, 204.
10. Holmes, *Unjust Enrichment*, 70.
11. Braun.
12. Chater, *Behind the Fence*, 207–208.
13. Braun.
14. Holmes, *Unjust Enrichment*, 66.
15. Chater, *Behind the Fence*, 205.
16. *Ibid.*, 206.
17. Holmes, *Unjust Enrichment*, 110–111, 180.
18. Chater, *Behind the Fence*, 207.
19. *Ibid.*, 209.
20. *Ibid.*, 207–208.
21. *Ibid.*, 209.
22. *Ibid.*, 208.
23. Braun.
24. Chater, *Behind the Fence*, 209.
25. *Ibid.*, 208.
26. *Ibid.*, 209.
27. *Ibid.*, 210.
28. *Ibid.*, 207.
29. *Ibid.*, 212.
30. *Ibid.*, 210, 212.
31. *Ibid.*, 212.
32. *Ibid.*
33. *Ibid.*
34. *Ibid.*, 213.
35. *Ibid.*, 216.
36. *Ibid.*, 215.
37. *Ibid.*
38. Holmes, *Unjust Enrichment*, 115.
39. Chater, *Behind the Fence*, 218–219.
40. *Ibid.*, 219.
41. *Ibid.*, 217.
42. E. Bartlett Kerr, *Surrender and Survival* (New York: William Morrow, 1985), 213–215.
43. Chater, *Behind the Fence*, 218.
44. Claire Guentz, Interview with author (Albuquerque, New Mexico, 5 February 2005).
45. Chater, *Behind the Fence*, 220.
46. *Ibid.*
47. *Ibid.*
48. *Ibid.*, 221.
49. *Ibid.*, 222.
50. Michael Gilewitch, *Moyeh* (ms in possession of author, 1990s), 4–95.
51. Chater, *Behind the Fence*, 223.
52. Mrs. H. Mark Earl to Mrs. L.G. Lujan, 13 April 1945 (copy in possession of author).
53. Washington, DC, to Mrs. L.G. Lujan, 17 April 1945 (copy in possession of author).
54. Chater, *Behind the Fence*, 223.
55. Richard Gordon, with Benjamin S. Llamzon, *Horyo* (St. Paul: Paragon House, 1999), 185.
56. Thomas B. Allen and Norman Polmar, *Code Name Downfall* (New York: Simon & Schuster, 1995), 82.
57. Chater, *Behind the Fence*, 223.
58. *Ibid.*, 224–225.
59. *Ibid.*, 225.
60. *Ibid.*, 225
61. *Ibid.*, 226.
62. *Ibid.*, 224.
63. Allen R. Bosworth, *America's Concentration Camps* (New York: Norton, 1967), 231–232.

Chapter 21

1. Les Chater with Elizabeth Hamid, *Behind the Fence* (St. Catharines, ON: Vanwell Publishing, 2001), 227.
2. *Ibid.*
3. *Ibid.*, 228.
4. *Ibid.*, 227.
5. Linda Goetz Holmes, *Unjust Enrichment: How Japan's Companies Built Postwar Fortunes Using American POWs* (Mechanicsburg, PA: Stackpole Books, 2001), 70.
6. Chater, *Behind the Fence*, 227–228.
7. Dorothy Cave, *Beyond Courage* (Las Cruces, NM: Yucca Free Press, 1992), 348.
8. Ivan Williams to W.F. Kelly, 30 March 1945, Washington, DC (NARA, RG 85, Immigration and Naturalization Service re: Demonstration at Santa Fe Internment Camp, file 1300/P).
9. Chater, *Behind the Fence*, 229–230.
10. *Ibid.*, 230.
11. *Ibid.*
12. *Ibid.*, 231.
13. *Ibid.*, 229.
14. *Ibid.*, 230.
15. *Ibid.*, 231.
16. *Ibid.*, 232.

17. *Ibid.*, 231.
18. Doris Kearns Goodwin, *No Ordinary Time* (New York: Simon & Schuster, 1994), 602.
19. Thomas B. Allen and Norman Polmar, *Code Name Downfall* (New York: Simon & Schuster, 1995), 87.
20. Chater, *Behind the Fence*, 232.
21. *Ibid.*
22. Michael Gilewitch, *Moyeh* (ms in possession of author, 1990s), 4–98 to 4–99.
23. Chater, *Behind the Fence*, 232–233.
24. *Ibid.*, 233.
25. *Ibid.*, 235.
26. *Ibid.*, 234.
27. *Ibid.*
28. *Ibid.*, 235.
29. *Ibid.*
30. Gilewitch, *Moyeh*, 4–95 and 4–96.
31. Harry E. Steen, *Experiences in WWII in the Far East* (Hamilton, ON: McMaster University, 1992; copy at NMMM; copy in possession of author), 55.
32. Allen and Polmar, *Code Name Downfall*, 225.
33. Captain Antonio Martin Report on Visit, 15–16 February 1945, Santa Fe Internment Camp, Washington, DC (NARA, RG 59, Special War Problems Division: Santa Fe folder, box 20, copy in Japanese American Internment Camps Research Material (AC304) at FACHL; W.F. Kelly, Department of Justice, 17 October 1945, re: Santa Fe Internment Camp, Washington, DC (AC304, FACHL).
34. Allen R. Bosworth, *America's Concentration Camps* (New York: Norton, 1967), 233.
35. Captain Antonio Martin Report on Visit, 20 and 22 April 1943, Washington, DC (NARA, RG 59, Special War Problems Division: Santa Fe folder, box 20, copy in Japanese American Internment Camps Research Material (AC304) at FACHL; *Albuquerque Journal*, 5 January 1944 AC304 FACHL).
36. Chater, *Behind the Fence*, 236.
37. *Ibid.*
38. *Ibid.*, 237–238.
39. *Ibid.*, 237.
40. *Ibid.*
41. *Ibid.*, 236.
42. *Ibid.*, 238.
43. *Ibid.*, 240.
44. *Ibid.*, 237.
45. *Ibid.*, 236.
46. Mine Takada to author, October 2009.
47. Chater, *Behind the Fence*, 238–239.
48. *Ibid.*, 238.
49. *Ibid.*, 239.
50. *Ibid.*
51. Allen and Polmar, *Code Name Downfall*, 220.
52. Chater, *Behind the Fence*, 240.
53. *Ibid.*
54. Holmes, *Unjust Enrichment*, 117.
55. Chater, *Behind the Fence*, 241.

Chapter 22

1. E. Bartlett Kerr, *Surrender and Survival* (New York: William Morrow, 1985), 268.
2. Thomas B. Allen and Norman Polmar, *Code Name Downfall* (New York: Simon & Schuster, 1995), 257.
3. Les Chater, with Elizabeth Hamid, *Behind the Fence* (St. Catharines, ON: Vanwell Publishing, 2001), 242.
4. Allen and Polmar, *Code Name Downfall*, 254.
5. *Ibid.*, 266.
6. Richard Rhodes, *The Making of the Atomic Bomb* (New York: Simon & Schuster, 1986), 651.
7. Dorothy Cave, *Beyond Courage* (Las Cruces, NM: Yucca Press, 1992), 354.
8. Robert S. Norris, *Racing for the Bomb* (South Royalton, VT: Steerforth Press, 2002), 420.
9. A.J. Baime, *The Accidental President* (New York: First Mariner Books, 2017), 314.
10. Jim Smith and Malcolm McConnell, *The Last Mission* (New York: Broadway Books, 2002), 99.
11. Rhodes, *The Making of the Atomic Bomb*, 734.
12. Smith and McConnell, *The Last Mission*, 108.
13. *Ibid.*, 106.
14. *Ibid.*, 107.
15. *Ibid.*, 117.
16. Rhodes, *The Making of the Atomic Bomb*, 740–742.
17. Smith and McConnell, *The Last Mission*, 129.
18. *Ibid.*, 148; Rhodes, *The Making of the Atomic Bomb*, 742.

19. Smith and McConnell, *The Last Mission*, 166.
20. *Ibid.*, 184.
21. Allen and Polmar, *Code Name Downfall*, 279.
22. William Manchester, *American Caesar* (Boston: Little, Brown, 1978), 437.
23. Smith and McConnell, *The Last Mission*, 164.
24. Chater, *Behind the Fence*, 243.
25. Harry E. Steen, *Experiences in WWII in the Far East* (Hamilton, ON: McMaster University, 1992; copy at NMMM; copy in possession of author), 57.
26. Chater, *Behind the Fence*, 243.
27. Rhodes, *The Making of the Atomic Bomb*, 744.
28. Allen and Polmar, *Code Name Downfall*, 286.
29. Chater, *Behind the Fence*, 243–244.
30. The Pacific War Research Society, *Japan's Longest Day* (Tokyo: Kodansha International, 2002), 328.
31. Chater, *Behind the Fence*, 243.
32. Allen and Polmar, *Code Name Downfall*, 285.
33. Chater, *Behind the Fence*, 244–245.
34. *Ibid.*, 245.
35. *Ibid.*, 245–246.
36. *Ibid.*, 246–247.
37. *Ibid.*, 246.
38. *Ibid.*, 247.
39. *Ibid.*, 247.
40. *Ibid.*, 248.
41. *Ibid.*, 248.
42. *Ibid.*
43. *Ibid.*, 250.
44. *Ibid.*, 250.
45. *Ibid.*
46. *Ibid.*, 250–251.
47. Steen, *Experiences in WWII*, 74.
48. Donnell Hester, Interview with author (San Antonio, Texas, 10 March 2020).
49. Chater, *Behind the Fence*, 251.

50. Betty Lujan, Interview with author (Santa Fe, New Mexico, 4 February 2002).
51. *Ibid.*
52. U.S. Army, "Bruns Annual Report, 1945" (Military Reference and Research Branch, Medical History Division, Ft. Detrick, Maryland; copy at Bruns General Hospital vertical files (AC704) FACHL).
53. John Pershing Jolly, *History, National Guard of New Mexico, 1606–1963* (Santa Fe: National Guard of New Mexico, 1964), 38.
54. Margaret Garcia, *Tell Me Another War Story* (Maitland, FL: Xulon Press, 2016), 98–100.
55. Doris Kearns Goodwin, *No Ordinary Time* (New York: Simon & Schuster, 1994), 436.
56. Saburō Ienaga, *The Pacific War 1931–1945* (New York: Pantheon Books, 1978), 152.
57. Brother Tim Coldwell, "A History of Bruns General Hospital and Its Subsequent Acquisition by St. Michael's College: 1942–1947" (FACHLPA: Research paper, 1977).
58. Betty Lujan, Interview with author (Santa Fe, New Mexico, 8 July 2002).
59. Franklin E. Miles, Adjutant General of New Mexico, retired, Interview with author (Santa Fe, New Mexico, 8 March 2007).

Epilogue

1. Betty Lujan, Interview with author (Santa Fe, New Mexico, 4 February 2002).
2. Richard Gordon, Telephone interview with author (New York, 14 July 2002).
3. Gavan Daws, *Prisoners of the Japanese* (New York: William Morrow, 1994), 373.
4. Betty Lujan, Interview with author (Santa Fe, New Mexico, 8 July 2002).

References

Allen, Thomas B., and Norman Polmar. *Code Name Downfall: The Secret Plan to Invade Japan and Why Truman Dropped the Bomb.* Simon & Schuster, New York, 1995.
Baime, A.J. *The Accidental President: Harry S. Truman and the Four Months That Changed the World.* First Mariner Books, Houghton Mifflin Harcourt, New York, 2017.
Billings, Richard N. *Battleground Atlantic: How the Sinking of a Single Japanese Submarine Assured the Outcome of World War II.* New American Library Caliber, New York, 2006.
Bodine, Roy L. "No Place for Kindness: The Prisoner of War Diary of Roy L. Bodine." Copy of ms. with author; original at Fort Sam Houston Museum, San Antonio, Texas, 1983.
Bosworth, Allen R. *America's Concentration Camps.* W.W. Norton, New York, 1967.
Brett, Edward, and Donna Brett. "Santa Fe's Shameful 'Jap Trap.'" *The Santa Fe Reporter,* 15 February 1984, p. 11.
Brown, Andrew. *Transatlantic Travails in The Manhattan Project: The Birth of the Atomic Bomb in the Words of its Creators, Eyewitnesses, and Historians.* Cynthia C. Kelly (editor). Black Dog & Leventhal New York, 2007.
Buckmeir, Jack R. *Coast Artillery Technical Manual.* Graphic Services and Manufacturing, Portland, Oregon, 1996.
Caraccilo, Dominic J. *Surviving Bataan and Beyond: Colonel Irvin Alexander's Odyssey as a Japanese Prisoner of War.* Stackpole Books, Mechanicsburg, Pennsylvania, 1999.
Cave, Dorothy. *Beyond Courage: Our Regiment Against Japan 1941-1945.* Yucca Press, Las Cruces, New Mexico, 1992.
Chang, Iris. *The Rape of Nanking: The Forgotten Holocaust of World War II.* Basic Books, New York, 1997.
Chater, Les, with Elizabeth Hamid. *Behind the Fence: Life as a POW in Japan 1942-1945—The Diaries of Les Chater.* Vanwell Publishing Limited, St. Catharines, Ontario, 2001.
Coldwell, Brother Tim. "A History of Bruns General Hospital and Its Subsequent Acquisition by St. Michael's College 1942-1947." FACHL (AC704) 1977.
Coleman, John S., Jr. *Bataan and Beyond: Memories of an American POW.* Texas A & M University Press, College Station, 1978.
Conant, Jennet. *A Covert Affair: Julia Child and Paul Child in the OSS.* Simon & Schuster, New York, 2011.
Conant, Jennet. *109 East Palace: Robert Oppenheimer and the Secret City of Los Alamos.* Simon & Schuster, New York, 2005.
Connaughton, Richard. *MacArthur's Defeat in the Philippines.* Overlook Press, Woodstock, New York, 2001.
Cox, First Sgt. Frank (Ret). *Enlisted Soldier's Guide, 4th Edition.* Stackpole Books, Mechanicsburg, Pennsylvania, 1996.
Cutler, Thomas J. *The Battle of Leyte Gulf 23-26 October 1944.* HarperCollins, New York, 1994.
Daly, Richard J. "Me—A Biography for My Children." Ms. in possession of the author; Veteran of the 200th/515th Coast Artillery (AA), interviewed, Santa Fe, New Mexico, 2002.

Daws, Gavan. *Prisoners of the Japanese: POWs of World War II in the Pacific*. William Morrow, New York, 1994.
Dickson, Paul. *War Slang: American Fighting Words & Phrases Since the Civil War*. Dover, Mineola, New York, 2011.
Egan, Timothy. *The Worst Hard Time: The Untold Story of Those Who Survived the Great American Dust Bowl*. Houghton Mifflin, New York, 2006.
Enright, Capt. Joseph F. (USN), with James W. Ryan. *Shinano! The Sinking of Japan's Secret Supership*. St. Martin's Press, New York, 1987.
Fort Detrick, Maryland. "Bruns Annual Report, Military Reference and Research Branch, Medical History Division, Fort Detrick, Maryland." Copy at FACHL, 1944.
Gabaldon, Guy. *Saipan: Suicide Island*. Guy Gabaldon, Saipan Island, U.S.A., 1990.
Garcia, Margaret. *Tell Me Another War Story: The Life of Evans Garcia Courageous Soldier, American Hero, My Dad*. Xulon Pres, 2016.
Gilewitch, Michael. *Moyeh*. Ms. in possession of author, n.d.
Gillespie, James O. *Recollections of the Pacific War and Japanese Prisoner of War Camps 1941-1945*. Ms. in the NMMM, 1975.
Goette, John. *Japan Fight for Asia*. Harcourt, Brace, New York, 1943.
Goldberg, Harold J. *D-Day in the Pacific: The Battle of Saipan*. Indiana University Press, Bloomington, 2007.
Goodwin, Doris Kearns. *No Ordinary Time: Franklin and Eleanor Roosevelt: The Home Front in World War II*. Simon & Schuster, New York, 1994.
Gordon, Richard, with Benjamin S. Llamzon. *Horyo: Memoirs of an American POW*. Paragon House, St. Paul, Minnesota, 1999.
Greene, Bob. *Duty: A Father, His Son, and the Man Who Won the War*. William Morrow, New York, 2000.
Hastings, Max. *Retribution: The Battle for Japan 1944-1945*. Alfred A. Knopf, New York, 2007.
Hersey, John. *Hiroshima*. Alfred A. Knopf, New York, 1946.
Hillenbrand, Laura. *Unbroken: A World War II Story of Survival, Resilience, and Redemption*. Random House, New York, 2010.
Holmes, Linda Goetz. *Unjust Enrichment: How Japan's Companies Built Postwar Fortunes Using American POWs*. Stackpole Books, Mechanicsburg, Pennsylvania, 2001.
Hook, Alex. *World War II Day by Day*. Grange Books, Kent, United Kingdom, 2004.
Hoyt, Edwin P. *How They Won the War in the Pacific: Nimitz and His Admirals*. Weybright and Talley, New York, 1970.
Ienaga, Saburō. *The Pacific War 1931-1945: A Critical Perspective on Japan's Role in World War II by a Leading Japanese Scholar*. Pantheon Books, New York, 1978.
Ishida, Jintaro. *The Remains of War: Apology and Forgiveness*. Lyons Press/Globe Pequot, Guilford, Connecticut, 2002.
Jenkins, Myra Ellen, and Albert H. Schroeder. *A Brief History of New Mexico*. University of New Mexico Press, Albuquerque, 1988.
Johnson, Forrest Bryant. *Phantom Warrior*. Berkley Caliber, New York, 2007.
Jolly, John Pershing. *New Mexico National Guard 1606-1963*. State of New Mexico, Santa Fe, 1964.
Keith, Agnes Newton. *Three Came Home*. Atlantic Monthly Press, Little, Brown, Boston, 1947.
Kelly, Cynthia (editor). *The Manhattan Project: The Birth of the Atomic Bomb in the Words of Its Creators, Eyewitnesses, and Historians*. Black Dog and Leventhal, New York, 2007.
Kerr, E. Bartlett. *Surrender and Survival: The Experience of American POWs in the Pacific 1941-1945*. William Morrow, New York, 1985.
Lawton, Manny. *Some Survived*. Algonquin Books, Chapel Hill, North Carolina, 1984.
Malkin, Michelle. *In Defense of Internment: The Case for "Racial Profiling" in World War II and the War on Terror*. Regnery, Washington, D.C., 2004.
Malloné, Col. Richard C. *Battle for Bataan*. Presidio Press, New York, 1980.
Manchester, William. *American Caesar: Douglas MacArthur 1880-1964*. Little, Brown, Boston, 1978.

References 241

Matson, Eva Jane. *It Told for New Mexico: New Mexicans Captured by the Japanese 1941-1945*. Yucca Press, Las Cruces, New Mexico, 1994.

Matson, Eva Jane (editor). *Heroes of Bataan, Corregidor and Northern Luzon*. Marcus Griffin, Carlsbad, New Mexico, 1994.

Mellnik, Stephen M. "The Life and Death of the 200th Artillery (AA)." *Coast Artillery Journal*, March 1941-April 1947.

Morton, Louis. *The Fall of the Philippines. United States Army in World War II—The War in the Pacific*. Center of Military History, United States Army, Washington, D.C., 1989.

Mosley, Leonard. *Hirohito Emperor of Japan*. Prentice-Hall, Englewood Cliffs, New Jersey, 1966.

Nelson, Craig. *The First Heroes: The Extraordinary Story of the Doolittle Raid—America's First World War II Victory*. Viking Penguin, New York, 2002.

Norman, Elizabeth M. *We Band of Angels: The Untold Story of American Nurses Trapped on Bataan by the Japanese*. Random House, New York, 1999.

Norris, Robert S. *Racing for the Bomb: General Leslie R. Groves, the Manhattan Project's Indispensable Man*. Steerforth Press, South Royalton, Vermont, 2002.

Okada, Koichiro Okada. "Significant Dates and Events of the Nikkei Ethnohistory." Appendix I of thesis. Copy in the Japanese American Internment Camps Research Material (AC304) at the FACHL, n.d.

Olson, John E. *O'Donnell: Andersonville of the Pacific—Extermination Camp of American Hostages in the Philippines*. John E. Olson, Lake Quivira, Kansas, 1985.

The Pacific War Research Society. *Japan's Longest Day*. Kodansha International, Tokyo, Japan, 2002.

Peck, Colonel Harry M. "200th and 515th Coast Artillery Regiments, New Mexico National Guard, Siege and Fall of Bataan, Life in Japanese Prisons." Ms. in the NMNGMA, n.d.

Rhodes, Richard. *The Making of the Atomic Bomb*. Simon & Schuster, New York, 1986

Russell, Lord (of Liverpool). *The Knights of Bushido: The Shocking History of Japanese War Atrocities*. E.P. Dutton, New York, 1956.

Sherman, John. *Santa Fe: A Pictorial History*. Donning Co., Norfolk, Virginia, 1996.

Sherrow, Victoria. *Hiroshima*. Silver Burdett Press, 1994.

Sloan, Bill. *Undefeated: America's Heroic Fight for Bataan and Corregidor*. Simon & Schuster, New York, 2012.

Smith, Holland M., and Percy Finch. *Coral and Brass*. Charles Scribner's Sons, New York, 1949.

Smith, Jim, and Malcolm McConnell. *The Last Mission*. Broadway Books, New York, 2002.

Snell, Roy J. *Secrets of Radar*. The Goldsmith Publishing Co., Chicago, Illinois, 1944.

Spector, Ronald H. *Eagle Against the Sun*. Macmillan Wars of the United States. Free Press, Macmillan, New York, 1985.

Steen, Harry E. "Experiences in World War II in the Far East: The Philippines and Niigata, Japan." Dictated reminiscences transcribed as Interview No. HCM 11-92 for the Oral History Archives Hannah Chair for the History of Medicine, McMaster University, Hamilton, Ontario, L8N 3Z5. Copy in the NMMM, 1992.

Takada, Mine. Letter to author, member of the Pow Research Network Japan, http://www.powresearch.jp, 2009.

Tobias, Henry J., and Charles E. Woodhouse. *Santa Fe 1880-1990: A Modern History*. University of New Mexico Press, Albuquerque, 2001.

Toll, Ian W. *The Conquering Tide: War in the Pacific Islands, 1942-1944*. W.W. Norton, New York, 2015.

Toll, Ian W. *The Pacific Crucible: War at Sea in the Pacific, 1941-1942*. W.W. Norton, New York, 2012.

U.S. Government Printing Office. *Abbreviated Firing Tables*. War Department, Washington, D.C., 1942.

U.S. Government Printing Office. *Basic Field Manual—Military Training*. War Department, Washington, D.C., 1941.

U.S. Government Printing Office. *Basic Field Manual—Soldier's Handbook*. War Department, U.S. Government Printing Office, Washington, D.C., 1941.

U.S. Government Printing Office. *Coast Artillery Field Manual—Antiaircraft Artillery.* War Department, Washington, D.C., 1933.
U.S. Government Printing Office. *Engineer Field Manual—Camouflage.* War Department, Washington, D.C., 1940.
U.S. Government Printing Office. *Gunnery Field Artillery.* War Department, Washington, D. C., 1936.
U.S. Government Printing Office. *Prisoners of War.* War Department, Washington, D.C., 1991.
U.S. Government Printing Office. *Technical Manual—Mess Management.* War Department, Washington, D.C., 1940.
Van der Post, Laurens. *A Bar of Shadow.* William Morrow, New York, 1956.
Vincent, Lynn, and Sara Vladic. *Indianapolis.* Simon & Schuster, New York, 2018.
Webber, Bert. *Silent Siege: Japanese Attacks on North America in World War II—Ships Sunk, Air Raids, Bombs Dropped, Civilians Killed.* Webb Research Group, Medford, Oregon, 1983.
White, W.L. *They Were Expendable.* H. Wolff, New York, 1942.
Whitman, John W. *Bataan: Our Last Ditch.* Hippocrene Books, New York, 1990.
Wirth, John D., and Linda Harvey Aldrich. *Los Alamos: The Ranch School Years: 1917–1943.* University of New Mexico Press, Albuquerque, 2003.
Wright, John M., Jr. *Captured on Corregidor: Diary of an American POW in WWII.* McFarland, Jefferson, North Carolina, 1988.
Young, Donald J. *Battle of Bataan.* McFarland, Jefferson, North Carolina, 2009.

Interviews

Braun, Matthew. Interview with author, 11 January 2004, Syracuse, New York. Veteran of the 192nd Tank Battalion and POW at Mitsushima and Kanose POW camps.
Daly, Richard. Interview with author, 1 September 2005, Santa Fe, New Mexico. Veteran of the 200th and 515th Coast Artillery (AA), instructor of antiaircraft height finder technology, and POW of the Japanese.
Gordon, Richard. Interview with author, 14 July 2002, via telephone call to New York. MP with the Philadelphia Division and POW at Mitsushima.
Guentz, Claire. Interview with author, 5 February 2005, Albuquerque, New Mexico. Errett Lujan's sister.
Lujan, Betty. Interview with author, 8 July 2002, Santa Fe, New Mexico. Errett Lujan's wife.
Miles, Gen. Franklin E. (ret.). Interview with author, 8 March 2007, Santa Fe, New Mexico. Formerly the Adjutant General of the New Mexico National Guard, son of Governor John E. Miles.
Mosely, John. Interview with author, May 2009, Santa Fe, New Mexico. Veteran of the 200th and 515th Coast Artillery (AA) and POW of the Japanese.
Overmeir, William. Interview with author, 2 May 2009, San Antonio, Texas. Veteran of the 200th Coast Artillery (AA) and POW of the Japanese. Interview conducted during the last ADBC held.
Reyna, Tony. Interview with author, 1 November 2005, Taos Pueblo, New Mexico. Veteran of the 200th Coast Artillery (AA) and POW of the Japanese.
Shillito, Winston. Interview with Air Force Captain Jonathan Cohen, 4 February 1997, El Paso, Texas, copy at the NMNGM. Veteran of the 200th and 515th Coast Artillery (AA) and POW of the Japanese.
VanBuskirk, Francis. Interview with author, 25 October 2006, Santa Fe, New Mexico. Veteran of the 200th Coast Artillery (AA) and POW of the Japanese.
Williams, Sally Atwell. Interview with author, 10 June 2004, Elkton, Virginia. Daughter of Corporal John Atwell, veteran of the 194th Tank Battalion and POW of the Japanese at Mitsushima and Kanose POW Camps.

Index

Abucay *see* Philippine Islands
Adams, Don 191
Adams, Dr. Lytle S. 150
Aiken, James 221, 223
aircraft: Australian 66; B-17 Flying Fortress 34, 41, 45, 176; B-24 Liberator 150; B-25 Mitchell 98-99; B-29 Superfortress 176, 192, 195, 197, 205-206, 211, 214; biplanes 198; *Bock's Car* 207; C-54 Skymaster 214; *Enola Gay* 205-206; *The Great Artiste* 205; *Jabbit III* 205; Japanese 11, 39, 47, 52, 59, 89, 115; *No. 91* 205; P-40 29, 34, 41, 43, 45, 49, 57-58, 66-67, 70-72; *Straight Flush* 205; United States 22-23, 29, 34, 41, 45, 98, 150, 185, 204, 206; Zeros 42-44, 49-50, 67, 70, 83
airfields: 63, 98-99; Bataan 56-57, 60, 66, 83-84, 86; Cabcaben 56, 58, 66, 85, 88-89, 90; Clark 32-34, 36-37, 40-45, 49-50, 54, 56, 77, 96, 105; Iba 43; Kirtland 215; Monte 52; Nichols 43-46, 50, 52-53, 77; Nielson 44; Pilar 70; Sangley Point 32; Zablan 53
airplanes *see* aircraft
Alamogordo Bombing Range 202, 207
Alaska 197, Kiska 150
Albuquerque *see* New Mexico
Albuquerque Journal 37
Alcatraz 27-28
American Defenders of Bataan and Corregidor 3, 73
Amori *see* Prisoner of War Camps
Anderson, Clinton P. 149
Angel Island 27-28, 32
Anzac Day 105
Aparri *see* Philippine Islands
US *Archer-Fish see* watercraft
Archey, James 223
Ardmore *see* Oklahoma
Army: British 184, 193, 201, 210; Japanese 48, 53, 62, 64, 67, 77-78, 86, 89, 93, 105-106, 112, 120, 132, 174, 178, 191, 200-201, 206, 208, 210; Philippine 45, 48, 63, 67, 70-71, 82, 86, 94, 108; United States 2, 6, 9, 11, 13-22, 27-28, 31-32, 34-35, 39-42, 47-48, 51, 59-63, 68-69, 71, 77-78, 80, 82-84, 86, 90, 97-98, 101, 105, 109, 114, 145-146, 150, 163-165, 177, 182, 190-191, 198, 201, 213, 216-219; U.S. Confederate Army 88
Army Air Corps (U.S.) 32, 103
Army Day 21
Artesia *see* New Mexico
Atimonan *see* Philippine Islands
Atnip, Bill (P. Beverly F.) 223
atomic bomb 209, 217; Fat Man 207; Hiroshima 205-207; Kokura 205, 207; Little Boy 204-207; Nagasaki 205, 207; Niigata 205; pursuits in Germany 204; pursuits in Japan 195, 206; pursuits in U.S. 204; targets 207
Attlee, Clement 201, 208
Atwell, Jack 223
Australia 66-67, 71, 73, 77, 90, 102, 105, 122, 130, 160, 167, 177
Austria, Vienna 194-195
Azuma, Hiroshi 173-176, 178-179, 184-185, 187, 190, 193-198, 200, 202, 209-211, 220

Bagac *see* Philippine Islands
Baggy Pants *see* Yoshio Tsuneyoshi
Baguio *see* Philippine Islands
Bandish, Kid (William E.) 223
Bangkok, Thailand 177
Barry, Jim (James) 223
Bataan *see* Philippine Islands
Bataan Airfield *see* airfields
Bataan Day 218
Bataan Death March 1, 55, 96, 102, 177, 191, 220

243

Index

Bataan Defense Force 60
Batangus *see* Philippine Islands
Battle of Midway 99, 106, 117, 203
Battle of Quinauan 66
Battle of the Java Sea *see* Java
Battling Bastards (of Bataan) 70
Bayard *see* New Mexico
Belen *see* New Mexico
Bell, Don 39
beriberi 102, 110, 125, 134, 162, 177
Berlin, Germany 195
Berry, Cullen W. 223
Big Glass Eye *see* Hiramatsu, Sadaharu
Bilibid *see* Prisoner of War Camps
biplanes *see* aircraft
The Bird *see* Watanabe, Mutsuhiro
Black River *see* New Mexico
boats *see* watercraft
Bock's Car see aircraft
Bodillo, Lucille 25, 50, 183–184
Boise City *see* Oklahoma
Bolin, (P) Bedford 223
Bolivia 197
bombers *see* aircraft
Boswell *see* Oklahoma
Bougainville 151
Boyer, Jack 72
Bradley, Omar 181
Brancaticano, Frank 176
Braun, E.D. (P. Matthew) vi, 172, 174, 223
Braun, Eva 195
Brokaw, Glenn 223
Brown, Betty 25
Brown, Bill W. 11–12, 17, 19, 23, 25, 45, 106, 108, 110, 127, 134, 141, 215, 220, 222
Brown, Mrs. 12, 25, 127, 222
Bruns, Earl Harvey 146
Bruns Army Hospital 13, 101, 144–146, 156, 165, 198, 215–218
Buchan, John 193
Buick *see* Kirishita, Takeo
Bulldog *see* Saito Kiromitzu
Burke, Arthur J. 142
Burma 130, 175; Burma-Thailand railway 177
Bushido 8, 10, 194

Cabanatuan *see* Prisoner of War Camps
Cabcaben *see* Philippine Islands
Cagayanos 48
Cain, Memory H. 45
Calumpit Bridge *see* Philippine Islands
camote 103, 112
Camp John Hay 32, 43
Camp Luna *see* New Mexico
Capas *see* Philippine Islands

carabao 63–64, 66
Carey, Ohio 223
cargo planes *see* aircraft
Carlsbad *see* New Mexico
Caroline Islands 176
Cartersville *see* Oklahoma
cassava 112
cavalry 23, 32; horses 63, 69
Cavite *see* Philippine Islands
Cavite Navy Base *see* Navy Bases
Celebes 130
Chang, Iris 9
Charlton, Gen. Russell 14, 47, 97, 101
Chater, Les 194
Chavez, Ben T. 191
Chavez, Joe D. 191
Chavez, Mike 115, 119, 149, 223
Chavez, Raymond 119, 129, 137, 142
Chicago 20, 223
China 7–11, 36, 53, 99, 117, 130, 132, 160, 168; Hankow 9; Hong Kong 39, 57, 177, 191; Nanking 9, 11; Shanghai 9, 103; Tientsen 44; Yangtze Valley 9
cholera 110
Churchill, Winston 10, 155, 175, 201
Civilian Conservation Corps camps 79–80, 128
Civilian Volunteer Corps (Japanese) 197
Clayton *see* New Mexico
Clovis *see* New Mexico
Coast Artillery 40, 45; 59th Regiment 40; 60th Regiment 40; 63rd Regiment 22–23; 91st 40; 92nd 40; 515th 45, 82, 87, 142; 200th 1, 3, 15–16, 19, 21, 23, 39–40, 45, 77, 82, 87, 90, 100, 142, 217, 219; 206th 23; 207th 14; 260th 23; Groupment A (AA) 82; Philippine Provisional Coast Artillery Brigade 87–88; Provisional Manila Group 45; Second CA 82
Coleman, William 42
College of Christian Brothers 217
USS *Conopus see* watercraft
USS *Coolidge see* watercraft
Cordillera *see* Philippine Islands
Corregidor *see* Philippine Islands
Cory, Allen 157, 223
Cosmoline 46
Coyote *see* New Mexico
Crowdell, Jack 193
cruisers *see* watercraft
Culo Bridge *see* Philippine Islands
Cupp, Burlin C. 179, 223
Czechoslovakia 206

Daly, Richard (Dick) vi, 11, 17, 41, 43, 58
Damortis *see* Philippine Islands

Davao *see* Philippine Islands and Prisoner of War Camps
de Haviland, Olivia 165
Dement, David A. 179, 223
Deming *see* New Mexico
dengue fever 29
Denmark 196
Denver, Colorado 190
Derr, Roger 141–142
destroyers *see* watercraft
diphtheria 111, 134
Doho Japanese-American newspaper 75
Domei News Agency 208
Dominican Republic 197
Don Esteban see watercraft
Doolittle, James 98–99, 151
Drummon, Orville 191
Duncan, Joe 119
Dunkirk 11
Dunn, Eugene C. 183–184, 211, 223
Dust Bowl 5, 7, 9, 12
dysentery 29, 65, 72, 109–111, 121–122, 125, 134, 137, 199
Dyson, Bessie 186

Earl, Mrs. H. Mark 185
Eaton, Bill (William) 223
ECR 268 49
Eisenhower, Dwight D. 181
El Nido 218, 220
El Paso, Texas 6, 16, 19, 21, 25, 193
enemy aliens 80, 188
England *see* Great Britain
Engle, Elmer 154
Eniwetok 188
Ennis, Earle 223
Enola Gay see aircraft
USS *Enterprise see* watercraft
Exclusion Act 8
Executive Order 9066 78, 188

Fat Man *see* atomic bomb
Faulkner, Ace E. 140, 223
Fay, Burnise L. 191
Fernandez, V.R. 145, 181
Field Orders No. 13 205
Fields, Bernard A. 223
59th Coast Artillery (antiaircraft) *see* military units
Findley, William J. 164
Fisser, L.F., 150
515th Coast Artillery (antiaircraft) *see* military units
fleas 159, 178, 203, 214
flying fortress *see* aircraft
Formosa 36, 39, 122, 130, 164, 191

Fort Bliss 1, 6, 16–27, 33–34, 49, 101, 184
Fort Dodge, Iowa 223
Fort McDowell 27
Fort McKinley 32, 44
Fort Mills *see* Philippine Islands
Fort Sam Houston 218–219
Fort Santiago 45–46
Fort Stotsenburg 30–34, 36–37, 39–40, 43–44, 47, 49, 59, 105
Fortress Monroe 14
Foster, John 193
Foy, Thomas 163
Foy, Tom 119, 125, 163
France 9, 175; Burgandy 177; Dunkirk 11; Normandy 177; Paris 181; Rheims 196
Franklin Mountains *see* New Mexico
Fujii, Shuji 75
Fulford-Williams, Henry Charles Ralph "Pinky" 129

Gachupin, Gregorio 49
Gallup *see* New Mexico
Gamble, John 43
Garcia, Evans 17, 217
Gavord, Charles 119, 180, 223
Gearhart Mountain 115
Geneva Convention 8, 90, 100, 114, 182, 184
Germany 10, 37, 49, 145, 185, 193, 196, 204; POWs 12, 168
Gilewitch, Michael 35, 88, 93, 195
Gilroy, California 78
Ginther, Garth 142
Globe, Arizona 223
Gobunko 208
Goff, Marshall W. 223
Golden Boy 221
Golden Gate Bridge 28, 204
Gomez, Frank 22
Gone with the Wind 17, 45
Gonzales, Rubel 191
Gordon, Richard (Albert Gordon) vi, 221
USS *Grant see* watercraft
Grassick, Paul A. 153, 223
Great American Depression 7, 9, 12, 79
The Great Artiste see aircraft
Great Britain 10–11, 29, 39, 49, 57, 67, 77, 119, 130, 136, 157, 164, 166, 193, 201, 208, 210, 223; army *see* army; Dorset 223; High Wycombe 223; Leicester 193; Liverpool 180; London 11, 223; Middlesex 193; POWs 67, 77, 102, 105, 122, 129–130, 134, 137, 139, 142, 152, 155, 159, 160, 163–164, 169, 174, 177–181, 184, 190, 193–194, 201, 211, 213–214, 223; uniforms 210, 213, 224

Great Plains 12, 33
Greater East Asia Co-Prosperity Sphere 9–10, 17, 37
Gross Kelly 221
Groves, James 153
Groves, Leslie R. 144
Guadalcanal 136, 188
Guam 39, 44, 168, 208

Hagerman *see* New Mexico
Hague Treaty 8
Haiti 197
Hamada, Major 175
Hankow *see* China
Hashimoto, Ruth 80
Hawaii 2, 27, 28–29, 32, 36–37, 197; Honolulu 28–29; Pearl Harbor 1–2, 10, 12, 26, 34, 36–37, 39–40, 75, 78, 98, 119, 151
Hayes, Albert 191
Hayes, Winfred D. 142
Hendrickson, Clarence 142
Hester, Betty McDaniel 218, 220; *see also* Lujan, Betty
Hewitt, Walter J. 119–120, 136, 140, 157, 159, 184, 196, 212, 223
Higgins, Don 19
Hiramatsu, Sadaharu 130, 164, 170, 220–221
Hiraoka *see* Prisoner of War Camps
Hirohito 8–9, 36, 38, 90, 105, 111, 136, 141, 184, 193, 207–210, 212
Hitler, Adolf 10, 181, 195
Holstein, A. Jay 223
Homma, Masaharu 36, 39, 48, 53, 62, 70–71, 82–83, 94
Hong Kong *see* China
USS *Hornet see* watercraft
Houk, Howard 145, 153, 168
Howden, Frederick 69
Hull, Cordell 37
Hunter, Kenneth 137, 142
Hyde, Revis C. 223

Idaho Falls, Idaho 185
Igorots 48, 70
Imperial Palace 186, 207–209
Imperial Rescript 208–209; *see also* surrender, Japan
US *Indianapolis see* watercraft
internment camps: German 80; (Japanese) Heart Mountain 80; Santa Fe 13–14, 80, 100, 128, 189, 198, 217; U.S. 80, 100;
Intramuros *see* Philippine Islands
Iowa National Guard *see* National Guard

Ishibe, Kiyoji 172, 221
Issei 79–80
Italy 160, 196
Ivey, James 48
Ivy, John B 223
Iwanaka, Major 115
Iwatia 132
Iwo Jima 191–193

Jabbitt III see aircraft
Jackson, Asa A. 142
Japan: army *see* army; Hiraoka 124; Hiraoka Dam 132; Hiroshima 205–207; Honshu 99, 122, 126, 169–170, 200; Kobe 99, 192, 197, 200; Kokura 205, 207; Kyushu 213, 247; Ministry of Health 217; Mitsushima 1, 124–172, 174, 176, 186, 190, 211, 221; Moji 122, 125–126, 197; Nagano Prefecture 125; Nagaoka 203; Nagasaki 205, 207, 215; Nagato 122; Nagoya 99, 167, 192, 200; Niigata 134, 187, 195, 200, 205, 208, 211–212; Niigata Bay 197; Niigata Prefecture 170; Okinawa 167, 177, 194–195, 197, 203, 209, 214–215; Osaka 123–124, 167, 185, 191–192, 197, 200; Takao 122; Tanagawa 123; Tenryū River 125, 129, 132, 138, 141; Tokyo 98–99, 106, 135, 139, 142, 151, 154, 157, 159–165, 167–168, 170–171, 175, 191–193, 195–197, 200–201, 205, 207, 209–210, 215; Tokyo Bay 212–213; Toyama River 125; Umbeda 124; Yokohama 99, 191–192, 197, 200, 213; Yokosuka 99
Java 129, 197, 201; Battle of the Java Sea 77
Johnson, Leo L. 223
Jones, Bob 223
Jones, Eugene 223
Jones, Verble 147, 179–180, 192, 194, 224
Jornada del Muerto *see* New Mexico

kamikaze 202, 253
Kamijo 132
Kanagawa, Shotaro 3, 172, 199, 200, 212–213
Kaneyama, Hisao 192, 194, 196, 220
Kanose *see* Prisoner of War Camps
Kawane, Yashikanda 94
Kawasaki Camp *see* Prisoner of War Camps; steamers 119; steel 201
Keller, Helen 165
Kentucky, Lexington 154; St. John's 223; West Point 223
Kimura, Tamotsu 130, 162, 220
King, Edward P. 71–72, 87–89, 102
Kingen 177
Kirishita, Takeo 130, 168, 220

Index 247

Kirtland Army Air Base *see* airfields
Klamath Falls, Oregon 201, 225
Klassen, Ray 224
Koiso, Kuniake 177
Kojima, Captain 182
Kolilis, P. Fred 224
komodi 161
Kondō, Hisaku 7
Korea 7–10, 117, 129, 138, 158–159
Krause, Gusta R. 142
Kumagai Engineering Company 132
Kumi Electric Company 155
Kwajalein 188

Lamao *see* Philippine Islands
Lane, Dr. 177, 191
Las Vegas *see* New Mexico
Legaspi *see* Philippine Islands
Letterman General Hospital 215
Leyte *see* Philippine Islands
Liberator *see* aircraft
Lily, Donald 224
Limay *see* Philippine Islands
Limpert, Daniel C. 191
Lindbergh, Charles 177
Lingayen *see* Philippine Islands
Lisbon Maru see watercraft
Little Boy *see* atomic bomb
Little Glass Eye *see* Tsuchiya, Tatsuo
Lobe, John A. 224
Logan Heights 19, 101
Lopez, Genaro (Jimmy) 11–12, 17
Lordsburg *see* New Mexico
Los Alamos *see* New Mexico
Los Alamos Ranch School 145
Los Baños *see* Philippine Islands
Louisiana 24, 179; Collinston 225; Elm Grove 223
Lufkin, Texas 223
Lujan, Andres 35
Lujan, Betty vi, 218, 220, 221 *also see* Hester, Betty McDaniel
Lujan, Carlos 146
Lujan, Claire vi, 5, 26, 75–76, 153, 165–166, 183, 190–191, 215
Lujan, Ernie 146
Lujan, Jake 221
Lujan, Jess 5, 12, 15–16, 25–26, 47, 67, 75–76, 100, 136, 141, 144, 149, 153, 156, 160–161, 165, 173, 176, 178, 180, 186, 190, 214–215
Lujan, Louis 5, 15–16, 19, 25–26, 47, 75–76, 101, 143, 145, 153, 156, 160, 176, 191, 215–216
Lujan, Manuel, Sr. 98
Lujan, Merle 5, 22, 25–26, 31, 34–35, 47, 50–51, 68, 72, 75–77, 85, 114, 153, 156, 160–161, 165–166, 168, 173, 180, 183, 186, 190, 194, 202
Luzon *see* Philippine Islands

MacArthur, Douglas 9, 15, 28, 40, 48, 57, 59, 66, 68, 71–73, 90, 105, 155, 181, 182, 190–191, 203, 205, 208
Macheta 158, 160, 162, 164–165, 168
Makin atoll 163
malaria 29, 60, 65, 72, 102, 110
Malaya 130, 145, 169
Malaysia 129, 169
Malinta Tunnel *see* Philippine Islands
Manchuko 37
Manchuria 7, 9–10, 130
Manhattan Project 144–145, 204; *see also* atomic bomb
Manila *see* Philippine Islands
Mann, Willie 224
Mansfield, Ohio 223
Marble, Verner 224
Mariana Islands 176–177, 205
Mariveles *see* Philippine Islands
Marshall, George C. 11, 203, 205
Martindale, Don A. 192, 194, 224
Matsu, James 80
Matsumoto Hospital 134
Matsuzaki 130, 220
McAfee, Larry B. 146
Meem, John Gaw 13
Mexhoma *see* Oklahoma
Meyers, Bill 45
Michishita, Masanobu 221
Middle Kingdom 7
Middlesex, England 193
Midway *see* Battle of Midway
Miles, John E. 13–14, 20, 75–77, 79, 98, 100, 101, 218–219
military units: Eleventh Airborne 191; First Cavalry 229; 14th Bombardment Squadron 29; Twenty-sixth Cavalry 53, 56, 69; Fifty-first Infantry Battalion 157; 59th Coast Artillery (antiaircraft) 40; 60th Coast Artillery (antiaircraft) 40; 63rd Coast Artillery (antiaircraft) 22–23; 91st Coast Artillery (antiaircraft) Philippine Scouts 40; 92nd Coast Artillery (antiaircraft) Philippine Scouts 40; 111th Regiment of Cavalry 15; 192nd Tank Battalion 67; 200th Coast Artillery (antiaircraft) 1, 3, 15–29, 32–34, 37–47, 49, 56–59, 61, 63, 65, 69, 71, 77, 85–91, 96, 100, 111, 142, 150, 161, 191, 215–217, 219; 206th Coast Artillery (antiaircraft) 22–23; 207th

248 Index

Coast Artillery (antiaircraft) 14; 260th Coast Artillery (antiaircraft) 22; 515th Coast Artillery (antiaircraft) 45–49, 54–60, 62–63, 65, 69, 71, 77, 82, 84–85, 87–89, 91, 96, 142, 180, 215; Philippine Provisional Coast Artillery Brigade (Scouts) 87–88; Philippine Scouts 40, 53, 57, 63, 71, 84–85, 87; Provisional Manila Group 45; Reserve Force 40
Minagawa, Tokio 172, 221
Mindinao *see* Philippine Islands
USS *Mindanao see* watercraft
Mindoro *see* Philippine Islands
USS *Missouri see* watercraft
Mitchell, Arthur (Archie) J. 115, 201, 224
Mitchell, Elsye 115
Mitchell, B-25 *see* aircraft
Mitsushima *see* Prisoner of War Camps
Mongolia 10
Montezuma Hotel 17
Montoya, Tony 217
Mori, Shigeji 105, 109, 114–115
Morris, Janis 177, 181, 188
Moulmein 177
Mount Arayat *see* Philippine Islands
Mount Natib *see* Philippine Islands
Mount Pinatubo *see* Philippine Islands
Mount Samat *see* Philippine Islands
Mount Santa Rosa *see* Philippine Islands
Mount Silanganan *see* Philippine Islands
Mount Suribachi 192
Mush Mouth *see* Macheta
Mussolini, Benito 195

Nagato Maru see watercraft
Nakajima, Sukeo 127, 130, 137, 140, 142, 156, 158–159, 164, 166, 169, 171, 220
Nakajima factory 186
SS *Nankin see* watercraft
Nanking *see* China
Nashville, Tennessee 196, 225
USS *Nashville see* watercraft
National Guard 6, 12, 14, 18, 224; Iowa 217; Santa Fe Armory 2, 12, 47; New Mexico vi, 3, 13–16, 21, 76, 144, 217; New Mexico National Guard Regiments (111th Cavalry; 200th Coast Artillery (antiaircraft); 207th Coast Artillery; 515th Coast Artillery [antiaircraft] *see* military units)
National Reclamation Association 79
Navy Bases 34; Cavite 32, 43- 44, 62
Naylor, Sam 26
Nazi 10
Negritos 31, 44
New Berlin, New York 223
New Cross, London 223
New Guinea 155, 163, 168
New Mexico 3, 6, 11–12, 14, 19–20, 22, 24, 26–27, 31, 33, 35, 38, 75, 78–81, 98, 119, 125, 129, 136, 142, 145, 149, 160, 167, 204, 214, 217, 221; Albuquerque 16, 18, 21, 24, 45, 85, 134, 191, 215; Artesia 16, 191; Bayard 119 224; Belen 191; Black River 22; Camp Luna 15; Carlsbad 16, 24, 42, 150; Clayton 5–6, 191; Central 119; Clovis 16, 80, 119, 191; Coyote 191; Deming 14, 16, 24, 119, 191, 223; Española 119; Franklin Mountains 24; Gallup 16, 119; Hagerman 44; Jornada del Muerto 204; Las Vegas 14; Lordsburg 191; Los Alamos 144–145, 204; McDonald 119; National Guard *see* National Guard; Pajarito Plateau 145; Regina 119; Roswell 44, 69, 165; Santa Fe 1, 3, 5, 7, 12, 14–17, 19, 21, 25, 33, 36, 42, 58, 75, 77, 80, 85, 89, 97–101, 110, 141, 143–145, 153, 156, 160–161, 163–164, 166, 180, 184, 191, 197, 215–218, 220–221; Santa Fe Inn 165; Seboyeta 191; Silver City 16, 119; State Archives 3; State Penitentiary 80, 101; Taos 16, 218; Taos Pueblo 24, 83; University of 80; Zia Pueblo 49
Newport, Tennessee 223
Nichols Airfield *see* airfields
Nielson Airport *see* airfields
Niigata *see* Japan and Prisoner of War Camps
Niigata Bay *see* Japan
91st Coast Artillery (antiaircraft) *see* military units
92nd Coast Artillery (antiaircraft) *see* military units
Nippon Times 150
Nisbeth, Abbie 47, 76, 161
Nisbeth, John 76, 161
Nisei 80, 193
Nishina, Yoshio 206
Nishino 130, 170, 185
Nishiyama, Corporal 109
Nitto Maru see watercraft
No. 91 *see* aircraft
Nobuhiro, Satō 7, 9
Nojima, Mineo 221
Normandy, France 177
North Luzon Force 40

USS *Oahu see* watercraft
O'Donnell *see* prisoner of war camps
Oh, Fair New Mexico 26
Oiwa 132
Ojinaga, Vincente 17

Index 249

Okinawa *see* Japan
Oklahoma 6, 33, 153; Ardmore 225; Boise City 5; Boswell 223; Cartersville 223; Mexhoma 5; Oklahoma City 225; Tulsa 225
Olongapo *see* Philippine Islands
One Arm *see* Nishino
Operation Downfall 203, 205
Operation Iceberg 167
Operation Mike I 182
Operation Olympic 203
Operation Overlord 175
Operation Vengeance 151
Operation Victory 182
Oppenheimer, Robert 144–145, 204
Organ Mountains 24
Origasa, Etsu 172, 212–213
Orion *see* Philippine Islands

P-40 *see* aircraft
Pajarito Plateau *see* New Mexico
Palau 177
Palawan *see* Philippine Islands; prisoner of war camps
Pampanga *see* Philippine Islands
Panama 197
Panay *see* Philippine Islands
USS *Panay see* watercraft
Paracale *see* Philippine Islands
Parker, Albert 191
Parker, George 40, 66
Pasay *see* Philippine Islands
Pasty Face 130, 148
Pearl Harbor *see* Hawaii
Peck, Harry M. 45, 71
Peleliu 177
pellagra 110–111
People's Rights movement 7
Perry, Admiral Matthew 7
Peru 197
Philippine Islands 1–2, 9–10, 12, 14–15, 18–19, 22–25, 29–37, 39–40, 44, 46, 50, 52, 59–60, 65, 67–68, 70–72, 75–77, 89–90, 94, 97–98, 106–107, 117, 119, 126, 130, 142, 160–161, 168, 177, 182, 190–191, 196, 198, 202, 214–215, 217, 222; Abucay 64; Aparri 43–44, 48, 50, 54; army *see* army; Atimonan 57; Bagac 64, 71; Baguio 32, 43, 48, 57; Bataan Peninsula 15, 24, 26 29, 32, 40, 54, 56–57, 59–67, 69–73, 77–78, 82–91, 97–100, 105, 114, 167, 216; Batangas 50; Cabcaben 91, 94; Calumpit Bridges 54, 56, 59, 105; Capas 95–96, 102; Cavite 32; Cavite Navy Base *see* Navy bases; Cebu 53, 59; Cordillera Central Mountains 32; Corregidor 1, 32, 57, 66–67, 71, 83–84, 87–88, 90–91, 100, 105, 109, 119, 191, 216; Culo Bridge 60; Damortis 53; Davao 43, 53; Fort Mills 32, 66, 71; Ilocanos 48; Intramuros 45; Laguna 60; Lamao 84; Legaspi 52, 57; Leyte 181–182; Limay 58, 71; Lingayen 50, 52–53, 57, 190; Los Baños 191; Luzon 30, 32, 39–40, 44, 47–50, 52–53, 55–56, 59, 62, 64, 87, 97, 102, 105, 182, 191; Malinta Tunnel 66; Manila 10, 15, 20, 22, 24, 26, 28–30, 32, 34–35, 40, 43–49, 52, 54, 56–57, 59–60, 62, 67, 72, 77, 105, 115, 118, 122, 191, 214, 218; Manila Bay15, 30, 32, 49, 56, 59, 61–62, 65, 70, 105, 119; Mariveles 32, 86–88, 91, 94; Mariveles Mountains 24, 57, 83–84, 92; Mindanao 40, 52–53, 87–88, 184–185; Mindoro 40; Mount Arayat 32; Mount Natib 56, 64; Mount Pinatubo 32, 40, 44; Mount Santa Rosa 64; Mount Silanganan 24; Olongapo 50; Orion 64, 71; Palawan 182; Pampanga River 54; Panay 53; Paracale 52; Pasay 44; San Fabian 53; San Fernando 50, 53, 91, 94–96; Silaiim 67; Subic Bay 49, 191; Sunken Gardens 45; Tarlac 43, 105, 108; Vigan 44, 50, 52–53, 57
Philippine Military Academy 48
Philippine Provisional Coast Artillery (antiaircraft) *see* military units
Philippine Scouts 40, 48, 53, 57, 63, 71, 84–85, 87
Phillips, Connie 19
USS *Phoenix see* watercraft
Piel, George 148, 154
Poland 12, 168, 181
Potsdam Declaration 204
Pratt, Dorris (Bob) 224
USS *President Pierce see* watercraft
prisoner of war camps (Japanese) 3, 5, 67, 91, 93, 98; Amori 211; Bilibid Prison 1, 44, 72, 105, 108, 115–118, 191; Cabanatuan 1, 106, 108–115, 117–118, 139, 190–191; Davao 69; Hiraoka 124; Kanose 1, 3, 126, 149, 157, 170–203, 207–213, 221; Kawasaki 197; Mitsushima 1, 124–172, 174, 176, 186, 190, 211, 221; Niigata 211; O'Donnell 1, 91–92, 94–96, 102–109, 111–112; Palawan 182; Santo Tomas 191; Shinagawa 211; Tokyo Branch Camp #16-D 170; Tokyo Camp #2 157; Tokyo Camp #3 124, 157
Project Tokyo 98
Provisional Minala Group *see* military units
The Punk *see* Tamotsu Kimura
Pyle, Ernie 194–195

quinine 46, 60, 65, 71–72, 110–111, 140
Quintero, Joe 134

Red Cross 110, 114, 135–136, 138, 141, 152, 154–155, 159, 162–163, 165–166, 169, 172, 186–187, 192, 196, 210; American 14, 47, 74, 97, 100, 161, 168, 173, 175; Geneva Convention 8; nurses 214
Reyna, Antonio (Tony) 12, 24, 39, 42
Richardson, William 119
Riken Laboratory 195
Rivera, Gabby 12
Roberts, Albert H. 142
Robertson 162
Robinson, Donald 191
Rogers, Harold 193
Rogers, Joel (Jack) 19, 85, 119, 224
Romania 80, 177
Rome, New York 223
Rommel, Erwin 217
Romulo, Carlos 59
Roosevelt, Eleanor 118
Roosevelt, Franklin D. 2, 10–11, 16, 22, 38, 52, 71, 73, 75–76, 78, 80, 97, 100, 105, 150, 175, 194, 195
Roosevelt, Theodore 15
Rosenthal, Joe 192
Roswell see New Mexico
Rouse, Samuel J. 225
Roy, John C. 196, 225
Ruiz, Eloy 11–12
Russia POWs 217

Saddler, Carmen 26
Saddler, Jim 26
Safford, Charles 11, 19
Sage, Charles G. 14, 22, 24, 82, 87–88
St. Clara Orphanage 190
St. Johns, Kentucky 223
St. Paul, Minnesota 223
St. Peter's Ward 104
St. Scholastica 72
Saipan 177–178, 198
Saito, Kiromitzu 171, 220–221
Sakamoto, Sergeant 130, 154
Salina, California 223
Salt Lake City 192, 224
San Antonio, Texas 3, 219
San Fabian see Philippine Islands
San Fernando see Philippine Islands
San Francisco, California 27–28, 59, 78, 213, 215
San Francisco Chronicle 78
San Pedro, California 10
Sanchez, Alfredo G. 191
Sanders, Douglas 44

Sangley Point Hospital 32
Santa Fe see New Mexico
Santa Fe Council on National Defense 98
Santa Fe Inn see New Mexico
Santa Fe National Cemetery 1, 14
Santa Fe New Mexican, The 36, 97, 136, 141, 176, 191, 198, 206, 216
Santo Tomas see Prisoner of War Camps
Scar Face see Matsuzaki
Schmid, Roy 44
Scotland 130, 193
scurvy 102, 111, 125
Seboyeta see New Mexico
Selective Service Bill 15; Board 17
Serrano, Earnest S. 191
Sharp, William F. 40
Sherwood, Francis B. 142
Shichino, Shichinobu 221
Shillito, Winston 42, 45, 63, 111
Shinagawa see prisoner of war camps
Shinano see watercraft
ships see watercraft
Shoidisan, Sgt. 130, 154
Shropshire, Reverend 218
Silaiim see Philippine Islands
Silva, Jesus 11, 45
Silver, Alvin 225
Silver City see New Mexico
Simmonds, Osmond H. 225
Simpson, Gerald M. 142
Singapore 67, 71, 77, 129, 210
Singapore Technical Corps 139, 169
Sister Gloria 190
60th Coast Artillery (antiaircraft) see military units
63rd Coast Artillery (antiaircraft) see military units
Skymaster, C-54 see aircraft
smallpox 110, 194
Smiling Sergeant see Sgt. Shoidisan
Smith, Alfred G. 142
Smith, Frank 180
Smith, James M. (Jake), Jr. 119, 142
Smith, Joseph S. 42
The Snake 130
Snodgrass, Clifton 225
Solomon Islands 136, 140, 151, 155
South Luzon Force 40
Spain 39
Spanish-American War 39, 77m 161
Speedo 109, 130
Spencer, Paul R. ("Emo") 225
Spiller, Oliver 22–23
Spruance, Raymond A. 191
Stanford, Kenneth 225
Stimson, Harry L. 77–78, 144

Index

Steele, Arvil L. 225
Steen, Harry H. 21, 39–41, 54
Stockton, California 223
Straight Flush see aircraft
Subic Bay see Philippine Islands
submarines see watercraft
Sunken Gardens see Philippine Islands
Superfortress, B-29 see aircraft
Supreme Council for the Direction of the War 207
surrender: British 57, 67; Denmark 196; Filipino 130; Germany 196; Italy 196; Japan 8 10, 168, 204, 206, 207–209, 211–212; Japanese rescript 208–209; U.S./allies 44, 53, 59–60, 73–74, 78, 80, 82–90, 94, 97, 99, 102, 105, 115, 118, 130, 141, 161, 165, 218
Suterfield, James 225
Sweeney, Charles 207
Swift, Innis P. 22

Tacoma, Washington 224
Taos see New Mexico
Taos Pueblo see New Mexico
Tarlac see Philippine Islands
Tashimitsu, Colonel 94
Teas, Robert G. 137, 142
Texas, El Paso 6, 16, 19, 21, 25, 193
Tibbetts, Paul 205–206
Timor 77, 102
Tinian 177, 204–205, 207
Tofuku Maru see watercraft
Tōjō, Hideki 9–10, 35, 71, 98, 105–106, 175, 177
Tokyo Camps #2, #3, #16-D see prisoner of war camps
Tokyo Times 150
Trejo, Felipe 23, 58, 62
Trinity Site 204
Truman, Harry S. 204–208
Tsuchiya, Tatsuo 130, 150, 158, 220–221
Tsuneyoshi, Yoshio 120, 131
Tule Lake 188, 193, 197
Tulsa see Oklahoma
Turner, John W. 52
200th Coast Artillery (antiaircraft) see military units
206th Coast Artillery (antiaircraft) see military units
260th Coast Artillery (antiaircraft) see military units
typhoid 174, 199
typhoon 29–30, 32, 207; Louise 215

U-boat see watercraft
Uchida, Kanemasu 173, 221

Umeda Maru see watercraft
United States Army see army

Valdes, Bailio 48
Vallerga, Simone (Sam) 225
VanBuskirk, Francis vi, 11, 17, 24, 42–43, 58, 89, 114, 218
VanBuskirk, Jeri 218
VE Day 167
Vicksburg, Mississippi 223
Vigan see Philippine Islands
Visayan-Mindanao Force 40
Vitelli, James A. 142

Waco, Texas 26
Wainwright, Jonathan 37, 40, 45, 60, 63, 71, 73, 82, 84, 88, 105
US *Wake* see watercraft
Wake Island 39, 53, 77, 130, 168
War Plan Orange 15, 54
War Relocation Authority 78
Warm Springs, Georgia 195
Wartime Civil Control Administration 78
Washington, D.C. 10, 15, 22, 36, 52, 66, 79, 167, 175, 203, 207–208, 224
Wasson, Wayne 119
Watanabe, Mutsuhiro 130
watercraft: US *Archer-Fish* 185; USS *Conopus* 87; USS *Coolidge* 28, 32; *Don Esteban* 71; USS *Enterprise* 98; German U-boat 185; USS *Grant* 20; USS *Hornet* 98–99, 150; US *Indianapolis* 204; Japanese 14, 47, 56, 66–67, 71, 76, 83–84, 88–8, 102–104, 123, 131–132, 143, 147–148, 150–151, 164, 199, 203, 214, 219–220, 223, 238, 245, 249; *Lisbon Maru* 160; USS *Mindanao* 84; USS *Missouri* 212; *Nagato Maru* 118–119, 121–122, 125–126, 163, 221; SS *Nankin* (British) 177; USS *Nashville* 99; *Nitto Maru* 98–99; USS *Oahu* 84; USS *Panay* 11; USS *Phoenix* 29; USS *President Pierce* 28–30, 32–33, 119, 218; *Ryuho* 99; *Shinano* 185; *Tofuku Maru* 129; *Umeda Maru* 118; U.S. 34, 38–39, 42, 50, 57, 67, 78, 83, 88–89, 103–104, 107, 122–123, 150–151, 197, 199, 220, 223, 235, 242, 246, 255, 259, 260; US *Wake* 44; *Yaifuku Maru* 119; *Yamato* 167
West Point 9
West Point, Kentucky 223
Wight, John 79
Wilhemina, Queen 211
Wilkinson 177
Wilson, Frank 119, 184
Wilson, Lucy 114

Womack, Paul 42
Woodring, Henry 11
Works Project Administration 79
World War I 8–9, 21, 47
worms 54, 82, 111

Yaifuku Maru see watercraft
Yamada, Asataro 80
Yamamato, Isoruko 119

Yamato see watercraft
Yangtze Valley *see* China
Yawata Steelworks 176
Yoshizawa, Kunio 127, 130, 137, 147, 220
Yuma, Arizona 27

Zero Ward 103–104, 108
Zeros *see* aircraft